"MAXIMUM CLARITY" AND OTHER WRITINGS ON MUSIC

MUSIC IN AMERICAN LIFE

A list of books in the series appears at the end of this book.

"MAXIMUM CLARITY"

AND OTHER WRITINGS ON MUSIC

Ben Johnston

EDITED BY BOB GILMORE

First Illinois paperback, 2022

1 2 3 4 5 C P 5 4 3 2 1
∞ This book is printed on acid-free paper.

The Library of Congress cataloged the cloth edition as follows:
Johnston, Ben. [Literary works. Selections]
"Maximum clarity" and other writings on music / Ben Johnston; edited by Bob Gilmore.
p. cm. — (Music in American life)
Includes bibliographical references (p.), discography (p.), and index.
ISBN-13: 978-0-252-03098-7 (cloth : alk. paper)
ISBN-10: 0-252-03098-2 (cloth : alk. paper)
1. Johnston, Ben—Criticism and interpretation. 2. Music—History and criticism. I. Gilmore, Bob, 1961– . II. Title. III. Series.
ML410.J67A25 2006
780—dc22 2006000325

PAPERBACK ISBN 978-0-252-08671-7

CONTENTS

II. ON MUSICAL AESTHETICS AND CULTURE

III. SOME COMPOSITIONS

EDITOR'S ACKNOWLEDGMENTS

For the initial encouragement to compile this edition of his writings (more years ago now than I care to remember), my warmest thanks go to Ben Johnston, who has been unfailingly patient throughout the long process of gathering and selecting the texts included here. I also want to extend special thanks to Brian Belet of San Jose State University for considerable help in the early stages of work on this volume, for help with permissions and publication subventions, and for many valuable hours of discussion.

The manuscripts of most of the previously unpublished texts in this book are located in the Music Library at Northwestern University, Evanston, Illinois. I am grateful to Don Roberts, then head music librarian, and to Deborah Campana, then music public services librarian, for access to the holdings of the Ben Johnston Archive and for their assistance on my visit to Evanston.

My thanks to the following journals for permission to reprint previously published materials: *Arts in Society; 1/1: The Journal of the Just Intonation Network; Percussive Notes Research Edition;* and *The Composer.* Special thanks must go to the editors of *Perspectives of New Music,* in which no fewer than eight of the texts included here were first published. "On Context" is reprinted by permission of *Source: Music of the Avant Garde,* Larry Austin, editor. "The Genesis of *Knocking Piece*" is reprinted by permission of the Percussive Arts Society, Inc. "Rational Structure in Music," "Tonality Regained," and "Three Attacks on a Problem" were originally published in *ASUC Proceedings,* a journal (now out of print) published by the American Society of University Composers, and are here reprinted by permission of the Society of Composers, Inc., New York (formerly the American Society of University Composers). "Microtonal Resources" is copyright © 1974 by E. P. Dutton & Co.; the copyright was reassigned in 1994 to John Vinton and is here reprinted by permission of John Vinton. The extracts from Johnston's *Knocking Piece* and his second and fifth string quartets are reprinted courtesy of Smith Publications, 2617 Gwynndale Ave., Baltimore, Maryland. My thanks also to the editors and publishers of the following anthologies for permission to reprint material contained therein: the *Encyclopaedia Britannica;* Da

Capo Press, New York (Elliott Schwartz and Barney Childs with Jim Fox, eds., *Contemporary Composers on Contemporary Music,* expanded edition, 1998); Harwood Academic Publishers, London (David Dunn, ed., *Harry Partch: An Anthology of Critical Perspectives*).

Research for this book was facilitated by a travel grant from Dartington College of Arts and publication underwriting by two grants from San Jose State University (from the Graduate Studies and Research Committee and from the College of Humanities and the Arts). I am grateful to my colleagues at Dartington College of Arts, whose support made work on this book possible, in particular Professor Kevin Thompson, Professor Edward Cowie, and Dr. Trevor Wiggins.

The figures in this volume were copied and processed respectively by Patrick Ozzard-Low and Paul Swoger-Ruston, both fine composers with a developed interest in microtones, and I am deeply grateful to them for their hours of painstaking work. Kyle Gann, Patrick Ozzard-Low, and Larry Polansky offered useful comments on an early version of my introduction. I would like to offer sincere thanks to my copyeditor, Angela Buckley, and to Judith McCulloh at the University of Illinois Press, for her advice, her encouragement, and her belief in this project.

The writings contained within this volume have enriched my musical life over more than two decades, as they have that of many other musicians. I would like to thank Ben Johnston for his music, for his writings, and for many forms of personal help and inspiration.

INTRODUCTION

Bob Gilmore

For the past fifty years Ben Johnston has been the most genuine kind of radical: a composer who has made a mark on American music in the late twentieth century not by loudly espousing a cause but by the persuasiveness of his thought and the appeal and fascination of his music. He has been described by critic Mark Swed as "probably our most subversive composer, a composer able to make both radical thinking and avant-garde techniques sound invariably gracious."[1]

Born in Macon, Georgia, in 1926, Johnston studied in Virginia, Ohio, and northern California, and taught for over thirty years at the University of Illinois at Urbana-Champaign. He now lives and works in Rocky Mount, North Carolina. He is proof positive—if proof be needed—that much of the most inventive and refreshing music of the composers of his generation in the United States was created away from the urban centers, in the supposed backwater of university towns. His large body of compositions includes opera and musical theater, music for dance, orchestral and chamber works, choral and solo vocal works, piano music, tape pieces, and indeterminate works. And although his music is still not as widely known as it deserves to be, it has an ever-increasing number of committed advocates among performers, composers, musicologists, and the general public.

Johnston's output as a whole defies easy classification. The entry on his work in the 2001 *New Grove Dictionary of Music and Musicians* states that "Johnston's reputation has rested primarily on his work in microtonality":[2] while this statement is true, it offers only a partial view of his overall compositional achievement. His work indeed took the direction that most strongly characterizes it as a result of his period of study (in 1950–51) with the American composer, instrument builder, and theorist Harry Partch. Johnston is, together with Lou Harrison and James Tenney, one of the small but significant number of American composers whose work was crucially transformed through their encounter with Partch.[3] But just as Johnston's music sounds nothing like Partch's, neither does it much resemble that of Harrison or Tenney; the listener in search of some degree of stylistic consistency in these composers' music will be disappointed. Nonetheless, because of the lineage from Partch and Johnston's subsequent commitment to extended just intonation as a tuning practice, Johnston has often been bracketed together with other American microtonalists roughly his age, such as Ezra Sims and Easley Blackwood. But this association is also misleading: Johnston has never been a card-carrying microtonalist, and such affinity as he feels with other composers exploring extended pitch materials does not necessarily extend to an identification with their aims or overall aesthetic standpoint. In being close to but always somewhat apart from most of the main directions in American composition in the second half of the twentieth century, Johnston perhaps more closely resembles composers of his generation such as Robert Erickson, Kenneth Gaburo, Roger Reynolds, and Alvin Lucier; their careers were, like his, forged in a university milieu, but their unorthodox music has operated freely from the fashions and constraints of that milieu. Another form of kinship might be with the various nonconformists who were his colleagues at the University of Illinois, such as Herbert Brün, Lejaren Hiller, or Salvatore Martirano.

Johnston belongs equally to another tradition: that of the truly literate composer, able to write and speak about his own music (and that of others) with great eloquence and charm. Throughout his life he has acceded to requests to contribute a variety of texts—technical articles, discussion papers, position statements, studies of other composers—to a wide range of publications. Some of these were written for small-circulation journals or were published in books of conference proceedings and have until now been difficult to obtain, especially outside the United States. This volume gathers together, for the first time, all of Johnston's significant writings, together with a body of texts of more modest scope that help illuminate other aspects of his work. As editor I have tried to be as inclusive as possible, placing informal lecture texts alongside technical articles, personal reminiscences alongside texts that ask searching questions about the role of the composer in the modern world. I have included also a sheaf of Johnston's program notes for his own compositions, to point the reader more directly to the body of music that is Johnston's primary achievement.

The papers collected in this volume span more than forty years, from Johnston's earliest writings on music theory and the rational proportions of pitch and rhythm to recent texts such as "Maximum Clarity," the title of which indicates a quest that has characterized the whole of his life and art. They cover a broad spectrum of issues, from the minutely technical through the personal to the broadly humanistic. Their greatest appeal will surely be to those already interested in the composer's music; by collecting them in book form I hope to fuel the growing interest in Johnston's work and to raise awareness of the issues it addresses.

In this introduction I aim to present some of the main outlines of Johnston's thought for those encountering it for the first time. Because the most technical articles in this collection make for demanding reading (particularly those on tuning theory and the structure of the microtonal scales employed by Johnston in his compositions from 1960 onward), some preliminary discussion of the ideas contained within them may be of use.

∽ ∽ ∽

It has never been Johnston's intention to build up a systematic body of music theory, and the writings in Part One of this volume must be considered as a collection of snapshots of unfamiliar terrain rather than as a full-scale map. And yet the value of these texts is enormous, presenting as they do a new conceptual milieu and a vocabulary in which matters of harmony and subtleties of musical pitch relations can be addressed. Johnston's work continues that of his teacher Harry Partch in reaffirming a connection between music theory, number, and acoustics, the roots of which stretch back to antiquity—in the Western world to Pythagoras, to whom is accredited the discovery that proportional lengths of a vibrating string, in small-number ratio relationships, produce basic musical intervals. But Johnston's theoretical work goes further, refining and generalizing Partch's investigations, and proposing starting points of more general applicability.

The core of Johnston's thought on matters of tuning theory is contained in three texts: "Scalar Order as a Compositional Resource," first published in 1964; "Proportionality and Expanded Musical Pitch Relations," first published in 1966; and "Rational Structure in Music," first presented as a lecture in 1976. Alongside these I have included several others that now seem, in retrospect, like background papers. Some are relatively well known and have had some degree of circulation in the new-music community ("Tonality Regained"); others are previously unpublished early texts in which we see Johnston's characteristic ideas beginning to take shape ("Aesthetic Theory; Philosophical Background for Mathematical Theory; Musical Background for Application of Mathematical Theory," "Divergence of Traditions"). Still others carry the discussion into areas of practical application ("A Notation System for Extended Just Intonation"). On occasion Johnston positions his own theoretical concerns with regard to those of other composers ("Microtonal Resources," "Music Theory").

The tuning system described in these writings, and employed in Johnston's music since 1960, is *just intonation,* the principle of tuning by pure intervals (in acoustical terms, those intervals without "beats"). This is a wholly different system from the equal temperament of the piano keyboard. Just intonation is the tuning system of the later ancient Greek modes as codified by Ptolemy; it was the aesthetic ideal of the Renaissance theorists; and it is the tuning practice of a great many musical cultures worldwide, both ancient and modern. These acoustically pure intervals are compromised and distorted in equal-tempered tuning. Twelve-note equal temperament sacrifices purity of intonation in favor of a system with a small number of fixed pitches and artificially creates equivalences between pitches that had previously been intonationally distinct (for example, between C♯ and D♭, or between F♯ and G♭). The main advantage of equal temperament, historically, was the freedom it gave to modulate from one key to another (so that a piano sonata in C major can modulate, say, to A♭ major and later to E major without needing different black keys for A♭ and G♯). The main drawback was the sacrifice of the pure intervals that had existed in earlier forms of temperament (in the various meantone temperaments, and in the well temperaments, such as those of Werckmeister, Kirnberger, Valotti, and others). A further disadvantage, as Johnston has pointed out, is the limited pitch resources that twelve-note equal temperament offers contemporary composers, resources that he feels have long since been explored to the point of exhaustion.

By the early 1960s—the heyday of total serialism, tape music, and indeterminacy—Johnston had come to feel that pitch, and its musical correlatives melody, harmony, and counterpoint, had become devalued as a musical parameter in contemporary composition. The increasing emphases placed on explorations of rhythm and timbre (to name only two areas), while refreshing in themselves, were often necessarily carried out at the expense of pitch interest; pitch relationships were being relegated to a position of lesser importance. Feeling that pitch listening "was too basic a parameter to be allowed to fall into disuse," and not wishing to see the art of music split into "an art of tone and an art of noise," Johnston felt the need to work toward a revivification of pitch relationships from a fresh standpoint. He felt, as Harry

Partch had, that as long as music continued simply to exhaust the resources of the equal-tempered scale, no significantly new advances were possible.

At the core of Johnston's response to this situation is his adoption of the ancient practice of describing musical pitch relations as *ratios*—that is, in mathematically precise, quantitative terms. Throughout the texts in this book he uses both the familiar system of letter names (A, B, C♯, etc.) and frequency ratios, a system in which the octave is represented by the ratio 2/1, the just perfect fifth by 3/2, the just perfect fourth by 4/3, the just major third by 5/4, the just minor third by 6/5, and so on, literally ad infinitum. The rationale for this adoption is provided first in his article "Scalar Order as a Compositional Resource" and is restated and developed in subsequent texts.

Johnston's music does not simply revivify an ancient conception of tuning but extends that conception of pitch materials to previously unexplored realms. His use of the term *extended just intonation* (which first appears in the 1967 text "Three Attacks on a Problem") implies a pitch system in which intervals deriving from the relatively unfamiliar seventh partial of the harmonic series (in ratio terms, 7/4) and/or higher partials—the eleventh, thirteenth, seventeenth, and so on—are used together with the more familiar intervals that form the basis of conventional triadic tuning. This concept, as Johnston has been at pains to stress, is evolutionary rather than revolutionary; he joins with other twentieth-century theorists, notably Schoenberg, in the belief that the ear is able to make much finer discriminations in its perception of pitch than is conventionally assumed, and that there is a slow but continual progress in our perceptual abilities toward ever-greater refinement.

This concern with extended just tuning leads to the use of *microtones,* intervals smaller than a semitone that are now common currency in new music but were still considered strange and exotic when Johnston began to use them at the beginning of the 1960s. (A contemporary perspective on this subject can be found in his 1967 article "Microtonal Resources.") He has been an important leader in this domain, both in his actual compositions and in the theoretical underpinnings he has given such materials in the texts collected in Part One of this book.

Far from being a purely technical matter, the use of just tuning is a matter of great symbolic import for Johnston. His ideas provide a refreshing new perspective on music history, especially on the crisis of tonality of the early twentieth century. In several of the texts collected here, Johnston offers a diagnosis of this crisis: the difficulty of forging new nontriadic harmonic relationships and the ultimate unsustainability of the atonal language overall are, he argues, the consequences of a conceptually exhausted pitch framework—twelve-note equal temperament—that was incapable of realizing them. Johnston takes the position that Schoenberg, "in tacitly accepting as an arbitrary 'given' the twelve-tone equal-tempered scale . . . committed music to the task of exhausting the remaining possibilities in a closed pitch system" ("Three Attacks on a Problem"). A different path was suggested by Debussy, "whose harmonic language approximates as well as can be in equal temperament a movement from overtone series to overtone series, with an emphasis upon higher partials . . . Schoenberg is an example of a radical thinker motivated strongly by a claustrophobic sense of nearly exhausted resources. Debussy, in sharp contrast, seems motivated by an expansion of harmonic resources and a greatly widened horizon" ("A.S.U.C. Keynote Address"). By the mid-1980s, Johnston had come to see his own work retrospectively as an attempt "to connect Debussy and Partch, to complete the revolution [begun earlier in the century] and connect it with a redefinition of older values" ("A.S.U.C. Keynote Address").

It was to be nearly ten years after Johnston's six-month "apprenticeship" with Harry Partch in Gualala, on the far northern California coast, in 1950–51, before he himself began to compose music in extended just intonation. Once he had decided to confront head-on the challenge of writing music for conventional instruments using complex microtonal tunings and to work with performers in finding these new pitch materials, the transformation in his musical language was rapid. The breakthrough works were the *Sonata for Microtonal Piano* and *String Quartet no. 2*, both completed in 1964 (Johnston discusses both these compositions in Part Three of this book). This music aligns his radically new approach to tuning with the concepts and concerns of "new music" as a whole. The language of these works is complex, their tone of voice intense. In 1963 Johnston wrote: "If contemporary music produces . . . images of tension and anxiety (and worse states) we cannot deny it is holding up a mirror . . . A habitual psychological state of high tension such as contemporary life tends to produce is a matter for serious concern. Art can help us by bringing to recognition, analyzing and making intelligible the complex patterns of these tensions . . . To extend musical order further into the jungle of randomness and complexity . . . that is perhaps the fundamental aim of contemporary serious music" ("Musical Intelligibility: Where Are We?").

The concern with systems of order within complexity is the hallmark of Johnston's compositions of these years. Indeed, regardless of the changing stylistic orientation of his eclectic output, the underlying aesthetic agenda of all his work has remained how "the extreme complexity of contemporary life [can] be reconciled with the simplifying and clarifying influences of systems of order based upon ratio scales" ("Extended Just Intonation: A Position Paper"). This concern is parallel to the explorations of complexity in the 1960s by composers such as Xenakis, Stockhausen, and Cage, with the difference that Johnston was interested primarily in "the kind of complexity needed to understand the intricate symbiotic interdependence of organic life on earth" and much less in "the kind which clarifies the statistical behavior of inanimate multitudes" ("On Bridge-Building").

Johnston found in the writings of the Harvard psychologist S. S. Stevens the materials from which to establish a formal hierarchy of types of perceptible order. In his 1964 article "Scalar Order as a Compositional Resource," Johnston contended that we listen to music from moment to moment on changing levels of this hierarchy. At the lowest level of perceptible order is the apprehension of distinctions as basic as *same* and *different*. At the next, more discerning level is the apprehension of the distinctions *more than* and *less than;* by application of this type of measurement we make such distinctions as louder or softer, higher or lower (with respect to pitch), longer or shorter, and so on. Taking his cue from Stevens, he termed these two types of measurement *nominal* and *ordinal*, respectively. At the higher levels of perceptible order are complex *proportional* relationships of pitch and rhythm—*interval* and *ratio* scales. Johnston argued that our perception of pitch especially is sufficiently acute and discriminatory that we can make much more complex judgments than those in common practice.

In his *String Quartet no. 2* the pitch relationships stem from a fifty-three-note scale, the second of the two different fifty-three-note enharmonic scales Johnston describes in "Scalar Order as a Compositional Resource." In that article he offers a notation of the scale, in a system designed to be as little different as possible from conventional notation. It might seem that the notation of a fifty-three-note scale would prove a formidable problem, but Johnston solved it by redefining the symbols of conventional staff notation to make them clear and unambiguous as a representation of just intervals. First, the seven notes on the staff without accidentals (from C to B) are assigned precise ratio values that represent the interval they make with C—1/1, 9/8, 5/4, 4/3, 3/2, 5/3, 15/8. Then, sharps and flats are also assigned a precise value: a sharp raises a note by the same interval by which a flat lowers it, but because that interval is not an equal-tempered semitone—in Johnston's system it is the ratio 25/24 (71 cents)—enharmonically equivalent notes are kept distinct. (Taking C as 1/1, C♯ will therefore be the ratio 25/24, whereas D♭ will be 27/25—9/8 divided by 25/24, or 9/8 x 24/25 equals 27/25.) Johnston also uses double sharps and double flats. The only "new" notational symbols needed in this fifty-three-note scale are pluses and minuses, which symbolize respectively raising and lowering a pitch by a syntonic comma, the ratio 81/80 (22 cents).

In his more recent music, Johnston has expanded his notation system to make provision for intervals derived from the higher prime numbers of the harmonic series—7, 11, 13, 17, 19, 23, 29, 31. He has needed to devise only one new symbol for each new prime number; from 7 upward Johnston calls these symbols *chromas.* (A full list of these symbols is given in Figure 36 in this volume.) These accidentals are used in combination for the more complex ratios: in his recent music it is not uncommon to find three such symbols applied to one note. A full discussion of the symbols and their meanings is found in "A Notation System for Extended Just Intonation." The fact that the notation system has become infinitely expandable makes it an aesthetically appropriate correlate to the tuning system itself. The notation system helped Johnston move toward an expandable pitch "space" free from the constraints of a fixed scale; by the beginning of the 1980s he could say of his elaborately microtonal *String Quartet no. 5* (see Part Three of this book), "I have no idea as to how many different pitches it used per octave."

There was one other important component in this freedom: Johnston's use of *lattice* models to represent the pitch relationships of just intonation scales. Of all the satisfactory models of ratiometric tuning systems, lattices are perhaps the most straightforward geometrically, yet they have the great advantage of being capable, like Johnston's notation system, of great mutability and of infinite expansion. He began working with lattices around 1970, taking his cue from an acquaintance with the writings of the Dutch microtonal theorist Adriaan Fokker; his most developed discussion of the lattices is found in his article "Rational Structure in Music." The lattice is a way of modeling the tuning relationships in a just intonation system. It is an array of points in a periodic, multidimensional pattern. Each point on the lattice corresponds to a ratio (i.e., a pitch, or an interval with respect to some other point on the lattice). The lattice can be two-, three-, or *n*-dimensional, with each dimension corresponding to a different prime-number partial. Thus a Pythagorean scale—one built exclusively from multiples of 2/1 and 3/2 (octaves and perfect fifths)—would be represented in a lattice of two dimensions only, since the integers of its ratios involve only powers of 2 and 3. The lattice implied by a just diatonic scale, with the ratios 5/4 and 6/5 as the just major and minor third and 5/3 and 8/5 as the just major and minor sixth, is three-dimensional (2, 3, 5). A twelve-note "chromatic" scale can be represented as a two-dimensional (3, 5) projection plane within the three-dimensional (2, 3, 5) space needed to map the scale. (Octave equivalents would appear on an axis at right angles to the other two, but this arrangement is not really necessary graphically.)

Johnston provides an extensive rationale for his use of lattices, both technical and aesthetic, in "Rational Structure in Music," where he explains: "Extrapolating the basic logic from the harmonic practice of traditional Western music is only a first step. A much more challenging and interesting follow-up is the generalization of this logic so that it becomes applicable to unfamiliar pitch materials." The lattices provided Johnston with the theoretical model he needed to help in the exploration of relationships based on partials higher than the sixth. It also gave him a method of making sophisticated comparisons between triadic systems and larger ones. "I became interested in the morphological analogy between structures, such as scales based upon triadically generated bases and the much more complex ones generated by using higher overtone relationships" ("Extended Just Intonation: A Position Paper").

A further advantage of lattices was that they demonstrated what Johnston terms *harmonic neighbors.* Ratios in near proximity on the lattice are simpler relationships aurally than those farther away. A more complex relationship, such as the septimal minor triad 1/1–7/6–3/2, can be "explained" by examining its geometrically more elaborate configuration on the lattice. This opened up the possibility of specifying closer or more distant harmonic areas: "patterns or 'paths' in the lattice may be used to give a sense of harmonic direction even to passages that lack entirely any conventional tonal or harmonic 'logic'" ("Rational Structure in Music"). *String Quartet no. 7* (1984), written with close adherence to a lattice model, contains some of the most microtonally complex writing in Johnston's output. (As of this date the piece remains unperformed: it provides an example of how some of his compositional designs are less in need of further analysis than they are of performance.)

∽ ∽ ∽

At the beginning of the 1970s, as Johnston's music began to explore harmonies derived from the higher partials of the harmonic series, a new and apparently contradictory impulse began to manifest itself: a desire to have the music speak clearly and be intelligible to a wide audience, particularly to listeners who had no particular investment in avant-garde music. The choral work *Rose* (1971) and the *Mass* (1972) were the first manifestations of this tendency. Perhaps the most compelling instance is *String Quartet no. 4* (1973), a set of variations on the hymn "Amazing Grace." The quartet traverses three different tunings in its twelve-minute span, from Pythagorean (3–limit) through just (5–limit) to extended just (7–limit). From this pitch world, partly familiar and partly unfamiliar, and in a rhythmic language of great complexity employing proportional rhythms and metric modulations, the piece creates an impression of unified and luminous beauty.

Several of the more recent papers in Part Two of this volume speak to this new tendency, which has continued to characterize Johnston's compositional output to the present day. He has grown less inclined in recent years toward the type of "hard" theoretical thinking manifested in some of his earlier writings. It is not that such work has come to seem meaningless to him: on the contrary, he retains a lively interest in work in this domain being pursued by younger theorists and composers. Rather it is that, having developed and refined a theoretical basis for his compositional practice, and having articulated that theoretical position verbally, he has moved on to a consideration of other aspects of his art.

One of these aspects is a reassessment of the whole purpose and value of such theory. "When in my teens I first heard about the discrepancy between traditional music theory and acoustical research," he writes, "I had no hesitation in siding with acoustics. But as time went on and I became more mature, I recognized that the real value of this emphasis lies in its aptness as a symbol of honest self-knowledge and therefore as a tool to help in seeking this."[4] The theory, in other words, is a means to an end: that of reaffirming, from a new standpoint, art as a human expression, and of reconsidering and reassessing the aptness of its symbols as expressive of the life of our times. This reassessment is in keeping with Johnston's idealistic (and, in the way he has put it into practice in his own life, altruistic) view of the function of art: "I think of any art as a way to help develop a better, more whole human being."

Johnston is, by temperament and inclination, reticent about biographical inquiry as a means of approaching his music. Partly from modesty, he has always claimed that his work is the important thing, not the life of the man who brought it about. He deplores the indiscretion and sensationalism of much contemporary biography while, characteristically, setting equally little store by the straitjacket of "authorized biography": a middle course between tabloidism and censorship, the aim of any serious biographer, is the only one he respects. For this book, with his active cooperation, I have written a chronology of his life, with the goal of establishing a firm factual basis on which subsequent work in this area may build.

Johnston's life has not been free of difficulties. Since he was a young man, he has suffered intermittent periods of mental illness and behavior patterns characteristic of manic depression. He has concluded from intense periods of self-observation that dry periods in composing, together with obsessive playing of card games and other forms of escape, are linked to the depressed phase of his illness. He has not, as far as possible, resorted to medical science to help him control the problem, using only very small and temporary doses of medication at the most intense phase of the "up" cycle. He takes no form of "leveling" medication; and his condition has become better, not worse, with time, the opposite of the usual prognosis.

One may perhaps speculate as to whether or not the voice of this "other" Ben Johnston—the one known only to close family and friends—can be heard in his music. Certainly his compositional voice ranges at times to music of disturbing intensity and to outbursts of violent energy. But such speculations are futile and entirely miss the point: that it is his art *as a whole* that has proved so effective a source of inner strength over many years. It is astonishing that a man burdened with these difficulties has maintained over a long and active lifetime such a steady and consistent rate of production. One suspects this has been achieved only by an immense inner determination, as well as by the support of those close to him. And while at various times psychiatry, meditation, esoteric belief, and a profound religious conviction have sustained that inner determination, his art testifies to the fact that Johnston has been seeking not merely personal solace but a medium in which he can convey something of his struggle, to make his own overcoming of obstacles a source of hope and inspiration for others. It is perhaps in this sense—as a record of an individual surmounting considerable difficulties, outer and inner—that the facts of his life are most relevant and his life story most affecting.

For Johnston, as for any real composer, the truest record of that inner life is to be found in his compositions, which, more than the writings collected here, have formed the real center of his productivity. In Johnston's view, these writings convey the same sorts of issues as does his music, but in a much less richly expressive medium; they are the bold statement of issues that the music evokes. Likewise, biography (even in terms of the necessarily brief chronology of his life presented in this book) is of value only to the extent that it can serve as a framework within which to view the compositions, which in turn, looked at with sufficient insight, provide a better indication of the "inner" life story than any reportage of facts, events, and comments could ever achieve. It is my hope that this volume will serve as a stimulus to more widespread performance of Johnston's music and to a deepening appreciation of the richness of the inner life contained within it.

In closing, a brief word on editorial method. The texts included in this volume represent perhaps ninety percent of Johnston's total output. I have respected his wishes regarding the selection of texts, just as he has readily supported my decisions regarding the inclusion or noninclusion of specific pieces. The main criterion governing the selection process was nonredundancy. In texts written over a period of more than forty years I found that Johnston had occasionally covered similar territory, or discussed the same musical example, in different contexts. While this is a common enough occurrence in texts written as separate items, in assembling them in book form we did not want to duplicate material unnecessarily. Occasionally (for example, in his program note to *String Quartet no. 6*), Johnston himself decided to excise some material to avoid repetition. The attentive reader will nonetheless find that some central ideas or explanations recur in several texts. I have endeavored to keep such repetition to the minimum, while acknowledging that a certain amount is unavoidable and may even, especially in the more technical articles, be welcome. In any case, I do not expect that this volume will be read from cover to cover, nor need it be (although there is much to be gained from reading the texts in Parts One and Two, especially, in the order in which they are presented here).

The writings themselves have required very little editorial intervention. Such textual editing as was necessary, as well as the final decisions regarding the selection and sequencing of the individual items, was done by me. The very occasional changes in interests of clarity or factual accuracy, even to previously published versions of these articles, have all been approved by Ben Johnston.

NOTES

1. Mark Swed, "Ben Johnston," *Chamber Music* (March–April 1995).

2. Richard Kassel, "Ben Johnston," in the *New Grove Dictionary of Music and Musicians* (London: Macmillan, 2001), vol. 13, 170.

3. I have written about this subject at greater length in two articles: "Changing the metaphor: ratio models of musical pitch in the work of Harry Partch, Ben Johnston, and James Tenney," in *Perspectives of New Music,* and "The Climate Since Harry Partch," in *Contemporary Music Review* (see bibliography).

4. Ben Johnston, e-mail to Bob Gilmore, April 12, 2000.

BEN JOHNSTON: A CHRONOLOGY

Bob Gilmore

1926, March 15 Benjamin Burwell Johnston born in Macon, Georgia, eldest child of Benjamin Burwell Johnston Sr. (1894–1960) and Janet Ross Johnston (1899–1975). Johnston's father at that time was managing editor of the Macon *Telegraph.*

1931 Birth of sister, Janet. This year, thanks to the tutelage of his mother's friend Augusta Worsham, Johnston enters Vineville School in Macon a year ahead of normal schedule.

1932 At the age of six Johnston begins piano lessons with Mrs. A. E. Reese.

1935 His mother (who is a Sunday school teacher), his sister, and Johnston himself attend Vineville Baptist Church, which he joins on his own initiative. He is baptized there. (Johnston's father, in contrast, is an agnostic.) With the Great Depression worsening, his mother goes to work as a stenographer; the care during the day of the two children and Johnston's invalid grandmother is entrusted to a series of servants, one of whom Johnston particularly likes because she plays phonograph records of Duke Ellington and Jimmie Lunceford. Almost the only classical music concerts he experiences as a child are a recital by the Brazilian pianist Guiomar Novaes and the operas *Carmen* and *Hansel und Gretel.* He collects phonograph records of the popular music of the day and plays most of the songs by ear on the piano, and he attends every movie musical he can (using his father's newsman's pass to the local theaters).

1937 The family moves to Richmond, Virginia, where Johnston's father becomes city editor and later managing editor of the *Richmond Times Dispatch.* Johnston attends Albert Hill Junior High School and has piano lessons with Eleanor K. Greenawalt.

1938 While visiting Macon for his grandmother's funeral, Johnston is taken by a family friend to a lecture at Wesleyan College on Debussy and the relationship of his music to the acoustic theories of Helmholtz. The lecture sparks an interest in music theory and acoustics, which continues to grow in the years ahead.

1939 Begins to compose at the age of thirteen. Attends Thomas Jefferson High School in Richmond: during this time he studies piano with Florence Robertson and attends lectures and master classes by the pianist, composer, and folklorist John Powell. Befriends the young piano student Donald Pippin.

1942 During his senior year Johnston is editor-in-chief of the school newspaper, the *Jeffersonian.* Writes poetry.

1943 Wins first and second prizes in a competition sponsored by *Scholastic Magazine* for his song "Homeward" and *Fugue in D Minor* for piano. Plays trombone in the school orchestra. Wins a state scholarship to study French at the College of William and Mary, where he majors in liberal arts.

1944, January 30 A concert of Johnston's compositions is given at the College of William and Mary as part of the Student Music Club's Sunday Afternoon Concert Series. The works performed include songs and piano pieces, a sonata for clarinet and piano, *Theme and Variations* and *Ballade in E major* for violin and piano, and a *Concerto in E* for two pianos. A feature on the seventeen-year-old Johnston in the *Richmond Times Dispatch* quotes him as looking forward to a musical future in which "there will be new instruments with new tones and overtones." Later that year, with war raging, Johnston enters the navy and is sent to the Chicago Great Lakes Naval Training Center and later to the Navy School of Music in Washington, D.C. He studies analysis, harmony, counterpoint, and orchestration for dance bands, and pursues his studies of piano and trombone; he even briefly considers a career as a dance-band arranger. His duty is on the USS *Augusta,* flagship of the Atlantic fleet. After some months he begins to experience serious psychological stress that is diagnosed decades later as a variety of manic-depressive illness.

1946 His composition *All the King's Horses* wins second prize in a competition sponsored by the National Federation of Music Clubs. He is discharged from the navy suffering from psychiatric difficulties. Later he falls ill with a collapsed lung, caused by using incorrect breathing techniques on the trombone. Upon leaving the navy he makes a living playing piano at the National Theater in Richmond and later with dance bands in Norfolk, Virginia, and Mason City, Iowa. In Mason

City he marries Dorothy Haines, a dance-band singer whom he had met in Richmond. Although neither is sure about the commitment, they do not wish to defy American Midwest conventional mores to the extent of living together unmarried. She suggests going west to Big Sur, California, to be part of the bohemian lifestyle and artistic culture flourishing there: Johnston persuades her that such a move without any funds or support is impractical. After about six months the marriage breaks up, and Johnston obtains a divorce. The whole experience upsets him greatly, and he falls ill with pleurisy. Sensing the young Johnston's lack of direction, his father flies out to rescue him and persuades him to return to college.

1947 Johnston returns to the College of William and Mary, graduating in 1949 with a B.A. in Fine Arts. There he befriends the young playwright and director Wilford Leach, with whom he collaborates on several projects in the years ahead. Their first project is a musical, *Carry Me Back,* which wins the Broadcast Music Incorporated prize for student musicals. Johnston travels to New York to meet Carl Haverlin, then head of the popular music division of BMI, who advises him that he could make a successful popular song composer, but Johnston tells him that his heart lies in the world of concert music.

1948 In the summer he follows a dancer, Mary Harrington, from William and Mary College to the American Dance Festival. Although not formally enrolled, Johnston is befriended by Louis Horst, Martha Graham's music director, who invites him to audit his class in composition for the dance. (Later, Horst's support is crucial to Johnston's application for a job at University of Illinois at Urbana-Champaign.) Later in the year he meets Betty Ruth Hall, then a painting student at Richmond Professional Institute.

1949 With some difficulty (because his degree is in fine arts rather than music), Johnston finally gains a place at graduate school, at the Cincinnati Conservatory of Music. Although disappointed with his composition studies, he finds the class on atonal counterpoint taught by Mary Leighton highly valuable. Under her tuition he composes his first serial work, the *Etude-Toccata* for piano. At the conservatory he befriends Ward Swingle, later the director of the Swingle Singers.

1950 Johnston's master's recital at Cincinnati features a woodwind quintet, piano pieces, and a setting of E. E. Cummings's "somewhere i have never travelled." Another legacy of his year there is his encounter with Harry Partch's book *Genesis of a Music,* which makes a profound impact. Johnston writes to Partch in care of the University of Wisconsin Press inquiring about studying with him. This plan has profound consequences for his personal life; in April he and Betty Hall are married by a justice of the peace in Lexington, Kentucky.

In August he begins a six-month "apprenticeship" with Partch on a ranch in Gualala, northern California. Johnston and Betty are pressed into service undertaking repair work around the ranch, a novel experience for both. Johnston helps Partch tune his instruments every morning and occasionally succeeds in discussing matters of music theory with him. He and Betty perform in recordings of Partch's *Eleven Intrusions, The Letter,* and *Dark Brother.* Partch and Johnston collaborate on incidental music for Wilford Leach's *The Wooden Bird,* a tape of which is used in the production at the University of Virginia in January 1951.

1951 While still in Gualala, Johnston attends musicology classes at the University of California, Berkeley, studying the Baroque forms. When Partch leaves Gualala for health reasons in March, Johnston becomes a student of Darius Milhaud at Mills College in Oakland. He finds Milhaud to be an exceptional teacher. Because composition lessons are conducted with all the students together in one large class, each student is witness to the others' lessons: Johnston recalls that Milhaud could be "devastating" when he disapproved of someone's work. While studying with Milhaud, Johnston composes the John Donne setting "A Nocturnall Upon Saint Lucie's Day" for baritone and piano, and a Concerto for Brass.

September: begins teaching at the University of Illinois at Urbana-Champaign, where he will remain for more than thirty years. Initially his appointment is half-time in Music and half in the Dance Department, where he is an accompanist and composes for dance.

1952 Graduates from Mills College with a master of fine arts; his thesis piece is a Concerto for Percussion. Meets John Cage at the Festival of Contemporary Arts at the University of Illinois. Cage invites him to come to New York to work with him during the summer and, in preparation, asks him to analyze the Webern *Symphony.* Although his teaching commitments leave him no time to prepare adequately, he goes to New York nonetheless and, together with Earle Brown, helps Cage with work on the tape piece *Williams Mix.* Following this experience he seriously considers applying for a Fulbright Scholarship to study in Paris with Pierre Schaeffer, but the idea is dropped.

1954 Composes incidental music for Wilford Leach's play *The Zodiac of Memphis Street.*

1955 On commission from the University of Illinois's Festival of Contemporary Arts, Johnston composes the cantata *Night,* setting a text by Robinson Jeffers. He also writes music for the ballet *St. Joan,* devised by Sybil Shearer, a former member of the Doris Humphrey studio in New York who is teaching in Illinois, but the work is never choreographed; Johnston makes a piano suite from the score. The same year he composes *Three Chinese Lyrics* for soprano and two violins, setting Ezra Pound's renderings of the Chinese poet Li Po. The songs mark a departure from his otherwise largely neoclassical idiom and seem prophetic of the music of the next decade.

1956 Johnston's next large-scale work is the chamber opera *Gertrude, or Would She Be Pleased to Receive It?* a further collaboration with Wilford Leach, who is then a doctoral student at the University of Illinois. Musically the opera draws on idioms both serious and popular, with satirical undercurrents; it is performed that year at the University of Illinois.

Johnston arranges for Harry Partch to come to the university to prepare the first performance of Partch's "dance-satire" *The Bewitched* in collaboration with the choreographer Alwin Nikolais at the 1957 Festival of Contemporary Arts.

1958 Completes the *Septet* for wind quintet, cello, and double bass, the culmination of his neoclassical idiom.

1959 Johnston's next large-scale composition is the dance work *Gambit,* commissioned by Merce Cunningham, which he composes on a summer fellowship at Yaddo in Saratoga Springs, New York. The score juxtaposes serial movements with tonal ones, modernist textures with jazz-derived ones, and marks an important step away from the concentration on neoclassicism. It is followed by the fully serial *Nine Variations,* his first string quartet.

He is on sabbatical in the academic year 1959–60, and with the award of a Guggenheim Fellowship spends the year in New York. His original intention was to work with Milton Babbitt at the Columbia-Princeton Electronic Music Center on composing microtonally by electronic means, but Babbitt is not encouraging and the experience is a largely negative one. Instead, he finally has the opportunity to study with John Cage.

While in New York Johnston and his wife, Betty, also study at the Gurdjieff Foundation; for a time they are both deeply involved in the writings of Gurdjieff and his follower Ouspensky.

1960 In New York he makes sketches for a work for retuned piano, which will occupy him on and off for four years; also, at the prompting of Edward Cone, who is also working that year at Columbia-Princeton, he begins writing what will turn out to be his first major theoretical article.

Following his return to Urbana, he receives tenure in the School of Music at the University of Illinois. This is partly a result of a letter of recommendation from Otto Luening and Vladimir Ussachevsky at Columbia University: his main supporters in the School of Music itself are John Garvey, violist of the Walden Quartet and chairman of the music committee for the Festival of Contemporary Arts; the pianist Claire Richards; and the head of Collegium Musicum, George Hunter. During the previous years, Johnston had undertaken a course of study leading toward a Ph.D. in musicology, doctoral degrees having become a near necessity for career advancement; but after two years he gives it up, gambling instead (on advice from Lejaren Hiller, then in the process of founding the Experimental Music Studio) on establishing a reputation outside the university.

The first completed composition following the frustrating year in New York is *Five Fragments,* settings of texts by Thoreau for alto voice, oboe, cello, and bassoon. This is Johnston's first work to use just intonation, which is combined with serial techniques. The work restricts itself to 5–limit tuning, as do most of his compositions for the rest of the decade; but the ultrachromatic complexity results nonetheless in a score of considerable difficulty. Also this year, but in a quite different vein, he produces two pieces for the University of Illinois jazz band, *Ivesberg Revisited* and *Newcastle Troppo.*

1961 Composes *Sonata for Two* for violin and cello. This four-movement work does not pursue his use of just intonation, but rather combines serialism, tonality, and improvisation in an original manner.

Johnston is asked to chair the Festival of Contemporary Arts planning committee and assumes responsibility for the 1963 and 1965 festivals.

1962 Composes *A Sea Dirge,* a setting of words from Shakespeare's *The*

Tempest for mezzo-soprano, violin, flute, and oboe. This again uses just intonation in its treatment of serial techniques.

1963 Composes *Knocking Piece* for two percussionists. Originally conceived for Wilford Leach's play *In Three Zones,* the music was to be part of Leach's retelling of the Faust legend: the musicians perform percussive sounds inside a grand piano, to portray a soldier who has sold his soul to the devil and returned home only to find he cannot enter his locked house. The piece, at first thought to be unplayable, is a compositional tour de force, a virtuoso treatment of proportional rhythms demanding intense concentration from the players. *Knocking Piece* and *A Sea Dirge* are premiered on December 14 at a Round House concert at the home of the composer Salvatore Martirano in Urbana. Also this year, for Bertram and Nancy Turetzky, he composes the serial *Duo for flute and string bass.*

1964 Johnston's first major theoretical article, "Scalar Order as a Compositional Resource," is published in the journal *Perspectives of New Music.* This year also sees the completion of two major works: the *Sonata for Microtonal Piano,* for a piano retuned in extended 5–limit just intonation, which he had begun in New York in 1959; and *String Quartet no. 2,* written for the LaSalle Quartet. Both works continue his exploration of serialism but create a distinctive sound-world unlike that of the music of his contemporaries. They testify to the fact that, as he had written in the program book for the previous year's Festival of Contemporary Arts, the fundamental aim of his music was now "to extend musical order further into the jungle of randomness and complexity," mirroring a need that he comes increasingly to feel is of social as well as musical urgency.

1965 The *Sonata for Microtonal Piano* (which also exists in an alternative version, with the order of movements changed, under the title *Grindlemusic*) is premiered by Claire Richards at a Round House concert in Urbana. During the year Johnston delivers the lecture "Proportionality and Expanded Musical Pitch Relations" at Illinois Wesleyan University, and it is published the following year in *Perspectives of New Music.*

1966 Tours in the summer with the University of Illinois Contemporary Chamber Players to Europe, where they perform in Darmstadt, Paris, London, Cologne, and Warsaw; *Knocking Piece* is included on the programs. Composes *Ci-Gît Satie,* for chorus, bass, and drums, written for the Swingle Singers but not performed by them.

Johnston is on sabbatical in the academic year 1966–67, on a grant from the National Council on the Arts and the Humanities. On commission from the St. Louis Symphony Orchestra, composes the orchestral work *Quintet for Groups,* and, at the end of the year, composes *String Quartet no. 3.*

1967, March 24–25 *Quintet for Groups* is premiered by the St. Louis Symphony Orchestra under Eleazar De Carvalho. Although one of Johnston's most ambitious and imaginative compositions to this time, the work is a mixed success and meets with some lack of cooperation from the orchestral players, not because of its tuning demands but because of the sections of graphic notation. An extended article on the piece by Barney Childs appears in *Perspectives of New Music* in 1968.

Some winds of change blow into his life in the person of John Cage, who becomes composer-in-residence at the University of Illinois in 1967–69; the Johnstons spend much time with him. Johnston even uses the *I Ching* in composing *One Man* for solo trombone (which also marks the first use of the seventh partial in his just intonation works).

1968 Johnston makes a brief foray into tape composition to realize *Museum Piece* (in collaboration with Jaap Spek), a commission from the Smithsonian Institution. Around this time he begins to write a series of articles and conference papers that ask searching questions about the nature and relevance of contemporary composition, and call for a less ivory-tower and more humanistic approach. These writings—"On Context," "How to Cook an Albatross," "Art and Survival," and others—do not signal an abandonment of his theoretical work in tuning theory but concern themselves with broader issues of which his theoretical work is but one part. They present disturbing recurrent images—of the chaos of modern life and the necessity of building a bridge over the chasm—and hint at "a private season in hell," which is part of Johnston's personal experience in these years. (Another factor in the shift of emphasis in these writings is Johnston's contact with Larry Austin, editor of *Source* magazine, which publishes his articles "On Context" and, in 1970, "Phase 1–a," an early attempt at the systematic modeling of his microtonal pitch resources.)

1969 Begins a collection of indeterminate pieces: *CASTA* *, *RECIPE for a* *, *CONFERENCE: a telephone happening for John Cage,* and *KNOCKING PIECE II.* He also has the idea for a fifth piece, not realized until 1979, *Age of Surveillance.* These are text pieces that are in keeping with the experimental temper of the times; but they also reflect Johnston's increasing interest in music making as a form of social interaction.

1970 Nonesuch Records in New York releases an LP of *String Quartet no. 2,* in a performance by the Composers Quartet, coupled with Cage's *HPSCHD.* The recording, with liner notes by Johnston's musicologist friend Peter Yates, helps bring his music to a wider public.

Collaborates with Wilford Leach on the rock opera *Carmilla,* a vampire tale adapted from a novella by Sheridan Le Fanu. It is produced by ETC of La MaMa in New York and recorded on Vanguard Records.

In this year, on the Feast of Corpus Christi, Johnston is received into the Catholic Church. Concomitant with this is a strong impulse in a new direction musically: a turning of his back on doctrinaire avant-gardism and a concern to "humanize" his music, letting "every work be a religious intention."

1971 The first manifestation of this new direction is a short choral work, *Rose,* setting a poem by his daughter, Sibyl Johnston. Although intended for the choir at Champaign Central High School, the piece does not involve any simplification of his idiom: on the contrary, it employs a 7–limit just tuning and demands fine discriminations of pitch. This exemplifies a new aesthetic: the use of ever more complex tuning goes hand in hand with a desire to have the music speak clearly and to "explain itself" to a nonspecialist audience. The *Mass* for SATB choir, ten trombones (or organ), string bass, and drums, completed the following year, continues this tendency.

1973 Composes *String Quartet no. 4,* a compelling example of his new compositional direction and, thanks to recordings by the Fine Arts Quartet and later by the Kronos Quartet, his best-known work. A set of variations on the hymn "Amazing Grace," the work traverses three different tunings, Pythagorean (3–limit), just (5–limit) and extended just (7–limit) in its twelve-minute span. From this unfamiliar pitch world, and in a rhythmic language of great complexity employing proportional rhythms and metric modulations, Johnston creates music of unified and luminous beauty. The master Indian musician Pandit Pran Nath, on hearing a tape of the work, understands immediately the tuning and tells Johnston the music is like the "voices of angels."

This year, at the instigation of Lejaren Hiller, he is guest composer at State University of New York at Buffalo. He receives a grant from the University of Illinois Research Board to purchase the Scalatron, an electronic organ capable of extended just intonation: the instrument resides in his office for many years.

1974 Johnston's scores begin to be published by Smith Publications in Baltimore, Maryland, which remains his principal publisher from this time onward. He studies the work of Joseph Campbell, whose *The Masks of God* makes a profound impression.

1975, January Lectures at the University of California, San Diego, on Harry Partch, who had died the previous September; the lecture is transcribed and is subsequently published as "The Corporealism of Harry Partch." Johnston's *In Memory, Harry Partch* is performed at a National Association of Schools of Music convention in San Diego. Receives a research grant from the Graduate College Research Board of the University of Illinois for the collection of biographical data and materials about Partch and a research grant from the Center for Music Experiment at the University of California, San Diego. Also this year he composes *Songs of Innocence,* settings of Blake for soprano and four instruments.

1976 Composes the semi-improvised work *Visions and Spels* on Native American texts, which he performs (as vocalist) with a vocal group in Urbana; the work is later released on CRI Records. On March 15, his fiftieth birthday, *String Quartet no. 3* is performed in a pairing with *String Quartet no. 4* under the title *Crossings* by the Concord Quartet at Alice Tully Hall, Lincoln Center, New York.

1977 Guest composer–lecturer at Yale University, Connecticut, and Dartmouth College, New Hampshire. Participates in the International Conference on Microtonal Music at Webster College, St. Louis, Missouri. Lectures about Harry Partch in Yugoslavia, West Germany, Scotland, and England. Randall Shinn's article "Ben Johnston's Fourth String Quartet," the most extended analytical article on his music to that time, appears in *Perspectives of New Music* (Spring–Summer 1977).

1978 Spends much time this year and next conducting, together with the young musicologist Thomas McGeary, an oral history project on Harry Partch, and this project forms a substantial part of the Harry Partch Archive, which Johnston establishes at the University of Illinois Music Library.

At the National Meeting of the American Society of University Composers at the University of Illinois he presents "Rational Structure in Music," a new substantial theoretical paper first given two years previously and published in the *American Society of University Composers Proceedings.* This paper outlines the concept of *lattices* as models of the tuning "spaces" of extended just intonation systems, a concept he has been developing throughout the 1970s. The compositions of this year, notably the *Suite for Microtonal Piano, Two Sonnets of Shakespeare* for bass-baritone/countertenor and ensemble and the *Duo for two violins,* all take extended just intonation well beyond the point reached by Harry Partch.

Guest composer and award winner at the ISCM American Music Festival in New York City and guest composer at the Warsaw Autumn Festival, Warsaw, Poland.

1979 Composes *String Quartet no. 5,* originally at the suggestion of the Concord Quartet, but the work is not premiered until 1983 (by the Tremont Quartet). A set of variations on the Appalachian hymn "Lonesome Valley," it uses 13–limit just intonation and makes the most extreme tuning demands of any of his pieces to date. Also composes *Diversion* for eleven instruments.

1980 Completes *String Quartet no. 6,* an 11–limit work based on the Schoenbergian principle of continuous melody. It is premiered by the New World Quartet in 1983 and recorded by them for CRI Records. Composes *Sonnets of Desolation* for the Swingle Singers, setting poems by Gerard Manley Hopkins, and *Twelve Partials* for flute and microtonal piano for the flautist Ruben Lopez-Perez. Becomes a member of the Executive Board of the American Music Center.

1981 Lectures in the summer in Bonn; in Hamburg, for György Ligeti's class; and at IRCAM in Paris, where he presents "Rational Structure in Music" and the young pianist Deborah Richards plays the *Sonata for Microtonal Piano.* Composes a *Trio* for clarinet, violin, and cello.

1983 Retires from full-time teaching at the University of Illinois and is appointed emeritus professor.

1984 Completes *String Quartet no. 7* in a complex 13–limit tuning on commission from the Concord Quartet, but the work is not performed. Becomes a member of the Review Board for the Fromm Foundation. Teaches briefly as guest professor at Northwestern University in Evanston, Illinois. Attends the Zen Center in Chicago.

1986 Publication of Heidi Von Gunden's *The Music of Ben Johnston* (Metuchen, NJ: Scarecrow Press), the first monograph devoted to his music. Composes *String Quartet no. 8,* which is premiered by the

Kronos Quartet at Kennedy Center in Washington, D.C., in 1988 in a concert consisting of his second, fourth, and eighth quartets.

1987 Composes *Songs of Loss,* settings of John Donne for tenor and string orchestra.

After thirty-six years in Illinois, Johnston moves with his wife Betty to Rocky Mount, North Carolina. The move away from Illinois provokes mixed feelings: a concern that any further career developments may not be possible (he has no institutional attachment of any kind), and, in contrast, a feeling of great relief—"not only a retirement but a liberation."

He joins the Tar River Chorus and sings bass with them for about a decade, and serves on the Board of the Tar River Chorus and Orchestra. He makes arrangements of jazz standards for string quartet in just intonation (*Set for Billie Holiday, Concentrate on You,* and *Revised Standards*) and composes *Journeys,* a choral-orchestral work written on commission for the Governor's Awards Ceremony in Springfield, Illinois, in memory of the patron Paul Fromm.

1988 The summer sees the completion of the *Symphony in A* for the Tar River Symphony Orchestra in North Carolina and of *String Quartet no. 9,* which is premiered and recorded by the Stanford Quartet. Both works consciously evoke earlier classical idioms as part of a new emphasis that becomes increasingly apparent in Johnston's music of these years, and which he discusses in a "Position Paper" published in *Perspectives of New Music:* that of exploring how European music might have developed had it been freed of the constraints of equal temperament. This is a form of musical revisionism, distinct in technique and intent from the neoclassicism of his earlier work.

1989 Completes the song cycle *Calamity Jane to Her Daughter* for soprano and small ensemble, which is premiered by Dora Ohrenstein in New York to great acclaim. A recording is released on CRI.

1990 Completes the *Chamber Symphony* for small orchestra, premiered in Richmond, Virginia, by the ensemble Currents.

1991 Compositions this year include a *Sextet* for flute and strings, commissioned by the ISCM and premiered at Columbia University in New York; *Legacy* for soprano and violin, setting passages from letters from Wilford Leach, who had died a few years previously; and *Ma Mie qui Danse,* a song cycle for voice and microtonal piano juxtaposing poems by Emily Dickinson with texts "dictated" by Johnston's two-year-old granddaughter Mie Inouye into her father's voice-interactive computer.

1993 New World Records in New York releases *Ponder Nothing,* a CD of Johnston's chamber and vocal works from the 1950s and 1980s, in performances by Music Amici. Composes *Progression* for string bass, for the bassist Robert Black, and a percussion ensemble work, *Sleep and Waking,* for the percussionist Ron George, who builds and tunes instruments especially for the piece.

1994 At the suggestion of the Kronos Quartet, Johnston makes arrangements for string quartet of works by Harry Partch. He first undertakes Partch's *Two Studies on Ancient Greek Scales* and then *Barstow* (the latter for voice and string quartet). Both works are performed and recorded by Kronos (*Barstow* with Johnston himself as vocal soloist), but they meet with strong resistance from Partch's heir, Danlee Mitchell, and others, for their supposed betrayal of authentic Partch performance practice. These criticisms do not deter Johnston and Kronos from undertaking a bigger project, an arrangement of Partch's *U.S. Highball,* premiered in 1997.

1995 Completes *String Quartet no. 10* and, later in the year, arranges *Calamity Jane to Her Daughter* for voice and string quartet.

By this time Johnston's religious life has undergone change and he no longer adheres to the Roman Catholic faith. He practices meditation and reads regularly in religious/spiritual literature. He feels an increasing determination to point his music even more definitely in this direction, regarding his music as a manifestation of his spiritual convictions.

1997 Koch International releases a CD of the piano works *Saint Joan,* the *Sonata for Microtonal Piano,* and the *Suite for Microtonal Piano* performed by Phillip Bush. Completes *Invocation* for soprano and chamber orchestra, which is premiered in Cleveland, Ohio, in May 1998 by Cheryl Marshall with the Cleveland Chamber Symphony, conducted by Edwin London.

1999 Completes several works for the New Century Saxophone Quartet, on a commission from the National Endowment for the Arts: a "meditation piece," *Nightreach;* a set of variations on the British folk song "O Waly, Waly"; and two sets of arrangements from the first two volumes of piano music by G. I. Gurdjieff and Thomas De Hartmann. Also composes *Octet* for the ensemble Music Amici and the song cycle *The Tavern* for voice and microtonal guitar for John Schneider.

2000 Serves on the committee to choose the Alpert Award–winning composer in Santa Monica. Travels to Cleveland, Ohio, to prepare *Songs of Loss* for recording and concert, with the Cleveland Chamber Orchestra conducted by Edwin London. Attends the premiere in New York of *Nightreach* and three arrangements of piano pieces by Gurdjieff and De Hartmann by the New Century Saxophone Quartet. Lectures at William and Mary College in Williamsburg, Virginia, his undergraduate alma mater.

2002 A new string quartet named the Kepler Quartet, comprising four players from Present Music in Milwaukee led by Eric Segnitz, comes together to perform and record all ten of Johnston's string quartets. Segnitz enlists the help of Andreas Stefik, a young guitarist and composer who has been studying privately with Johnston, to make microtonally exact MIDI realizations for the Kepler Quartet to use in preparing performances and recordings.

2003 *Carmilla* is revived by La MaMa in New York. Nonesuch Records releases a recording of Johnston's arrangement of Partch's *U.S. Highball,* performed by David Barron and the Kronos Quartet.

PART I

ON MUSIC THEORY

AESTHETIC THEORY; PHILOSOPHICAL BACKGROUND FOR MATHEMATICAL THEORY; MUSICAL BACKGROUND FOR APPLICATION OF MATHEMATICAL THEORY

1959–60

I. AESTHETIC THEORY

Beginning with the four physical characteristics of musical tone (pitch, timbre, duration, loudness), it is possible to develop an aesthetically well-grounded theory of music as a complex of rhythmic phenomena perceived at different rates of speed.

Suzanne Langer (in *Feeling and Form*) regards music as evocative of the subjective experience of time. This characterization of time is achieved through the interplay of various levels of rhythmic organization. The subjective experience of time is not simply an undifferentiated duration, but a duration characterized by moods or *states,* or perhaps by *events* involving changing states. The only difference between these two aspects is that in the perception of a duration as a subjective state, the events composing it are relatively undifferentiated.

Langer has described a rhythmic phenomenon as wave-like in its basic nature: as composed of events which follow on one another in such a way that the end of one prepares the beginning of the next. This description can be taken as a definition of what, in this context, is meant by *events.* In one aspect any event is like any other: each builds up a tension to a peak, after which there is a recession of tension, which is the gathering of tension for the next event. Events may differ widely in content, and also in durational proportions, but they may also recur almost identically, as in all periodic phenomena.

In music, duration is commonly organized into such event patterns as motives, phrases, sections, movements, etc. The metric pattern of recurring accents (a function of loudness and duration) is frequently periodic but not necessarily so. When not regular enough to create a periodicity of longer durational events, meter will often be found to be based upon a more rapid periodicity of duration grouped in accent patterns of irregular length. Occasionally this aspect of rhythm is almost entirely absent, and timing is based on events of a nonmetric character (not involving a continuity of accent patterns).

Pitch and timbre are largely used to characterize *states* in music. The event structure of pitch is microrhythmic (as is, therefore, that of timbre). The periodicity of pitch is perceived on a perceptual level greatly different in velocity from that of metric rhythm. The speed is vastly beyond our capacity to count, yet we are capable of an extremely sensitive degree of accuracy in recognizing analogous pitch relationships, which is to say similar ratios of vibration.[1]

Noise, usually said to lack pitch, can be viewed as a complex sound insufficiently periodic in behavior, or changing its pitch relationships too rapidly, or involving periodic relationships too complex to be perceived as pitch. Timbre, a function of pitch and loudness too subtle and/or too complex to be analyzed by ear into its pitch components, is a property of noise as well as tone. Thus, in dealing with noise, we are dealing with a phenomenon either less highly organized than pitch or else organized to a degree of complexity not analyzable by ear into simpler components. To relate noise to tone it would be necessary to subject the noise to a pitch analysis to reveal its tonal components, much as timbre can be analyzed, or else to increase its degree of organization to the point where this becomes possible. Even the differentiation by loudness and timbre into distinguishable sounds is a degree of organization, though nonperiodic.

To summarize: there are in music three possible levels of rhythmic organization, each of which is perceived in a distinctly different manner. These are: (1) the level of phrasing and sectioning, including, at one extreme, motivic construction and, at the other, the overall formal "architecture" of an extended composition; (2) the level of metrical rhythm, having to do with accent grouping and motor response (what is usually meant by "rhythm"); and (3) the level of pitch and timbre, involving microrhythmic phenomena, and the whole question of tonal relationships in music.

The musical purpose of this inquiry is to examine the time phenomenon of pitch quantitatively, for the purpose of discovering a more fruitful orientation to the problems of pitch organization than that commonly in use in music. A second purpose emerges in the development of mathematical problems necessitated by the quantitative basis of the investigation. A third possible purpose might be the application of the resulting theory to other areas.

II. PHILOSOPHICAL BACKGROUND FOR MATHEMATICAL THEORY

A recurring phenomenon is described as cyclic. Time is measured in cycles. All vibratory phenomena are cyclically perceived.

The only definition possible of *equality* of durations is in terms of measurement by cycles. There is no *absolute* way to determine the equality or nonequality of durations. The recognition of cyclic recurrence in any phenomenon depends upon the perception of the recurrence of *analogous patterns* of phenomena during its continuance. Thus the only method of determining the relative amounts of duration in these recurrent patterns is by using a more rapid series of cycles to measure them. This entails the fact of accumulation by multiples if we deal with cycles which turn out to be of equal duration when measured by other cycles. This makes possible the use of multiplication and division rather than addition and subtraction, rendering the use of the ratio scale a more legitimate (more accurate) device than the use of the interval scale, which is relevant and legitimate when only one series of cycles is under consideration.[2]

A common use of ratios is their application to a scale basically of the interval type, by considering the cycles created by taking every *n*th term of the interval series, thus transforming it into a ratio scale. In the case of ordinary chronometric time measurement, this is in fact the method used. In the case of natural cycles used in measuring time, however, the cycles given in nature (e.g., rotations of the earth, revolutions of the earth around the sun and of the moon around the earth) are not rationally commensurable (i.e., the day cycles, for example, do not fit an integral number of times into the year cycle, so that a compensation of one extra day must be made every fourth year).

Thus two contrasting uses of cyclic measurement of time are currently operative. In the case of chronometric time measurement, once the scale has been made into a ratio scale by the consideration of interrelated cycles, the problem of subdivision of the shortest cycle of time is handled in an exactly reciprocal manner as the compounding of several cycles to make a longer cycle. The number of subdivisions is thus arbitrary and gratuitous, as is the length of any given cycle.

Contrastingly, in the case of "natural" cyclic time measurement, the relative durations of the cycles are empirically given. The incommensurability of these cycles introduces a necessity for constantly compensating for the increment present at the points of near coincidence of any two cyclic series. This can be done either by adding all the increment to every *n*th cycle of the more rapid series, or by dividing up the increment into *n* equal parts, and adding one part to each of *n* rapid cycles found integrally within each of the slower cycles. In order to achieve any semblance of commensurability between such cycles, the problem of artificial "equal" division of some cycle or portion of a cycle has to be solved. This is a device proper to artificial chronometric measurement and possible only by means of it.

Implied in what has been said is the observation that the natural cycles of time are measurable in terms of a ratio scale rather than those of an interval scale. If cyclic repetitions are viewed as being numbered, not intervallically (1, 2, 3, 4, 5, etc.) as an arithmetic series, but cyclically (1, 2, 4, 8, 16, etc., or 1, 3, 9, 27, 81, etc.) as a geometric series, then "equal" subdivision of any cycle becomes a logarithmic derivation (e.g., to "divide" the period between 3 and 9 of the second above-mentioned series into 5 "equal" parts, one must multiply 3, five times successively, by the fifth root of 6 since all "addition," in ratio scales, is multiplication and all "subtraction" is division, so that "multiplication" becomes a process of raising to powers and "division" one of extracting roots).

That the application of the ratio scale interpretation of the numerical series to cyclic phenomena could be productive of a number of fruitful observations is one of the possible indications of this inquiry. The inquiry will be conducted along lines suggested directly by problems of musical theory, however, with parallel applications suggested or implied merely. The manner in which simultaneously progressing series of cycles (bearing definite numerical relationships to each other) mutually subdivide each other, though not with "equal" intervals, will be demonstrated mathematically and applied to music. This method will be shown to yield the derivation of various musical scales and other basic tonal relationships.

III. MUSICAL BACKGROUND FOR APPLICATION OF MATHEMATICAL THEORY

Musical tone is cyclic perception of the vibratory phenomenon of sound. Pitch relations are perceptions of relative velocities of vibration cycles. The resultant rhythmic patterns of these cyclic velocities constitute harmonic intervals which are expressible mathematically as ratios of vibrations. The simpler a ratio, the more consonant the interval, because the period of the resultant rhythm of the two velocities is shorter and less complex.[3] If a ratio closely approximates a much simpler relationship, the discrepancy is not easily perceived unless the duration of the interval is sufficiently long and the loudness of the tones sufficiently constant to allow perception of the rather long and complex resultant. (E.g., 81/64 is easily mistaken for 80/64 if the tones are not held sufficiently long and evenly.)[4]

Tonal hearing is based upon perceptual understanding of the degree of consonance implied by the contextual relationships of the intervals used. In general the more complex (dissonant) intervals are either understood as distortions of simpler ones or as compounds of simpler intervals.

Since the phenomenon of pitch is a cyclic one, and since the mathematical expression of intervals is as ratios, the use of a ratio scale is necessary for proper analysis of tonal relationships. This means that intervals must be multiplied and divided rather than added and subtracted. The common occidental view of the musical scale is that it is an interval scale composed of equal intervals arrived at by subdividing the "natural" cycle of octaves, based upon the interval ratio 2/1.

The octave ratio is so fundamental that pitches standing in this relation to each other are given the same name and are felt to be in a sense the same pitch in different "registers." The interval of the octave is fundamental in all music, and all intervals greater than an octave are usually considered as basically the same as the intervals obtained by "subtracting" as many octaves as possible, thus reducing them to intervals smaller than an octave (dividing the pitch ratio by 2/1 as many times as possible without lowering it past the pitch of the lower tone: e.g., 3/1 is reduced to 3/2, since all ratios greater than 2/1 are treated in the manner described).

The next-simplest interval to the octave (2/1) is the fifth (3/2), which can also be used cyclically. When the 2/1 series and the 3/2 series are combined, there is a near coincidence of pitches after seven octaves (or after twelve fifths). The increment (caused by the fifth series yielding a slightly larger interval after twelve cycles than the octave series yields after seven cycles) is the ratio (312/219, or 531441/524288, an interval of 23.5 cents, the "Pythagorean comma"). It is the adjustment of these cycles, by "subtracting" from each 3/2 of the twelve intervals of the series the irrational value that is the twelfth root of the comma, so that the "sum" of these twelve distorted fifths will coincide exactly with the "sum" of seven octaves. This adjustment, the "twelve-tone temperament" of European musical tradition, is usually described as dividing the octave into twelve equal intervals, each one of which is equal to the twelfth root of 2—certainly a simpler description, but one which does not explain why twelve divisions of the octave are adopted rather than some other number.

A system of pitches is organized cyclically by measuring off each interval from the previous one by some given ratio, usually a simple one; but in almost all cases any such cyclic series is then arranged within the octave, subdividing it into smaller intervals. These intervals are then expressed *syntonically* by computing the ratio of each tone to one given *tonic* (fundamental tone).

European music actually uses not merely the 2/1 and 3/2 cycles, by implication, but also the 5/4 cycle, to a more limited extent. The purpose of temperament is to fix the absolute pitch of any given scale tone in relation to others in use, instead of allowing each scale tone a *region* of pitch, its exact pitch in any instance depending upon its harmonic involvements in a given musical context. Variable pitch regions for each scale tone would be necessary to replace the approximations currently in use with accurate ratio expressions of the tonal function of each pitch.

The majority of musical scale patterns actually in use, in various cultural traditions, are not exhaustive systems of cyclically derived pitch relations but more selective patterns extracted from these complex cyclic series. Such is the case in all modal systems of monophonic music, where all tones of the mode are constantly related to the tonic. Thus also heterophonic systems of musical composition such as the Balinese use a constant and invariable selection of pitches. But European music, with its polyphonic and harmonic heritage, has developed a tradition of usage which at a certain point of its development (at the end of the Renaissance) came to be known as *tonality.* This usage can be shown to be implicit in the basic techniques of polyphonic music almost from its inception. It is this tradition which involves the implication for each scale tone of variable pitch depending upon tonal context. The need to solve this problem was the cause of the adoption of temperament. The subsequent development of extended modulation and chromaticism only intensified a tendency already fully developed in the European musical tradition.

NOTES

1. [Ed.: By "analogous pitch relationships" Johnston refers to our experience of perceiving, for example, the interval 5/4 (the just major third) as being the same "ratio of vibration," and thus the same interval, regardless of its actual frequencies (i.e., whether it is low or high in the auditory spectrum).]

2. [Ed.: The concept of interval scales and ratio scales, introduced in this early paper, is given a fuller and more detailed treatment in "Scalar Order as a Compositional Resource."]

3. [Ed.: The implied definition of *consonance* given here—"the simpler a ratio the more consonant the interval"—is consistent throughout Johnston's writings but is only one of several definitions that have been proposed, historically, to explain the phenomenon of consonance and dissonance. A lucid discussion of this subject is to be found in James Tenney, *A History of "Consonance" and "Dissonance"* (see bibliography).]

4. The only distinction commonly noticeable in such cases is the secondary phenomenon of beats (alternate interference and reinforcement of vibrations during the resultant period), which can be heard as a vibrato-like tremolo in the interval or in some cases as subjectively perceived "resultant tones." Beats are more rapid the more dissonant the tones.

SCALAR ORDER AS A COMPOSITIONAL RESOURCE

1962–63

When listening to music we hear changing sound qualities in rhythmic patterns which create an illusion of growth. Most people hear music most readily as rhythmic gesture. Their musical present moment is the beat, the bar, the phrase (or the equivalents of these in less traditional music).

Tone qualities, noise textures, and pitch combinations make up the musical "objects" which are composed into rhythmic gestures. These different kinds of phenomenal gestalts are, physically speaking, different modes of vibration. Qualities and relationships of sounds are our way of perceiving great numbers of tiny events (vibrations) on a molecular scale. We cannot hear these individual events, but we can easily detect order in the patterns they make.[1]

The rhythmic gestures composed of these qualities and relationships are in turn composed into larger patterns. These larger contexts are not directly perceptible. Memory reconstructs images of them once we have heard them. Even as we listen to a musical composition for the first time, expectations can grow in us which result from an intuitive grasp of the larger design patterns of the music. The act of musical composition relates the order and pattern of sound vibrations to the order and pattern of musical shapes of larger duration. A composer makes the two interdependent by means of his construction and deployment of musical order on the scale of ordinary rhythmic perception.[2]

When we listen for *practical* purposes, we identify objects and actions by their sounds. This recognition depends upon a recognition of similar patterns of sound vibration. To listen *musically* is to turn one's attention to details of the sound patterns and to interrelations of these patterns on different time scales. For everyday needs we usually need only to compare the similarity or difference of sounds or at most to classify them loosely in terms of their qualities; for aesthetic purposes we need to understand relationships more precisely. We need as a basis an intuitive grasp of more sophisticated systems of relationship. The depth of musical understanding depends upon the ability to hear orderly relationships and upon the precision of interrelationships implicit in the various kinds of scalar order used to organize the sounds.

S. S. Stevens presents four kinds of scales of measurement: nominal, ordinal, interval, and ratio.[3] A nominal scale is a collection of equivalent and interchangeable items. An ordinal scale is a collection which is rank-ordered in terms of some attribute. An interval scale is a rank-ordered collection in which the intervals of difference between items are equal. A ratio scale is a rank-ordered collection in which the items are related by exact ratios. A meaningful conception of zero value of the attribute in question is necessary before such a scale can be formed. Each of these scales includes all of the measurement possibilities of its predecessors, plus one more. "Thus an interval scale can be erected only provided we have an operation for determining equality of intervals, for determining greater or less, and for determining equality (not greater and not less). To these operations must be added a method for ascertaining equality of ratios if a ratio scale is to be achieved" (Stevens, *Handbook of Experimental Psychology*).

The assignment of letters to thematic sections in traditional musical analysis (e.g., ABA, ABACABA, etc.) is an example of analysis by nominal scale. We are here concerned with the determination of *same* and *different*. The conventional use of dynamic markings in music (*pp, p, mp, mf, f, ff*) is an example of ordering by ordinal scale, since it is in practice very difficult to decide what an "equal increment" of loudness is, and in musical scores all that is usually implied by *mf* is that it is louder than *mp* and not so loud as *f*. The *melodic* use of pitch (rather precisely stepped contours of pitch variation) is an example of ordering by interval scale. So also is the establishment of a regular metrical *beat* (recurring equal durations). The *harmonic* use of pitch (carefully tuned simultaneous pitch combinations) is an example of ratio scale ordering, as is, in general, the practice of tuning by ear.

The application made in this paper of Stevens's scale types is based upon musical usage rather than upon controlled psychophysical experiments. The assumption has been that much is to be gained by exploring the nature of the audible order employed in musical composition, from the dual viewpoint of traditional conceptions of musical order and of psychoacoustical theory. Perhaps this and other similar investigations may suggest new lines of inquiry which can be undertaken by psychoacousticians. Certainly, it can add to the understanding of musicians to apply to their field discoveries in this related discipline.

If a system of scalar order can be grasped intuitively, patterns easy to remember can be composed by rearranging it. The psychological tension between a particular scalar order and the pattern imposed upon it by composition stimulates attention, memory, and interest. The interrelation of many such patterns stimulates associations: memories and images having similar patterns. Whether I experience these associations as sensory images, as emotional affects, or as abstract patterns, the music has *meaning* because of them.[4]

A pitch scale is a complex system of ordered relationships. It is not merely one kind of scalar order but a combination of two different kinds: melodic and harmonic scalar order.[5] I can make patterns of melody or harmony by using pitches according to rules of composition which are based upon rearranging these two kinds of scalar order. I may choose not to use both kinds of pitch order, or even not to use either kind. But the order systems possible for pitches are greatly more refined than those possible for non-pitches, because the physical patterns of vibration that make up pitch are much more orderly. With pitched sounds, the possibility for interrelation is perceptibly more precise and more varied.

An extreme case of non-pitched sound is *noise*. If the vibrations of a sound have no discoverable recurrence of pattern, then the sound is classed as a noise. I can classify noises as similar and different, or compare them in terms of some sound quality such as loudness, "texture," or general pitch region. For more elaborate comparisons and relationships between sounds, I need to perceive a regularity of vibration pattern. Pitch provides this: a regular periodic pattern dominates a pitched sound. If this pattern is too simply repetitive, the sound is not only "artificial" sounding but also more difficult to relate to other sounds.[6] Most musical tones have a harmonious complexity. Acoustically, pitches are tempos of vibration. A *harmonious* sound is caused by an ensemble of tempos of vibration which measure off simple proportions of duration. Harmoniousness, or consonance, is the experience of simple proportionality in vibration patterns, whether of a single complex sound or of combinations of simultaneous sounds.[7]

Almost all cultures intuitively divide the pitch continuum into *octaves*. An octave, acoustically speaking, is the relation between a given tempo of vibrations and the tempo which is *double* or *half* of it (mathematically speaking, in the ratio 2:1). Tones an octave apart seem, apparently independently of cultural conditioning, the "same" tone transposed to different pitch levels. For this reason, music uses the octave cyclically, as the basis of scale formation.

Octaves are then divided by a scale of smaller intervals. The two conflicting criteria which condition this are simplicity and symmetry: that is, a preference for simplicity or consonance of harmonic pitch ratios, and a preference for dividing melodic intervals symmetrically, into "equal" smaller intervals.

Melodically, the pitch dimension is a linear succession of octaves, each internally subdivided into smaller intervals which we speak of adding and subtracting. But this view of pitch offers no explanation of the common harmonic experience of a gradual scale of consonance and dissonance. Listening harmonically to pitch intervals we are actually comparing tempos of vibration. Thus what we commonly call "adding" adjacent intervals is, in acoustics, multiplying their vibration ratios, and subtracting them is dividing their ratios. When we "divide" an interval into "equal" smaller intervals, we seek a smaller ratio which, when multiplied by itself a given number of times, equals the larger ratio: that is, we are extracting roots. This "division" produces "irrational" pitch ratios which seem dissonant or *out of tune* when compared to near equivalents which are simple ratios. (This procedure is the basis of equal temperament.)

Harmonic listening is too easy and too basic to be ignored, even in purely melodic music. Yet melodic preference for equal scale intervals is also strong. If a scale is derived harmonically, it must consist of intervals whose melodic sizes differ by what seems a negligible amount. What seems negligible depends mostly upon relative interval sizes but also upon cultural conditioning and upon "how good an ear" an individual listener has.

Different cultures have evolved different solutions to this problem. Western European music has evolved a melodic scale of twelve "equal" intervals per octave. This pitch distribution originated from a rationally derived scale. Historically, equal temperament (which is a melodic equalization of the scale intervals) gradually gained general acceptance during the eighteenth century, because it facilitated instrumental design and performance, particularly of keyboard instruments.[8] The selection of *twelve* notes per octave is due to the nature of rationally derived scales and to musical practices resulting from their use (cf. a thorough discussion of pitch ratio scales, below). Rational scales with other numbers per octave exist. The western European seven-tone and twelve-tone scales simply reflect a melodic preference for intervals approximately the size of "whole and half steps."

A sensitive musical performer tends naturally to play harmonically in tune except where instrumental design makes this impossible, as with keyboard and percussion instruments, or where such refinements are not audible due to speed or complexity. Playing harmonically in tune (listening to other performers to adjust the pitch) results in small melodic interval displacements. While these variations in the pitch of theoretically "fixed" scale tones are melodically insignificant, their use reduces equal temperament to an abstraction. It is these precisions, adjusted *by ear,* which give clarity and resonance to simultaneously sounding tone combinations. Actual use of equal temperament in performance obscures this clarity by introducing a blurring element of dissonance into every musical interval except the octave.

A more harmful, if more subtle, effect of temperament is the inadequate conceptual model it presents to the composer. So long as musical usages are based upon a rational scale, the out-of-tuneness of temperament is a largely negligible consideration. But when many of these usages become outmoded and a search for new principles of musical organization begins, as has happened in the twentieth century, the one-sided model provided by equal temperament becomes a serious but largely unrecognized limitation. When musical organization based upon a linear (interval) scale replaces that based upon a ratio scale, there is a net loss in audible intelligibility. For instance, rhythmic order based merely upon additive equal increments is less "organic" than that based also upon the division of wholes into proportional parts, though in a given instance either kind of order may predominate. Ordering procedures based simply upon contour (that is, upon a fluctuation of greater and less without regard even for equal increments), and those based merely upon a perception of similarity and difference are still less integrative.[9]

The functioning of a higher level of organization does not negate the importance of lower levels, but subordinates them. If a lower level of scalar order is intended to predominate, then the tendency of a listener to read a higher level of order into the composition must be counteracted. For example, if *general* pitch contour is the main design element, then *precise* melodic interval patterns should be relatively hard to measure by ear. Similarly, if the composer intends simultaneous interval combinations to be heard as "vertical melody," then it should be made hard to hear these combinations as chords subordinated to roots: blend should be underemphasized, rhythmic displacement, timbre contrast, and dissonance perhaps emphasized. Many of the devices (especially the prohibitions) of serial and "atonal" composition are explicable most satisfactorily by reference to this principle. Linear ordering (by intervallic contour, motif, serial pattern) lends itself to much more elaborate systems than does merely qualitative ordering, but even these often have too little mnemonic power to integrate complex music so that its interrelations on a large time scale are evident to the ear. Proportional organization has much more mnemonic power than this, but where pitch is concerned, western European tradition so far offers too limited a horizon on this front to satisfy contemporary aesthetic needs. This horizon is extensible, however. The rational pitch scale offers a hierarchy of relationships from the simplest (identity) to complexities beyond the analytical capabilities of human hearing. We are operating nowhere near these psychoacoustic limits at present. It is possible, with sufficient determination and effort, to extend rational intelligibility much farther into complex relationships.[10]

The most significant difference between proportional and linear organization is that the former makes possible the relation of all musical sounds to a *common reference point.* A group of pitches may be very complexly related to each other, but often all of them can be simply related to another pitch, which need not even be present. Thus, the missing pitch is strongly *implied* by the complex group. The *root* of a chord, the *tonic* of a tonality, the *principal tonality* of a modulating movement are all examples of this principle.

Before embarking upon a detailed derivation of pitch ratio scales, let us examine a parallel formal situation. Not only pitches but durations are proportionally relatable. A pattern of melodic rhythm has a "beat" if all its note durations approximate simple proportions and can, therefore, be related to a single tempo.[11] In a contrapuntal ensemble, it may be that no two melodic rhythms ever coincide and that each melody has a different tempo and beat grouping. But in the ensemble, a single beat may emerge, which is the overall tempo, the common denominator of all the different beats of the individual parts. Organization into periodic rhythmic divisions often applies also to beat groupings, to measures, and to phrases.

Durational proportionality exists on a note-to-note scale, on a beat-to-beat scale (since beats can have proportions other than equality), on a measure-to-measure scale, on a phrase-to-phrase scale, on a section-to-section scale, and even on a movement-to-movement scale. The composer's problem is to provide a variety of durations whose proportions to each other and also to larger durations, of which they are part, are intelligible to a listener. These relationships aid greatly in creating either the sense of a completed whole or else of a significantly uncompleted one. A predominance in rhythm of the simplest ratios (equality: 1/1; duple subdivision: 2/1; and triple subdivision: 3/1; or multiples of these) makes for ease in intelligibility. So long as all proportions are referred to unity, there is a single tempo. Secondary durational proportions (such as 3/2 or 4/3) create overall tempos both slower and faster than their member durations. These can result either from additive durations or from different simultaneous subdivisions of the same whole duration (Figure 1).

A linear scale of tempos exists in practice but is not customarily described as such. Between any two given tempos there can be a scale of gradually accelerated tempos. The normal way to perform such an increase is by graduating "equal" increments of tempo between the two limiting tempos. Except for this technique of *accelerando* and *rallentando,* successive tempos are usually proportional, or at least approximately so. There is no evidence that any perceptible interrelation exists between linear and proportional gradations of tempos. Tempo rubato can be described as fluctuation along this linear tempo scale.

Such an interrelation of linear and proportional relationships is of the essence in dealing with pitch scales, however, where it accounts for the conflict between melodic symmetry and harmonic simplicity. If we begin, in dealing with pitch, with the octave (2/1), cyclically dividing the pitch spectrum, the next question is how to divide each octave.[12] A desire for melodic symmetry suggests a division of the octave into two "equal" intervals. This would be the geometric mean (12). But this interval, the equal-tempered tritone, is

FIGURE 1. The creation of faster and slower common tempos by both addition-based and division-based rhythms.

harmonically extremely dissonant. If, instead, the arithmetic mean is selected, a melodically unequal division into a 3/2 (perfect fifth) and a 4/3 (perfect fourth) results. If this arithmetic division is taken, starting with the upper pitch as well as with the lower, an interval of difference, 9/8 (the diatonic whole step, or major second) results.[13] It separates the two disjunct tetrachords (4/3 intervals) of the octave (Figure 2).

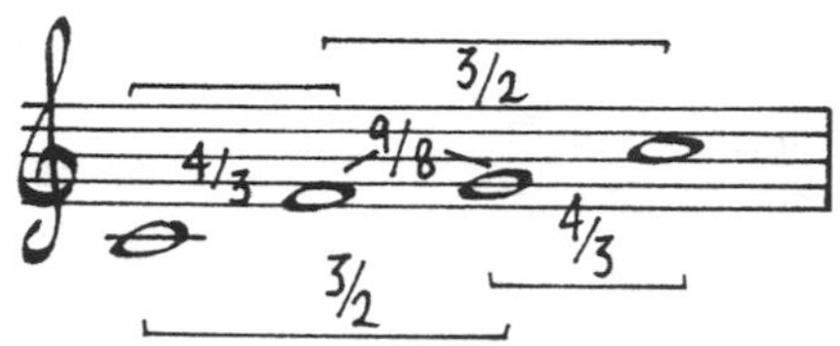

FIGURE 2. The two disjunct tetrachords (4/3 intervals) of the octave separated by the diatonic whole step (9/8).

If the two fifths are divided similarly, a pentatonic scale results (Figure 3).

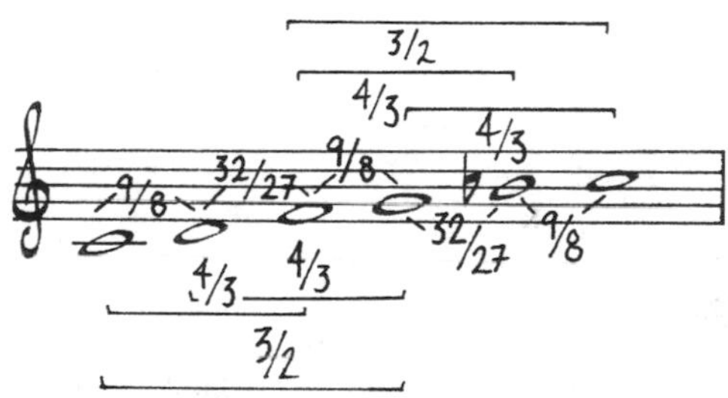

FIGURE 3. Pentatonic scale corresponding to the ratio sequence 1/1–9/8–4/3–3/2–16/9–2/1 (taking C as 1/1).

By the introduction of the new prime number, 3, the "cycle" of fifths as well as that of octaves is implied. If we take the lower pitch as 1/1 and the upper as 2/1, the arithmetic mean is 3/2. If we take the upper pitch as 1/1 and the lower as 1/2, the arithmetic mean is 2/3, which, raised an octave, is 4/3.

If instead the two tetrachords are similarly divided, either of two pentatonic scales results (Figure 4).

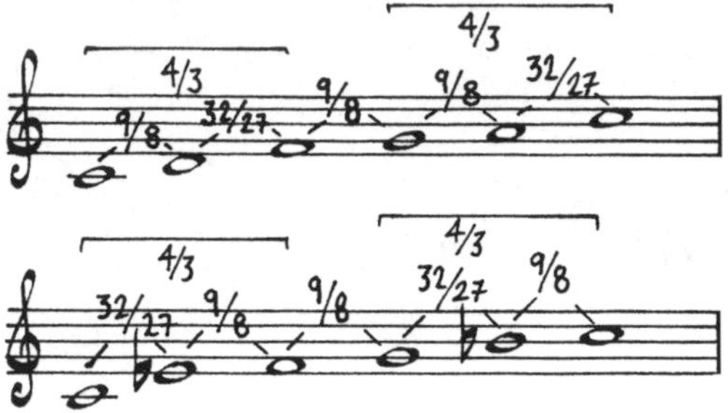

FIGURE 4. Two different pentatonic scales, the upper corresponding to the ratio sequence 1/1–9/8–4/3–3/2–27/16–2/1, the lower to the ratio sequence 1/1–32/27–4/3–3/2–16/9–2/1.

In all these cases the whole step is used to divide the tetrachords. The difference in size between the whole step and the minor third, the diatonic half step (256/243, or $2^8/3^5$), may be considered melodically negligible, in which case a pentatonic scale is melodically adequate. If this interval is considered melodically significant, a seven-tone scale can be derived (Figure 5).

FIGURE 5. Heptatonic scale in Pythagorean tuning, corresponding to the ratio sequence 1/1–9/8–32/27–4/3–3/2–27/16–16/9–2/1.

Scales which are not modes of this same diatonic scale are obtainable by melodically inverting the two 32/27 intervals of a pentatonic scale.

Pythagorean five-tone and seven-tone scales can be shown to be derived from cyclic tuning in perfect fifths (Figures 6 and 7). Each whole step (9/8) can be divided (factored) into a diatonic half step (256/243) and a chromatic half step (2187/2048 or $3^7/2^{11}$). The chromatic half step can be placed either above (as a sharp) or below (as a flat) a diatonic scale tone. The enharmonic

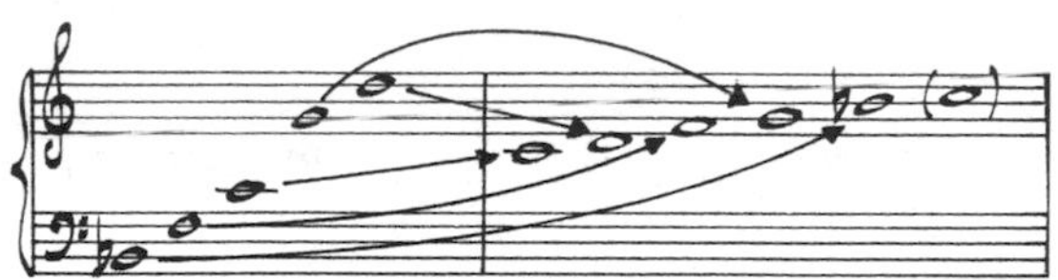

FIGURE 6. Pythagorean pentatonic scale, derived from cyclic tuning in perfect fifths; the scale in the second measure is, in ratios starting from C, 1/1–9/8–4/3–3/2–16/9–2/1.

FIGURE 7. Pythagorean heptatonic scale, derived from cyclic tuning in perfect fifths; the scale in the second measure is, in ratios starting from C, 1/1–9/8–32/27–4/3–3/2–27/16–16/9–2/1.

interval between these two alternative possibilities is called the Pythagorean comma. The Pythagorean twelve-tone scale can also be derived from cyclic tuning in perfect fifths (Figure 8). If cyclic tuning in perfect fifths is extended further, enharmonic equivalents are multiplied until we obtain a fifty-three-tone scale, all but eleven of whose adjacent intervals are Pythagorean commas (Figure 9).

The Pythagorean scale provides a very limited amount of consonance. Only its perfect octaves, its fifths and fourths, and its major seconds and minor sevenths have no near interval equivalents which are more consonant. If the first principles used in dividing the octave are extended further, a system of scales analogous to the Pythagorean system is possible, providing many near interval equivalents which yield a much greater number of consonances.

If the arithmetic mean is taken as before, this time within the perfect fifth (3/2), the major and the minor thirds in "just intonation" (5/4 and 6/5)

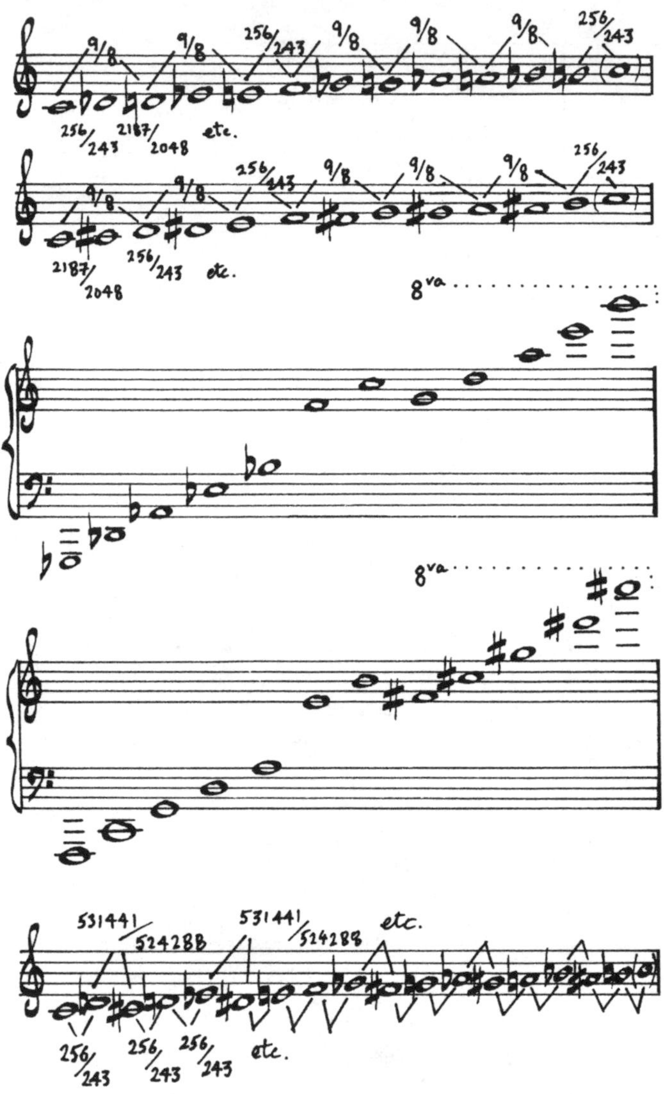

FIGURE 8. Two different possible derivations by cyclic tuning in perfect fifths of the twelve-tone (chromatic) scale; and, on the bottom staff, their combination into a seventeen-tone enharmonic scale composed entirely of diatonic half steps (256/243) and enharmonic Pythagorean commas (531441/524288 or 312/219).

FIGURE 9. Derivation of a fifty-three-tone enharmonic scale by cyclic tuning in perfect fifths and perfect fourths (first five lines). The next-to-last tone of the scale is higher than the last tone by approximately one-fourth of a Pythagorean comma. The second part of the figure shows the scale (except for this penultimate tone) in ascending order of pitch (bottom six lines). The derivation is carried out as far as possible without overlapping enharmonic regions.

are obtained. The chromatic half step (25/24) is the interval of difference (Figure 10).

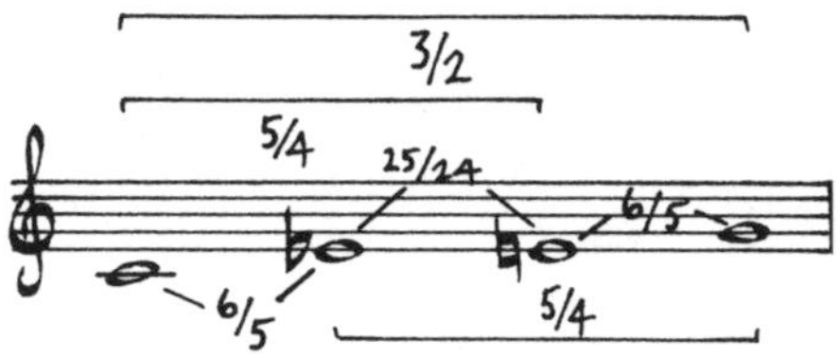

FIGURE 10. Major and minor thirds in just intonation (respectively 5/4 and 6/5). In ratios, the sequence of pitches from C is 1/1–6/5–5/4–3/2.

Similarly, if the arithmetic mean is taken within the major third, the two major whole tones of just intonation, sometimes called the major and the minor tone (9/8 and 10/9), are obtained. The diatonic comma or comma of Didymus (81/80) is the interval of difference (Figure 11).[14]

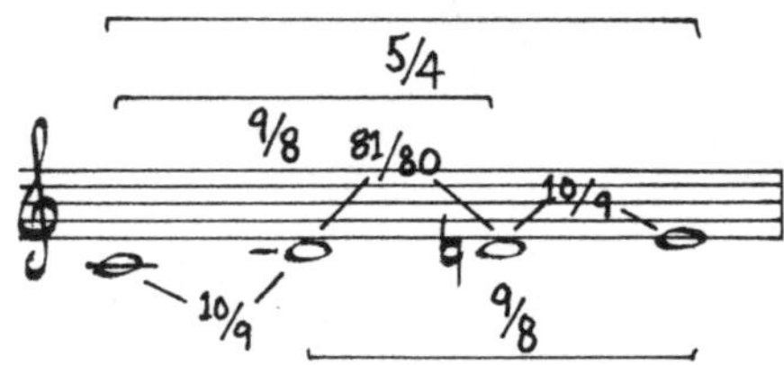

FIGURE 11. The comma of Didymus, also known as the syntonic comma (81/80), between the two different whole tones in just intonation. In ratios, the sequence of pitches from C is 1/1–10/9–9/8–5/4.

Just tuning, involving ratios based on prime numbers 1, 2, 3, and 5 (rather than on 1, 2, and 3 only, as in Pythagorean tuning), does not readily yield pentatonic scales but is extremely useful for heptatonic scales (Figure 12).

The harmonic basis of just intonation is the major third (4:5:6, which expresses the arithmetic division of the perfect fifth). The inversion of this is the minor triad. The arithmetic division within major thirds can be shown to result from triadic tuning (Figures 13 and 14).

FIGURE 12. An octave, divided into two tetrachords separated by a whole tone (9/8); the arithmetic mean of two perfect fifths, yielding major triads on C (1/1–5/4–3/2) and F (4/3–5/3–2/1); and the arithmetic mean of the major third, with two different whole tones, first 9/8 then 10/9. In the just major scale the internal structure of the two tetrachords is not identical: the order of the two whole tones is reversed in the second tetrachord (as can be seen from the last two measures of this figure).

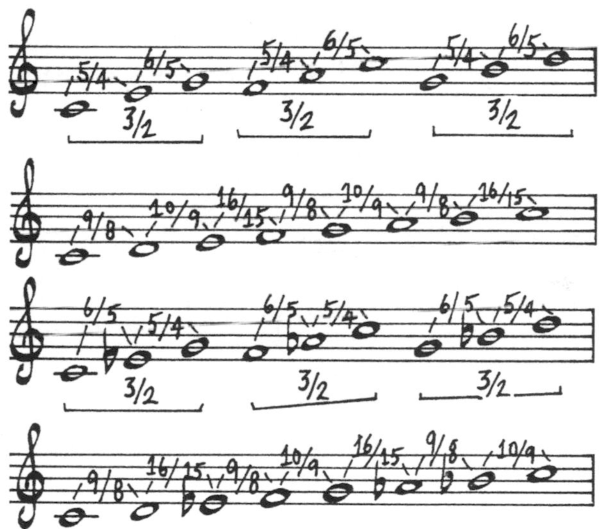

FIGURE 13. Triadic derivation of the seven-tone major and minor scales in just intonation. These two scales are modally related: that is, they have the same interval pattern, but from different starting points (in the case of the major, C, and of the minor, E♭).

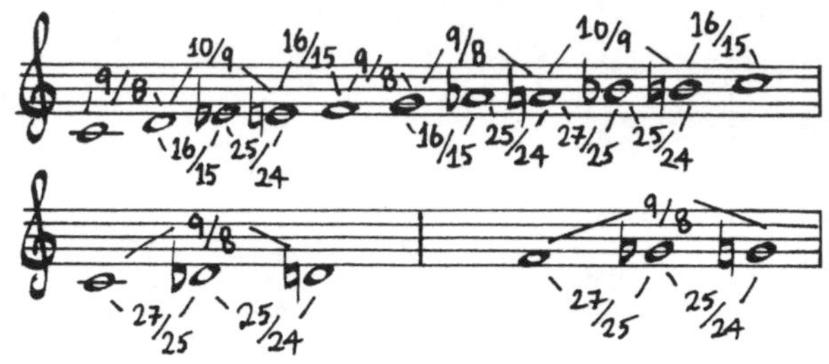

FIGURE 14. Mixture of the two scales derived in Figure 13, giving ten tones to the octave. The two undivided whole tones can be divided in a manner analogous to the other whole tones, as shown on the lower staff, which would in combination yield a twelve-tone (chromatic) scale.

A just intonation twelve-tone scale can be based upon a mixture of these two diatonic scales (Figure 15).[15]

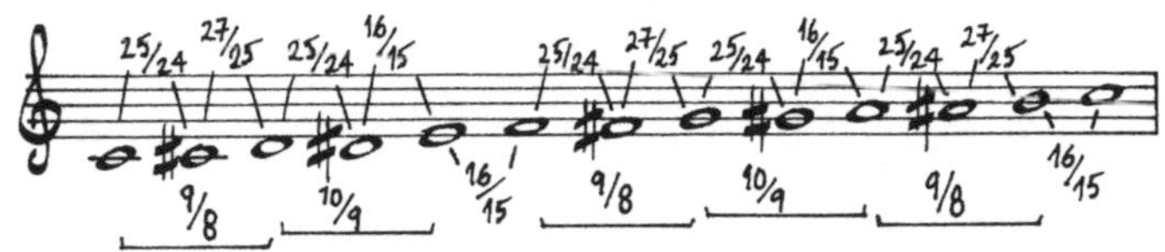

FIGURE 15. A twelve-tone scale in just intonation.

If these two scales are combined, enharmonic scales result. Between E and F, either E♯ or F♭ can be added. Similarly, between B and C, either B♯ or C♭ can be added (Figure 16).

If an interlocking system of triads is set up, such that every tone participates in four different capacities (as root, as fifth, as major third, and as minor third), and if this derivation is stopped at points where the twelve chromatic regions of the octave would overlap, a fifty-three-tone scale results[16] (Figures 17 and 18).

The ratio 81/80 and 2048/2025 are very close to the same size, but 3125/3072 is almost twice as large. If we add to the scale one of each of these pairs: D♭♭ or C♯-, D♭+ or Cx, E♭♭+ or D♯-, E♭+ or Dx-, F♭+ or E♯-, G♭♭ or F♯-, G♭+ or Fx, A♭♭+ or G♯-, A♭+ or Gx-, B♭♭ or A♯-, B♭+ or Ax, and C♭+ or B♯-, a sixty-five-tone scale of

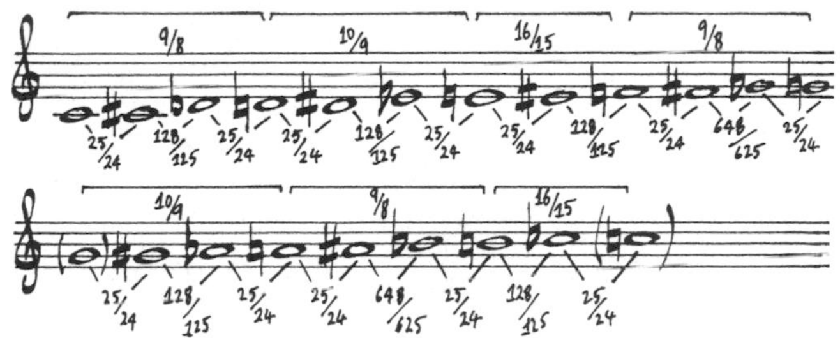

FIGURE 16. Mixture of the scales derived in Figures 14 and 15 into an enharmonic nineteen-tone scale. The 648/625 and 128/125 intervals are approximately equal to quartertones. The difference between them is a syntonic comma (81/80), which is the difference in size between the major (9/8) and minor (10/9) whole tones.

almost equal intervals results. Each 3125/3072 is thereby divided into an 81/80 and a 15625/15552, or $5^6/3^5$ multiplied by 2^6 (which is somewhat larger than half the size of an 81/80). If both of each pair were chosen, the chromatic regions would overlap (see Figure 19). Note that the *diatonic* regions overlap not only because of x's and 𝄫's, but also at the intervals F𝄫, E♯ and C𝄫, B♯. The choice between these alternative notes is clear from the triadic derivation,

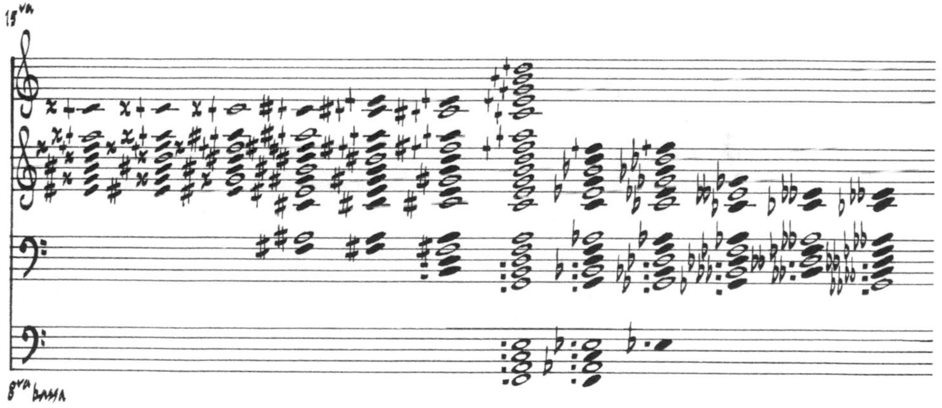

FIGURE 17. Fifty-three-tone scale in just intonation, expressed as a system of interlocking triads. Plus and minus signs indicate the raising or lowering of a pitch by the syntonic comma (81/80).

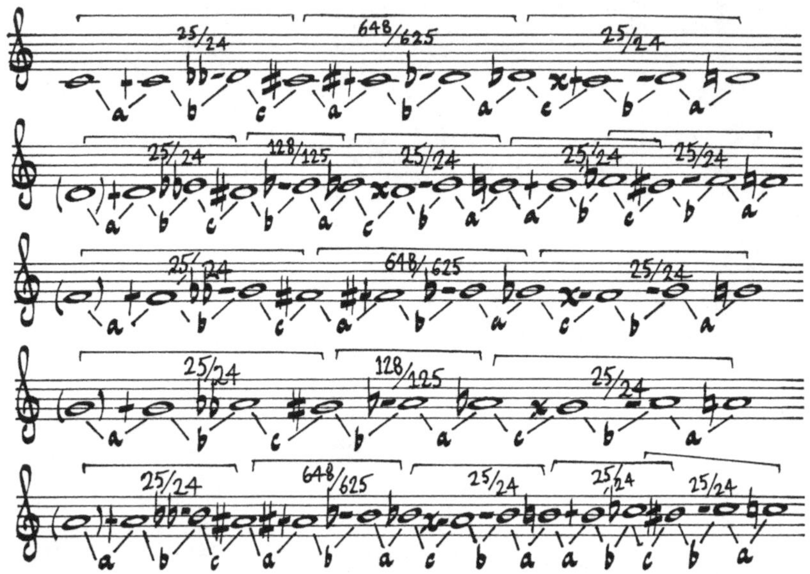

FIGURE 18. Fifty-three-tone scale in just intonation: a = 81/80, b = 2048/2025, c = 3125/3072.

except in the case of the F♭+, E♯- choice and the C♭+, B♯- choice. All the additions to the scale, however, spoil the regularity of the pattern of adjacent intervals within the larger diatonic intervals.

A comparison of these recurrent patterns with the whole- and half-step pattern of the seven-tone diatonic major scale is interesting. If the 9/8 is called A, 10/9 B, and 16/15 C, the seven-tone pattern is ABCABAC, where A and B are near the same size and C is not. Within the 9/8, if the 81/80 is called A, the 2048/2025 B, and the 3125/3072 C, the pattern is ABCABACBA, where A and B are near the same size and C is not. Within the 10/9, the pattern is ABCBACBA. Within the 16/15, it is ABCBA. In all cases, the C intervals are the first place where chromatic regional overlapping occurs in further derivation (Figure 19).

The triadic system of this derivation can theoretically be extended as far as desired, but the linear (melodic) intervals of adjacent notes of the resulting scale, at points where chromatic regions overlap, are at the largest only 2 cents wide. This interval (32805/32768) is the difference in size between the

C C+ Dbb- C# C#+ Db- Db Cx+ D- D D+ Ebb D#
1/1 81/80 128/125 25/24 135/128 16/15 27/25 1125/1024 10/9 9/8 729/640 144/125 75/64
ab a abbc ab a ab abbc a ab ab a abbc

(D#) Eb- Eb Dx E- E E+ Fb E# F- F F+ Gbb- F# F#+
(75/64) 32/27 6/5 625/512 100/81 5/4 81/64 32/25 125/96 320/243 4/3 27/20 512/375 25/18 45/32
a ab abbc a ab ab a abbc a ab ab a abbc ab

(F#+) Gb- Gb Fx+ G- G G+ Abb G# Ab- Ab Gx A- A A+
(45/32) 64/45 36/25 375/256 40/27 3/2 243/160 192/125 25/16 128/81 8/5 625/384 400/243 5/3 27/16
a ab abbc a ab ab a abbc a ab abbc a ab ab

(A+) Bbb- A# A#+ Bb- Bb Ax+ B- B B+ Cb B# C- C
(27/16) 128/75 125/72 225/128 16/9 9/5 1875/1024 30/27 15/8 243/128 48/25 125/64 160/81 2/1
a abbc ab a ab abbc a ab ab a abbc a ab

FIGURE 19. The fifty-three-tone just intonation scale as shown in Figure 18 with pitches expressed both by letter names (with accidentals) and by ratios. Intervals between adjacent pitches are denoted by lower case letters, where a = 2048/2025, b = 32805/32768, and c = 1600000/1574323. Accidentals have precise values: ♯ = x25/24, ♭ = x24/25, + = x81/80, – = x80/81. Note particularly the seven-tone diatonic scale tones, which are the only tones with ab (81/80) intervals on each side. Also note that the abbc (3125/3072) intervals delineate the borderlines between the twelve pitch regions.

81/80 and the 2048/2025. Its size is impractically close to the psychoacoustical threshold of linear pitch discrimination. By contrast, in most cases discrepancy of 2 cents in a *harmonically* played perfect octave, fifth, or fourth is easy to hear. Melodic intervals as small as diatonic commas (as in the fifty-three- or even the sixty-five-tone scale) are not difficult to discriminate.

Each prime number used in deriving a harmonic scale contributes to a characteristic psychoacoustical meaning. One to one is the relationship of identity; two to one, of recurrence or repetition. Three to one (or three to two) contributes polarity: a sense of gravity, of right-side-up and upside-down (e.g., the root–fifth relationship and the tonic–dominant relationship).[17] Five, in combination with the other prime relationships, contributes major–minor coloration.

In a manner analogous to the scale derivations discussed, other prime numbers can be introduced into rational pitch scales.[18] There would be no aesthetic point in introducing a new prime into harmonic usage unless its psychoacoustical meaning were quite distinct. To hazard a guess based on a *consonant* use of the dominant seventh chord (tuned in the ratio 4:5:6:7), prime number 7 may be said to contribute a sense of centralized instability, suspending the dominant–tonic (3 to 2) polarity. Its harmonic use provides a consonant tritone (7/5), a consonant minor seventh (7/4), and a consonant major second (8/7). The intervals 7/6 and 8/7 are the two arithmetic means of the perfect fourth (4/3) (derived as before).

Interval-scale thinking emphasizes symmetry of design. The harmonic and tonal meaning of symmetrical pitch structures is *ambiguity.* Chordally they produce either a sense of multiple root possibilities or of no satisfactory root possibility. Tonally they cause either a sense of several possible tonics or of no adequate tonic.

Ratio-scale thinking, on the contrary, emphasizes a hierarchical subordination of details to the whole or to common reference points. The harmonic and tonal meaning of proportional pitch structures is clarity and a sense of direction. Symmetrically repeating rational pitch intervals does not bring about a circular return to the original pitch, but progressively changing spiral approximations of it (cf. the "circle" of fifths; also the process of harmonic displacement by diatonic comma in triadic music). So long as music is designed by principles based upon ratio-scale order, distortion of its pitch proportions, whether by equal temperament or simply by imperfect performance, does not destroy its psychological effect of "progression" and change. Music designed by symmetrical principles systematically based upon an equal-interval scale (e.g., serial organization of pitch) does tend to destroy this effect.

In our time, the resources of ratio-scale pitch organization have come to seem exhausted and outmoded. Thus there has been a deliberate reliance upon less sophisticated organizational techniques: interval-scale, ordinal-scale, and nominal-scale methods of creating musical order. This research has produced, by implication, new orders of complexity in ratio-scale ordering, since we cannot entirely suspend the action of our intelligences on this level so as to attend exclusively to other kinds of order. In practice, we already use much more complex pitch ratios than are provided in traditional tonality. In order to make intelligible this implied complexity, an extension of ratio-scale techniques is needed. Typically, theory lags behind practice.

The "emancipation of the dissonance" did not solve the problem of harmonic freedom.[19] While rendering permanently obsolete the old black-and-white division into consonant and dissonant, it in no sense abolished the tonal hierarchy. On the contrary, it has made more urgent than ever the need for more basic principles of tonal order to integrate ever more complex pitch situations. Serial technique is only an interim solution. Its contributions to musical intelligibility and expressivity need to be subsumed under a larger and less restrictive whole.

Traditional tonality depends upon ratio-scale ordering: upon harmonic relations between chord roots, tonal centers, and principal tonics. Likewise, classical metricality and symmetrical phrasing depend upon proportional use of durations and tempos. Both these techniques are capable of very great extensions beyond present usage, while still remaining audibly intelligible and expressive.[20] There is no need to sacrifice the linear ordering methods of serial technique in order to achieve this. What must be given up is the limitation of equal temperament. The ordering potential of ratio scales includes that of linear scales, but not vice versa.

The adoption of a microtonal ratio scale does not imply a return to modal monophony. Such a scale is equally applicable to harmonic polyphony. The fact that our instruments are designed for equal temperament is not an insuperable obstacle. Except in the case of keyboard and percussion instruments with fixed tuning, sufficient control of the pitch by the performer can at present be expected. The new possibilities opened up by electronic instruments and electronic synthesis already begin to provide more flexible control of pitch than has hitherto been possible.

Great complexity in the materials of art calls for a compositional technique with maximum organizing power. To establish connection between the known and rational and familiar, on the one hand, and the unknown and irrational and unpredictable on the other, requires subjecting them to the same measure. Proportionality is such a common measure, if we bear in mind the modifying principles of variation and approximation. It is not incompatible with other modes of organization, such as serial ordering. It applies with equal effectiveness to formal, rhythmic, and pitch organization. It can be realized best by ear, in the case of pitch; by kinesthetic perception, in the case of rhythm; and by intuitive timing, in the case of formal divisions. Yet it is capable of intellectual formulation and manipulation. Most important of all, such a technique reestablishes a connection which has been broken, a connection with ancient and worldwide traditions of aesthetic order.

NOTES

1. Cf. Henri Bergson's *Matter and Memory* (authorized translation by Nancy Margaret Paul and W. Scott Palmer), p. 275: "In reality there is no one rhythm of duration; it is possible to imagine many different rhythms which, slower or faster, measure the degree of tension or relaxation of different kinds of consciousness, and thereby fix their respective places in the scale of being." Thus Bergson indicates the intimate connection between tempo and quality, or to be more accurate, between varying rates of development and the building up and relaxing of psychological tensions.

2. For some of the ideas on rhythm and tempo in this paper I am indebted to Robert Erickson's "Time Relations," a lecture given at the 1962 Illinois Wesleyan Symposium in Bloomington, Illinois.

3. S. S. Stevens, "On the Theory of Scales of Measurement." See also Stevens, "Mathematics, Measurement, and Psychophysics," in *Handbook of Experimental Psychology.*

4. For a thorough but one-sided discussion of the emotional imagery of music, cf. Suzanne Langer's *Feeling and Form.* [Ed.: This paragraph of "Scalar Order" was the focus of criticism by Ben Boretz in his "Metavarations" part 1 (originally published in *Perspectives of New Music* 8 no. 1, 23–29). Although in 1970 Johnston responded in print to Boretz's criticisms ("A Small Demur," *Perspectives of New Music* 9 no. 1 (1970), 155–56), he does not think it important to include the exchange in the present volume.]

5. Stevens, "On the Theory of Scales of Measurement." Stevens's *interval* and *ratio* scale types correspond to *melodic* and *harmonic* scales.

6. Analogously, a jigsaw puzzle, if all the pieces are congruent and regularly shaped, is much harder to put together than if less similar shapes are used.

7. Cf. Helmholtz, *On the Sensations of Tone.*

8. Cf. James Murray Barbour, *Tuning and Temperament.*

9. Cf. Stevens, "On the Theory of Scales of Measurement." Stevens's *nominal* and *rank order* scales are here in question.

10. To cite a single occidental example: Harry Partch's *Genesis of a Music.*

11. Cf. Erickson, op. cit.

12. Cf. Alain Daniélou, *Traité de Musicologie Comparée.* (Cf. also Daniélou, *An Introduction to the Theory of Musical Scales.*) Daniélou's approach to the subject of pitch scales is ethnic and historical. The present discussion is concerned only peripherally with those aspects of the subject. The scale derivations given below are not based upon a scholarly reconstruction of theories of Pythagoras, King Fang, ancient Sanskrit writers, or, for that matter, any other theorists. The application of these patterns of order in diverse musical systems of other times and places is a matter of great interest and importance, but it does not fall within the scope of the present inquiry. An attempt has been made, however, to lay the groundwork for an application of

these scales within our own musical tradition and to present them in the perspective of a more general theory of scalar order. Divergences between this presentation of scale theory and Daniélou's are traceable mainly to a difference of cultural musical context. Although he is attempting to transcend any specific musical tradition in his *Traité,* and although in it he has considerably moderated the harsh criticism of occidental musical traditions which he included in his earlier book on the same subject, Daniélou's sympathies are obviously with Asiatic musical traditions and practices. This writer, on the contrary, while making some of the same criticisms, views the occidental tradition as potentially a great one, but with serious flaws which can nevertheless perhaps be corrected both in theory and practice.

13. All tones are transposed by octave into the same pitch range.

14. The + sign means raised by a diatonic comma; the – sign means lowered by that interval.

15. The flat (♭) lowers by a chromatic half step (25/24); the sharp (♯) raises by the same interval.

16. Derivation of a just intonation fifty-three-tone enharmonic scale, showing the diatonic and chromatic scales contained within it. The pattern of adjacent intervals within each major whole tone, that within each minor whole tone, and that within each diatonic semitone is the same. There are only three kinds of adjacent intervals: 81/80, the diatonic comma; 2048/2025, which is a diatonic comma smaller than 128/125, the smaller of the two enharmonic intervals; and 3125/3072, which separates the twelve chromatic regions of the octave.

17. A pitch carries with it by implication, if not in acoustical fact, a system of overtones standing in the relation of a harmonic series to the fundamental (taken as unity). Thus if two pitches have the relation 3:1, the entire harmonic series of the higher pitch is contained in that of the lower one, while the reverse is not the case. Hence, the perfect fifth is traditionally consonant, while the perfect fourth is not. Hence also, dominant to tonic is a restful progression, since the new root contains the harmonic series of the former one entirely.

18. Cf. Partch, op. cit.

19. Arnold Schoenberg's term: cf. *Style and Idea.*

20. The mature works of Elliott Carter, to cite one outstanding example, extend rhythmic technique in this direction.

PROPORTIONALITY AND EXPANDED MUSICAL PITCH RELATIONS

1965

Before considering the problem of expanded pitch resources in contemporary composition of music, I shall contrast two different traditions for the realization of precise pitch relations in performance.

The first tradition may be represented by the practice of Gregorian chant.[1] In plainchant the melody is unaccompanied, or monophonic. Thus the relations of melodic tones to each other are the only intervals used. The perfect fifth and perfect fourth and the interval of difference between them, the major second, are the basis of pitch choice. The particular distribution of the seconds within the melodic distances of fifths and fourths, and the choice of cadence points, determine the "mode" of the music. All major seconds are always the same size, as are all minor seconds, since these are the remainder intervals when the largest possible whole number of major seconds subdivides either a perfect fifth or a perfect fourth.[2] All other intervals are likewise fixed in size, but are much more difficult to sing in tune.

A contrasting type of pitch usage is illustrated in East Indian monophonic musical practice.[3] This monophony "opposes" a line of fluctuating pitch against a fixed pitch, or drone. A specific emotional expression is achieved by means of a particular set of intervals measured against the drone. The "harmonic" relation of melodic pitches to the drone is primary to this expression, whereas the intervallic relations between melodic tones are less important. Possible relations to the drone are classified as consonant, dissonant, and out-of-tune—i.e., not an ingredient in the conventional expression of a particular *rasa* (emotional content).[4] There is a legitimate but subordinate use of "out-of-tuneness" in the practice of inflecting or "teasing" certain pitches microtonally. In other words, simpler intervals are deliberately distorted, for expressive reasons, into out-of-tune approximations of themselves. Viewed from the aspect of pitch alone, a performance consists of an improvised exploration of the interval content of a given set of preselected pitch relations. The number of expressively distinct interval relations used in different improvisations based upon *ragas* of widely ranging emotional expression is relatively very large. The number selected in a specific *raga,* for a particular *rasa,* is quite small.

It is immediately evident that Gregorian chant is a much simpler and also a much more restricted system of pitch order than East Indian monophony. First, the absence of a harmonic point of reference, the drone, makes the problem of singing in tune less crucial but more difficult to achieve. Even if we suppose that the final of the mode were kept in the aural imagination as a point of pitch reference, analogous to a "tonic," the monophonic idiom would preclude any very precise tuning by ear. Second, the ritual use of plainchant imposes a conscious and intentional restriction upon the emotional content of its expression.

Without any attempt to connect these examples historically, I shall contrast them to two contemporary usages of pitch which seem to be significantly analogous to them. The most obvious point of difference is that while the above examples are monophonic, the ones which follow are polyphonic. A more important difference is that the pitch vocabulary of the polyphony is significantly expanded beyond that of the corresponding monophonic examples.

Twelve-tone practice presupposes a pitch system where any octave is divisible into twelve half steps, all of equal size. Thus all intervals which subdivide into the same number of half steps are exactly the same size. There are, therefore, twelve different interval sizes to learn, not counting intervals expanded by the inclusion of one or more octaves. Musical usage assumes the ability to locate, given any tone, a second tone at a distance of any one of these intervals from the first tone. The twelve notes are, to quote Schoenberg, "related only to each other." Whether a linear (melodic) or a vertical (harmonic) interval is used, the method of finding the pitch is the same: to measure a known interval distance above or below another pitch in the context. There is not, for either performer or listener, a fixed point of pitch reference, as there is in tonal music.

As a tonic with its associated scale is analogous to a drone with its associated pitch intervals, so a piece of music without a tonic is analogous to a monophonic piece without a drone. It follows that the process of finding pitches in performing twelve-tone music is intellectually similar to that of finding pitches in plainchant.

To find the polyphonic analogy which I wish to suggest as a parallel to East Indian monophony, it will be necessary to examine some loopholes in contemporary twelve-tone musical practice and theory. For I do not propose traditional diatonic or even chromatic tonality as an alternative adequate to the expressive needs of present-day music.

In traditional triadic music, the functional meaning of an interval usually determines perfectly clearly its exact tuning. But in most twelve-tone music, the pitch organization obliterates this clarity. Triadic organization is usually irrelevant to such music, and there is seldom any alternative harmonic system clearly enough defined to imply unambiguous tuning. An unhappy result of this can be observed in playing such music in strict equal-tempered intonation, as, for instance, on an organ. A certain grayness results, a certain lack of variety in interval color, which is observable neither in tonal music played on the same instrument, nor in the *same music, really well played* upon instruments capable of pitch variation in each tone.[5] In other words, the muddy sound just mentioned can be cleared up by careful tuning *by ear.* Obviously something more than twelve fixed tones per octave is involved here. This something operates entirely outside twelve-tone organization, which deals only with twelve chromatic interval sizes and patterns of these. More accurately, it deals in patterns made from classes of intervals. What happens when a good string quartet, for instance, performs a nontonal work, especially if the piece contains a large proportion of simultaneous pitch combinations, is an inflection of each pitch according to its context. Thus, in practice, there are not twelve *notes* but twelve *pitch regions* per octave. Twelve-tone organization leaves this refinement unspecified, and twelve-tone theory has no place for it.

There are two musical reasons for such refinement of pitch discrimination. One is to gain clarity and focus in the pitch relations. The other is to distort what is simple for expressive purposes. But "what is simple," in this connection, is not the *average* interval size provided by equal temperament, but the most consonant interval within the size class called for, the exact tuning determined by the pitch context. Distortion is meaningful only if the norm is clearly evident from the harmonic involvements of the interval. Its nature may even be determined by ambiguities of harmonic function. Triadic function is only one among many possible systems of harmony, though its relatively high degree of consonance makes it one of the easiest to understand by ear. Given any such system, a norm of tuning is implied, and this may be used as a foil for inflected (distorted) intervals. The two motivations for inflecting pitch are thus mutually dependent.

From this standpoint the question of consonance and dissonance, gaining a new refinement of meaning, becomes once again relevant. What Schoenberg called "the emancipation of the dissonance" was actually an extension of the range of what we mean by "consonance."[6] Dissonance still functions outside this expanded sphere of consonance. The relativity of consonance and dissonance is obsolete only if you choose to ignore it.

The need for such a tension is reflected in much post-Schoenbergian music in the contrast between tones with easily identifiable pitch, and complex timbres and noises. A complex timbre may approach noise more or less nearly. It is not difficult to establish a spectrum of timbral changes from sine tones (with only a single pitch) to white noise (with completely random fluctuation of all possible pitches). But to deal rationally with such raw materials, at least a stepped contouring of this spectrum would be necessary. And for forming musical order from relations between complex timbres approaching noise, as distinct from using them coloristically, it would be necessary to establish analogous relationships between pairs of such tones. The effort to achieve this kind of musical order is in its earliest stages at present. Most music which extensively uses very complex tones relies still upon other means of ordering, such as rhythmic structure, serial ordering, and much more familiar techniques for ordering tones which have an easily perceived predominant pitch. Aleatoric and random selection are at present among the principal means for exploring unfamiliar sound materials.

If we are not to be faced eventually with the splitting apart of the art of music into an art of pitched sounds and a separate art of non-pitched sounds, we must greatly refine our understanding of pitch relationships. Such understanding must be not only theoretical (intellectual) but also practical (audible by ear in actual musical compositions). The relations between component pitches of very complex sounds include a great many with which our traditional pitch system is powerless to deal. We are, therefore, accustomed to hear, more and more, relationships which demand a more comprehensive vocabulary of pitch intervals than we now have.

Merely to multiply the number of available pitches, as with quartertones or any other system of temperament with more than twelve notes per octave, complicates the problem of harmonic organization without helping to solve it. Rather than to enlarge the pitch vocabulary by such artificial means, it is more desirable to expand the order we already perceive in it by means which we already understand in practice. To achieve this, two procedures are necessary. First, one must learn to tune precisely, *by ear,* a definite number of harmonic pitch relations, from which a great variety of others can be derived. For the harmonic awareness necessary to play triadic music accurately in tune (a degree of sophistication which can be generally expected), only three such intervals are needed, the octave, the perfect fifth, and the just major third. From combining and comparing these, all the other common intervals used in triadic music result, and in addition many variants of these which are microtonally related to them. These same three intervals are the basis of the entire East Indian pitch system, different as it is in so many ways from the modern Western musical tradition.[7]

Second, one needs a grasp of the microtonal scale pattern formed by adjacent pitches which are inflections of the larger intervals of the twelve- or seven-tone scale. The seven-tone scale still forms the basis of our traditional notation system. In fact, given this diatonic scale tuned in consonant triads, one needs only two different pitch inflections to achieve a microtonal scale the density of which can easily be proliferated to a point where the human ear can no longer discriminate between the resulting pitches.[8] Both of these inflections result naturally from playing in tune by ear, and one of them, the chromatic half step, is already reflected in our notational system. The other, the diatonic (or syntonic) comma, can be represented in notation by a + sign (meaning raise by one comma) and a - sign (meaning lower by one comma).

One way of explaining how the comma results is to point out that when triadically organized music is played so as to sound at its most consonant, two different major seconds result, a larger one, which is the difference in size between a perfect fifth and a perfect fourth, and a smaller one, which is the difference in size between a perfect fourth and a just minor third. For example, if I begin on C and want to find D, the progression C, G, D and the progression C, F, D give two different Ds. The comma is the difference in size between these two C–D intervals. It is about one-fifth the size of a half step (21.5 cents).

The inflection of the comma plays a part in traditional diatonic progressions even though it is not expressed in standard notation. Cyclic displacement by this tiny interval is a passive result of common diatonic chord patterns.[9] Similarly, cyclic displacement by a larger interval, the diesis which is approximately twice the size of the diatonic comma, results from extended chromatic modulation. This is reflected in standard notation by the use of enharmonic equivalents (e.g., the distinction between D♯ and E♭, between C and B♯, between A and B𝄫, etc.).

The use of chains of intervals of the same size is a basic principle of pitch usage. The octave, repeated cyclically in this manner, is the basic interval division of the audible pitch spectrum. The fifth, used in this way, generates the cycle of fifths. Although these two cyclic series are the most important ones, all the simple intervals are used in this way, to form what are sometimes called symmetrical chords or scales (e.g., the "chord of fourths," the augmented triad, the fully diminished seventh, the whole-tone scale, and the chromatic scale).

The most characteristic twentieth-century way of using chromatic pitch structures is in cyclic patterns, whether formed as chords, as scales, as successions of roots or tonics, or as twelve-tone rows (or less numerous row patterns). The simplest cycles, in which only one kind of interval is used, are less common than mixed types, in which two or more different intervals alternate in regular patterns. Due especially to pitch displacement by comma and by enharmonic equivalent, many cycles appear circular. A twelve-tone row beginning with a C, for example, may actually return to B♯ or to D𝄫, or to C- or C+, or to some more complicated combination of these intervals of pitch displacement. The cyclic repetitions of row forms can be so designed as to cause pitch displacement with each successive row form. This displacement itself can be made to follow a cyclic pattern on a larger time scale than that of the row statements. To control this process, the exact size of the intervals of the row forms must be determined unambiguously by the context of notes. The pitch displacements can then be calculated, shown in the notation, and formed into cyclic patterns. Furthermore, locating pitches only by intervals which can be tuned accurately by ear, dissonant intervals which are unfamiliar representatives of interval size classes can be made to occur in the musical texture, not only as distortions produced by melodic inflection, but also as necessary results of the harmonic process. This possibility includes many intervals smaller than half steps, generically called "microtones."

As a performer's relative pitch discrimination becomes more acute, even intervals other than the familiar consonances become part of his expanded vocabulary of intervals. He can learn, for example, after a period of familiarization, to distinguish accurately between triadically generated intervals (particularly seconds, thirds, tritones, sixths, and sevenths) and those of the same size classes produced by the use of "natural" seventh and eleventh intervals, such as occur in the "natural" overtone series. One does not have to look as far as ancient Greek theory or Arabic musical theory and practice to find such pitch relations. The contemporary American composer Harry Partch has been using them in his music for over thirty years.[10]

The main obstacle to learning new intervals by ear is the habit of listening only accurately enough to identify the correct size class. For example, if precise tuning is to result, when there is an interval C–E (a just major third) in the pitch context and an A♭ enters, the performer must decide whether to tune the A♭ to the C or to the E, in which latter case it is actually a G♯ and must be pitched slightly lower than an A♭. Common usage is too careless to make such distinctions audible. In a polyphonic texture it is desirable for each individual performer to know, at least for each harmonically functional tone, precisely to which note in the surrounding context he should adjust his pitch. Triadic music played in this way, with precise interval adjustment, gains enormously in clarity and in richness of interval color. If serial pitch organization is present, its effect is in no way vitiated by the absence of equal-tempered intervals; in fact, the grayness which often characterizes twelve-tone harmony is largely eliminated. Except for keyboard and pitched percussion instruments, the needed flexibility of pitch inflection is at present not prohibitively hard to achieve. It is not necessary to build new wind or string instruments to play music in this way.

So long as the intervals used to find the exact pitch levels are all familiar from traditional music, no extensive unfamiliar ear-training is necessary to make possible a great variety of microtonal intervals. And since the crucial intervals are precisely those which predominate in the pitch texture of triadic music, a single harmonic system includes combinations from the smoothest consonances to dissonances stronger than any possible in twelve-tone equal temperament. Twelve-tone and other types of serial pitch organization can be used in such a pitch system, as *optional* devices of partial or total thematicism. The thematic process is not expected to replace harmonic organization, but instead is freed from this responsibility to adopt a parallel role in the achievement of musical intelligibility. Thus we can avoid two of the most restricting characteristics of twelve-tone music: its banishment of simple consonance and the weakness of its large-scale harmonic logic.

It seems clear that we have long ago moved into a post-tonal period in the history of music. The possibilities of triadic tonality have been worked over for so long a time and in so many ways that the meanings once powerfully conveyed by its musical syntax are blunted and overfamiliar. Just as maxims and proverbs easily become truisms or platitudes through mere repetition, musical styles similarly deteriorate with overuse. Those who have most to do with originating musical meaning, composers, are always the first to notice the deterioration. The contemporary musical scene is now dominated by non-tonal, nontriadic music. Cultural lag has not yet brought audiences, performers, or impresarios to the point where this stylistic shift is manifest; but the willing acceptance of works in the immediately preceding style, neoclassicism, is no longer unusual.

Neoclassicism is like a retrospective summary of the past. In undeniably contemporary idioms it sums up an era of musical history: the tradition of European music since the medieval period. Thus it is a culmination rather than a new beginning. The revolutionary movement which began with atonality now seems to point in the direction of a music not basically pitch-oriented. If the use of pitch as a basis of musical organization is not to fall into eclipse in serious contemporary music, a considerably broadened horizon of possibilities must be explored.

I have felt for years that conventional tonal organization permits one only parody today, whether comic, serious, or unintentional; and parody is ultimately too restricting to be of lasting interest. But I have also felt that twelve-tone method has limited the emotional scope of musical composition rather drastically, and that many of its devices (especially some of the methods of so-called total serialism) are meaningless as audible organizational devices. An often-noted observation—that the musical results of "total organization" and those of "total chance" are not distinguishable without footnotes—indicates clearly that too many of the organizational devices of total organization are not being perceived. Perhaps they cannot be; perhaps time will change that. But I believe that the above-suggested methods supplement serial technique while neither denying its value nor interfering with its effectiveness nor functioning irrelevantly to it. I also believe that proportional organization can more easily do without serial organization than vice versa.

It is time we broke the magic—and vicious—circle created by the supposed polarity of total serialism and total chance. We do not really have to choose between a hair shirt and chaos.

NOTES

1. Cf. David Krahenbuehl and Christopher Schmidt, "On the Development of Musical Systems." This analogy presupposes the scale tuning of medieval plainchant to have been Pythagorean, following a hypothesis independently formed, which accords with that of Krahenbuehl and Schmidt. The theoretical approach adopted in this article is fully consistent with that adopted by these authors.

2. The 9/8 interval, the difference in size between a perfect fourth and a perfect fifth, is the Pythagorean whole tone. The size difference between two such tones and a perfect fourth (256/245) is the Pythagorean semitone.

3. Cf. Alain Daniélou, *Traité de Musicologie Comparée,* 93–122.

4. Cf. Hermann L. F. Helmholtz, *On the Sensations of Tone,* 182ff. The definition of *consonance* herein used is based upon Helmholtz's. Congruency of rates of vibration

between two tones produces reinforcement, heard as blend or consonance. Contrasting rates of vibration produce interference, which is experienced as dissonance. An out-of-tune interval is one which approximates a simpler relationship of which it is assumed to be an inaccurate version.

5. Peter Yates has commented to me, in relation to this question, that "three organists and a pupil of Widor are among the most original composers of modern times, particularly in creating new orchestral ensembles. Bruckner, who revived just intonation in the multiple octave, Ives, Messiaen, and Varèse . . . These composers work, organ style, by adding overtones, rather than Stravinsky style, by differentiating timbres . . ." Yates's basic point seems to me to be the interdependence of timbre with tuning, and the dependence of both upon the balance struck in a given composition between homogeneity and "independence" of "voices" or other sound elements. While this is a valid and important point, I maintain that when the partial relationships which make up a complex tone are *harmonic* (i.e., related in pitch by simple whole-number relationships), the use of *inharmonic* intervals in the simultaneous pitch relations between fundamental pitches results in a *blurring,* the consequence of *near*-congruences of vibrations among the partials. A certain amount of inharmonicity in tones or in tuning is negligible; a little more can be interesting; too much is confusing and "sour." These boundaries shift in different musical contexts and are always hard to delineate. A standardized uniformity in this aspect of sound is in my opinion aesthetically dull or "gray."

6. I am indebted again to Peter Yates for an important clarification: "You should make a clear distinction between Schoenberg's belief that each note of the tone row is an absolute of our musical speech, without any other acoustic or key reference—therefore not to be retuned in just intonation—and his subsequent practice of resuming traditional harmonic relationship or dropping it when he pleased. Slonimsky has shown that the traditional relationship is there all the time; e.g., by dropping the 'acciaccaturas' of Op. 33a."

7. Daniélou, *Traité de Musicologie Comparée.*

8. Cf. Johnston, "Scalar Order as a Compositional Resource."

9. Helmholtz, op. cit., p. 431. The common diatonic progression I, VI, II, V, I, if common tones are kept identical and if all harmonic intervals are tuned in just intonation, will lower the pitch of the tonic by one diatonic comma.

10. Cf. Harry Partch, *Genesis of a Music,* first edition, esp. Part III, "The Resources of Monophony" (pp. 109–251).

MICROTONAL RESOURCES

1969

The term *microtones* denotes musical scale intervals smaller than the semitones of twelve-tone equal temperament. The use of microtones provides so-called neutral intervals and unfamiliar near-equivalents of common intervals as well as the small intervals themselves. Hence, *microtonal* refers to music in which successive or simultaneous pitch relations lie outside twelve-tone equal temperament and outside traditionally used variations of just tuning or unequal temperament.

Microtones and microtonally distinct variations of common intervals have been introduced into Western music in four principal forms: in equal temperament within the octave, in equal temperament within some other interval, in extended just intonation, and as components of noise and other "irrational" pitch elements.

One form of equal temperament, first used in the early twentieth century, employs as a point of departure common twelve-tone equal temperament. Each semitone is divided either into two or four equal parts; or else each tone is divided into three equal parts. This provides so-called quarter, eighth, and sixth tones. Although offering the advantage of including within their compass the standard occidental twelve-tone scale, these microtonal scales otherwise diverge sharply from diatonic tuning, the acoustical basis of traditional Western music. While equal temperament at twelve tones per octave approximates a stage in the diatonic derivation of pitches by just tuning, scales with twenty-four, forty-eight, or thirty-six tones per octave do not have this advantage. Since there are other stages in just tuning at which equal temperament can be applied without gross interval distortion, these numbers of tones (e.g., nineteen tones, thirty-one tones, fifty-three tones) are preferable to multiples of six or twelve.

Composers of the early twentieth century employed such scales for a variety of reasons. For Charles Ives, such scale expansion was a way to get closer to sounds he heard in his environment—for instance, bells. For Béla

Bartók, these scales were a means of approximating eastern European and Asiatic folk usages of pitch. Similarly, Ernest Bloch sought in such tuning an approximation of traditional Hebrew usages. But in the music of these composers, microtones are the exception rather than the rule. Alois Hába, Ivan Wyschnegradsky, Julián Carrillo, and Hans Barth conducted much more systematic researches into the use of microtonal tempered scales. These latter composers, reacting to the post-Romantic breakdown of diatonic tonality, sought a way out of the impasse mainly in an expansion of pitch resources. The possibility of obtaining quarter or eighth tones simply by tuning twelve-tone instruments at pitch distances of quarter or eighth tones was the easiest practical method for getting more notes per octave.

It is also possible to subdivide some interval other than the octave into equal intervals; but before it was feasible to synthesize music electronically, such a procedure was impractical. Since the electronic breakthrough, such scales have occasionally been used (e.g., Karlheinz Stockhausen's *Gesang der Jünglinge;* also Toshiro Mayuzumi and Makoto Moroi's *Variations sur 7*). A systematic catalogue of such scales is being assembled by Józef Patkowski, head of the Experimental Music Studio of Radio Polskie in Warsaw. Perhaps the most extensive use of such scales is in John Cage and Lejaren Hiller's *HPSCHD,* in the magnetic tape components of which the pitches were derived, realized, and composed with the assistance of computers.

Tempered tuning is not acoustically the simplest kind. In just tuning, any interval is tuned so as to eliminate "beating" (the result of vibrations interfering with each other). Just intonation is the easiest to achieve by ear. In this kind of tuning, all intervals have vibration rates related by small whole-number ratios. The larger the integers of the ratio, the greater the dissonance.

One important property of integer ratios, however, creates insoluble problems for conventional fixed-pitch instruments: the octave cannot be subdivided equally by any other just interval, so an equal-interval just scale within an octave is an impossibility. Scales derived by just tuning have sometimes, in the course of history, been tempered so that their just intervals are replaced by evenly spaced ones which fit within the octave cycle. The occidental twelve-tone scale is the best-known example.

Harmonic progressions using scales based on just tuning result in many near-equivalent pitches. For instance, in C major, with just triadic tuning, the A of the subdominant triad is approximately one-fifth of a semitone—a diatonic comma—lower than the A which is the ninth of the dominant triad. Also, the difference between enharmonic equivalents (e.g., G♯ and A♭) is approximately double the size of a comma, or about two-fifths of a semitone. Just tuning produces ever-increasing series of these and other similar microtones.

As mentioned previously, scales derived by just tuning approximate at certain numbers of notes per octave the equal distribution of temperaments. Twelve tones per octave is only one such stage. Certain theorists, accordingly, have proposed temperaments with other numbers of notes than twelve. Two of the best-known such proposals in the twentieth century are Joseph Yasser's (nineteen tones per octave) and Adriaan Fokker's (thirty-one tones per octave), both of which theories show close resemblances to the tripartite but actually untempered division of the whole tone proposed in 1922 by Ferruccio Busoni. There has also been a revival of interest in Gerhardus Mercator's (sixteenth-century) proposed temperament at fifty-three tones per octave. Except for the group of composers associated with Fokker in the Netherlands, not much music has been written using these temperaments, for the obvious reason that both instrument design and performance practice stand in the way.

It is with the use of just tuning that the most extensive recent compositional results with microtones have been achieved. Harry Partch, rejecting all kinds of temperament, has designed and built his own instruments and has composed music for them. Although the number of pitches per octave—forty-three—on his Chromelodeon keyboard has become associated with Partch, each of his instruments has a different finite selection of pitches from the potentially infinite tuning system he uses. By means of just intonation exhaustively using the intervals provided by the first twelve partials of the overtone series, Partch is able to extend his harmonic field as far as he chooses. (Analogously, the modulations possible within the traditional diatonic system can extend infinitely far in either a sharp or a flat direction.)

Lou Harrison, using a similarly derived pitch system, specifies adaptation of conventional instruments to play many pitched just intonations, as does this writer. This is possible because performers have never abandoned just tuning of consonant intervals "by ear." String and wind instruments permit flexible pitch control by the performer, and many fixed-pitch instruments can be retuned as desired.

The music of La Monte Young, rigorously based upon just tuning, is perhaps the purest example of such music in Western art. Young's long sustained, slowly changing harmonies provide optimum chance for precise perception of pitch intervals. Such music, scarcely concerned at all with melodic use of pitch, can hardly be said to be concerned with a "scale," in the conventional meaning of the term. However, its precision is expressible in terms of pitch ratios, which themselves constitute a kind of scale.

The concept of scalar order has been generalized in recent years, as a result of psychophysical research, notably that of S. S. Stevens. Measuring a given domain of perception may require a nominal, an ordinal, an interval, or a ratio scale. A nominal scale distinguishes only *same* and *different.* An ordinal scale also distinguishes *more than* and *less than.* An interval scale distinguishes equal increments of change between greater and less. A ratio scale provides analogous relationships between different scale positions. The most important measurable dimensions of music, pitch and duration, are capable of analysis by both interval and ratio scale. Since these kinds of scalar order provide statistically the highest potential for predictability, the traditional predominance of pitch and rhythm in nearly all the music of "high cultures" up to the twentieth century is understandable. Recent musical preoccupation with less precisely differentiated aspects of sound reflects an interest in freer kinds of scalar order as well as in more organized kinds. Many recent compositions introduce microtones either as components in sounds incorporated together by nominal scale ordering (e.g., the "notes" on Cage's prepared piano) or by ordinal scale ordering (c.f. Christian Wolff's "indeterminate" instructions to performers to select pitches closer together than semitones).

Rhythm measured metrically (by equal time increments) uses only an interval scale. In its proportional aspect as variously used, for instance, in works by Pierre Boulez, Luigi Nono, Stefan Wolpe, Elliott Carter, Henry Weinberg, and the author of this article, it constitutes a ratio scale, thus providing in the time dimension the same infinite expansion from unity as do microtonal pitch ratio scales.

Use of noise and natural speech elements coupled with the use of electronic musical synthesis is rapidly bringing about a kind of music which simultaneously uses nominal, ordinal, interval, and ratio scalar order in various perceptual domains (c.f. works by Stockhausen, Luciano Berio, Kenneth Gaburo, and others). Nominal ordering, as in much indeterminate music, ordinal contouring, as in much "statistical" and stochastic music, interval ordering, as especially in serial composing, and ratio ordering, all play their roles. These techniques have been combined and applied to instrumental music (c.f. especially orchestral works by Iannis Xenakis, Krzysztof Penderecki, György Ligeti, and others). Much recent electronic music similarly combines all types of scalar organization (e.g., Hiller's *Seven Electronic Studies*).

NOTES

[Ed.: Cage's *HPSCHD,* composed in collaboration with Lejaren Hiller Jr. in 1967–69, consists of twenty-minute solos for one to seven amplified harpsichords and tapes for between one and fifty-one monaural tape machines; the performance duration is variable. The tapes each use a different scale, from five divisions of the octave up to fifty-six, omitting the conventional twelve divisions.]

TONALITY REGAINED

1971

It is now possible to say that the concept of tonality has been elucidated and generalized. Using just intonation of various kinds, it can be shown how traditional seven-tone triadic tonality expands to twelve-tone chromaticism and thence to scales of fifteen, nineteen, thirty-one, thirty-four, fifty-three, and sixty-five tones per octave (plus an indefinitely great number of still more numerous scales). Using this system as a model, alternative tonalities based on analogous but different triads, tetrads, pentads, or hexads (or still more numerous basic chords) can be constructed.

To have a tonal system with *n* notes in its basic chord (*n*th-ad), you need *n* prime numbers greater than 1. Normally 2 is the cycling number, since most scales extend to the compass of an octave and repeat their patterns in all octaves so that every note has octave equivalents. It would be theoretically possible to use 3 or any other prime number as the cycling interval. (In the case of 3 as cycling number, scale patterns would extend over the interval of a perfect twelfth, and each note would have twelfth "equivalents.")

Three is normally the *tonal* number when it is included in a system. The interval 3/2 (perfect fifth) provides the relation between tonic and dominant or between subdominant and tonic. Progressions analogous to these are traditionally called *tonal* progressions.

In a traditional triadic system, the prime numbers greater than 1 are 2, 3, and 5. Five (referring to major and minor thirds and sixths) is a *modal* number, traditionally so-called because it effects major–minor coloration. Progressions where the root moves a third or a sixth are called *third-related* (sometimes *tertiary*) progressions.

If the seventh or eleventh partials of the overtone series are introduced, they constitute new *modal* numbers, providing additional coloration in the harmony and the progressions. If any higher primes are present when 3 is not, normally the smallest of these becomes the tonal number. It is not possible to make any prime number the tonal number. In such a case, other primes greater than 2 become modal numbers and effect changes of chord color.

The Pythagorean (also medieval Western and ancient Chinese) system is a diadic system. Its basic chords are perfect fourths and fifths. Strictly speaking such a system provides no modal coloration. Pythagorean thirds and sixths can form triads in a distorted imitation of true triadic harmony, but normally these intervals are considered dissonances, since they are actually distant tonal notes rather than bona fide modal intervals.

In order to express graphically the harmonic relations possible in a given system, one needs an *n*-dimensional lattice of ratios, each ratio representing a note in the system. On each principal axis of the lattice, a particular prime and its powers are compared to powers of the cycling number.

Usable tonal scales are composed of neighboring ratios in a lattice, the ratios rearranged to be in ascending order of magnitude. Each acceptable scale in a system has the same number of discrete adjacency ratios as there are notes in the basic chord, one for each prime number greater than 1. This is one more than the number of axes in the lattice.

A basic major chord consists of a point in the lattice and one point in a positive direction on each of the axes. The parallel minor chord uses the same notes on the tonal axis and one step in a negative direction on the modal axis. This step is taken from the ratio one step farther in a positive direction on the tonal axis than the starting point.[1]

The first set of scales to be derived are diatonic major scales; the second set, parallel diatonic minor scales; the third and last set, chromatic and hyperchromatic scales. The chromatic scale is composed of the mixture of parallel major and minor diatonic scales plus whatever adjacent ratios are necessary to produce an acceptable scale. Hyperchromatic scales involve choosing additional notes in all directions in the lattice, rather than restricting choices in modal directions.

The notation assigns the note names C, D, E, F, G, A, B to the major diatonic scale of the traditional triadic system. The symbols + and - show the raising or lowering of notes by the syntonic comma (81/80), which is about 22 cents in size (approximately a 1/10th tone). Each new prime number introduces a new pair of inflectional ratio symbols. Prime number 7 introduces ∠ and 7, which indicate raising or lowering a pitch by 36/35, or about 49 cents (approximately a quartertone). Prime number 11 introduces up-arrow and down-arrow, ↑ and ↓, which indicate raising or lowering a pitch by 33/32 (somewhat more than a quartertone).[2]

Scalar systems can now be derived by computer, using a program in Fortran IV which was written by Ed Kobrin. An upcoming issue of *Source: Music of the Avant-Garde* will present this program along with all scalar systems involving prime numbers up through 11. The one involving 2, 3, 5, 7, and 11 entails using a four-dimensional lattice. The rules for deriving scalar systems can be understood from a study of the flow chart of this program.

The lattice of the 2, 3, 5 system, given in Figures 20 and 21, yields the scales given in Figure 22. Exactly analogous systems of scales may be obtained with other selections of prime numbers. A number of such systems will appear

9/8		D	
3/2	15/8	G	B
1/1	5/4	C	E
4/3	5/3	F	A

7-tone diatonic major

9/5	9/8	B♭	D
6/5	3/2	E♭	G
8/5	1/1	A♭	C
	4/3		F

7-tone diatonic minor

36/25	9/5	9/8			G♭	B♭	D		
	6/5	3/2	15/8			E♭	G	B	
	8/5	1/1	5/4			A♭	C	E	
		4/3	5/3	25/24			F	A	C♯

12-tone chromatic

FIGURE 20. Lattice representations of diatonic major, minor, and chromatic scales of traditional triadic tonality. Three-limit relationships (i.e., by chains of perfect fifths) are mapped on the vertical axes, 5–limit relationships (i.e., by chains of major thirds) on the horizontal axes.

			243/200	243/160				50625/32768			
				81/80	81/64			16875/16384	54375/32768		
			27/25	27/20	27/16	135/128	675/512	3375/2048	16875/16364	84375/65536	421875/262144
	1152/625	144/125	36/25	9/5	9/8	45/32	225/128	1125/1024	5625/4096	28125/16384	
	768/625	192/125	48/25	6/5	3/2	15/8	75/64	375/256			
		128/125	32/25	8/5	1/1	5/4	25/16	125/64			
	2048/1875	512/375	128/75	16/15	4/3	5/3	25/24	125/96	625/384		
2768/8125	8192/5625	2048/1125	256/225	64/45	16/9	10/9	25/18	125/72			
	32768/16875			258/135	32/27	40/27					
					128/81	160/81					

			E♭+	G+				Ax++			
				C+	E+			Dx+	F♯x++		
			D♭	F+	A+	C♯+	E♯+	Gx+	Bx+	D♯x+	Fxx++
	C♭♭	E♭♭	G♭	B♭	D	F♯+	A♯+	Cx+	Ex+	G♯x+	
	F♭♭	A♭♭	C♭	E♭	G	B	D♯	Fx+			
		D♭♭ -	F♭	A♭	C	E	G♯	B♯			
	E♭♭♭ -	G♭♭ -	B♭♭ -	D♭ -	F	A	C♯	E♯	Gx		
F♭♭♭-	A♭♭♭ -	C♭♭ -	E♭♭ -	G♭ -	B♭ -	D -	F♯	A♯			
	D♭♭♭-			C♭ -	E♭ -	G -					
					A♭ -	C -					

FIGURE 21. Lattice of the sixty-five-tone hyperchromatic triadic system (using prime numbers 2, 3, and 5), expressed in ratios (above) and in letter names (below). This is a two-dimensional lattice, showing the 3–axis vertically and the 5–axis horizontally; the 2–axis is omitted in this diagram and in all the other lattice diagrams in this book, as it merely shows 2/1 relationships (octaves) of the pitches in the other dimensions.

in the *Source* issue mentioned in the previous paragraph, under the title "Phase 1–B."[3]

The foregoing is a description of Phase 1 of a project undertaken by Ed Kobrin and me. Phase 2 will consist of computer programs aimed to generate compositional decisions based in part upon the scale systems of Phase 1.

3	C																				E														
4	C																				E														
5	C										D										E														
7	C										D										E						F								
3	C																Eb																		
4	C																Eb																		
5	C																Eb										F								
7	C										D						Eb										F								
12	C				C#						D						Eb				E						F							Gb	
15	C				C#			Db			D						Eb				E						F				F#			Gb	
19	C				C#			Db			D				D#		Eb				E		Fb				F				F#	F#+		Gb	
31	C		Dbb-		C#			Db		Cx+		D		Ebb		D#		Eb		Fbb		E		Fb		E#		F		Gbb-		F#	F#+		Gb	
34	C		Dbb-		C#		Db-	Db		Cx+		D		Ebb		D#		Eb		Fbb		E		Fb		E#		F		Gbb-		F#	F#+		Gb	
53	C	C+	Dbb-		C#	C#+	Db-	Db		Cx+	D-	D	Ebb-	Ebb		D#	Eb-	Eb	Eb+	Fbb		E	E+	Fb		E#	E#+	F	F+	Gbb-		F#	F#+	Gb-	Gb	
65	C	C+	Dbb-	Bx +	C#	C#+	Db-	Db	Ebbb-	Cx+	D-	D	Ebb-	Ebb	Fbbb-	D#	Eb-	Eb	Eb+	Fbb	Dx+	E	E+	Fb	D#x+	E#	E#+	F	F+	Gbb-	Ex+	F#	F#+	Gb-	Gb	Abbb-

		G																											C
		G										A																	C
		G										A																	C
		G										A											B						C
		G																											C
		G																	Bb										C
		G																	Bb										C
		G						Ab											Bb										C
		G						Ab				A							Bb				B						C
		G						Ab				A				A#			Bb				B						C
		G				G#		Ab				A				A#			Bb				B						C
Fx+		G		Abb		G#		Ab		Gx		A		Ebb-		A#			Bb		Cbb		B		Cb				C
Fx+		G		Abb		G#		Ab		Gx		A		Bbb-		A#		Bb-	Bb		Cbb		B		Cb		B#		C
Fx+	G-	G	G+	Abb		G#	Ab-	Ab		Gx	Gx+	A	A+	Bbb-		A#	A#+	Bb-	Bb	Cbb-	Cbb		B	Cb-	Cb		B#	C-	C
Fx+	G-	G	G+	Abb	F#x++	G#	Ab-	Ab	Fxx++	Gx	Gx+	A	A+	Bbb-	G#x+	A#	A#+	Bb-	Bb	Cbb-	Cbb	Ax++	B	Cb-	Cb	Dbbb--	B#	C-	C

FIGURE 22. Scales within a 5–limit just intonation system, culminating in a sixty-five-tone hyperchromatic scale.

These partly generate compositions in which the parameter of harmony is germane, as it is not in, for example, most serial or atonal compositions. Alternatively, one can say that consonance–dissonance becomes once more a significant compositional variable.

Phase 3 involves the design of an interface between a small computer and musical synthesizer equipment. The aim is to make possible real-time interaction between performers and the computer. A PDP-5 computer was donated for our use by Digital Equipment Corporation. The rest of the hardware is designed and built by Ed Kobrin. The computer will act not only as an instrument but also as a decision maker in the composition process. It will function onstage with performers and their traditional instruments. The contributions of the composer will have been made in preparing the available software (programs) for the computer, based upon Phases 1 and 2. We are aiming at a first composition, a commission from violinist Paul Zukovsky, using these means.[4]

As we near the completion of Phases 2 and 3, we plan a complete report on the project, which we have promised to *Perspectives of New Music.*

The project raises questions not only about the use of "artificial intelligence" in the production of music, but also about the nature of tonality and related questions of pitch usage in music.

NOTES

1. [Ed.: A gloss on this complex paragraph may perhaps be helpful. The "basic major chord" Johnston refers to is, in ratio terms, 1/1–5/4–3/2, which "consists of a point in the lattice" (1/1) and "one point in a positive direction on each of the axes," i.e., the 3–axis (giving 3/2) and the 5–axis (giving 5/4). The "parallel minor chord" (i.e., the tonic minor, in ratio terms 1/1–6/5–3/2) is made up of "the same notes on the tonal axis" (the tonal axis being the 3–axis, as defined in the text), hence 1/1 and 3/2, and the pitch that lies "one step in a negative direction on the modal axis" (in this case the 5–axis) from "the ratio one step farther in a positive direction than the starting point" (namely 3/2, the starting point being 1/1), i.e., 6/5.]

2. [Ed.: When Johnston writes that the symbols ∠ and 7 "indicate raising or lowering a pitch by 36/35, or about 49 cents," he is taking the just (5–limit) major scale as his starting point: for example, 36/35 is the amount by which 9/5 (the just minor seventh) must be lowered to give the 7/4 (the "septimal" minor seventh).]

3. [Ed.: The article "Phase 1–B" was never completed. Much of the intended content appears in more developed form in "Rational Structure in Music."]

4. [Ed.: Unfortunately, the violin piece for Paul Zukovsky was never realized.]

MUSIC THEORY

1973

A theory of music comprises acoustics, aesthetics, and stylistic practice. The musical theories of a culture reflect not only its attitude to the arts but also its religious, philosophic, and scientific biases. China, India, Greece, and Islam developed musical theories long before the modern era, and western Europe has, since medieval times, contributed extensively to this multiple heritage.

Acoustics connects with instrument design and musical-scale derivation and also with number theory and metaphysical symbolism. Aesthetics derives from the practice of artists and also from religious and philosophic theories of universal and social order. Although musical practice generates theories of composition and performance, fundamentally it springs from the religious, philosophic, and scientific thought of the culture that engendered it.

Chinese music theory, based acoustically on a system of relations of the numbers 2 and 3, connects symbolically with metaphysical theories of the interaction of yin (2) and yang (3), the two principal contrasting elements of the Chinese cosmos; and, by dint of a theory claiming causal effects on human behavior for musical sounds, it also connects with ethical, social, and political teachings. Indian music, based acoustically on numbers 2, 3, and 5, yields many seven- to nine-tone scales (called *ragas*), each with associated melodic patterns and each causing a specific emotional effect (called *rasa*). Varying interval tensions are produced against a fixed drone by the tones of the scale. The fixed pitches of the drone symbolize the *atman* (soul; the individual's participation in the universal Brahman), and the changing pitches of the *raga* represent life experiences. Indian music, therefore, is connected by tradition with meditation and self-transcendence. Other non-Western music is similarly based upon such religious and philosophical foundations.

Western European music is characterized by counterpoint and harmony and by its constant stylistic evolution. *Counterpoint* refers to the simultaneous unfolding of several melodic lines. The combinations of tones that result are harmonies, classified as *consonant* (bearing harmonic repose) and *dissonant* (bearing harmonic tension) and arranged since the seventeenth century in hierarchical families called *tonalities* (relationships between tones). Since the Renaissance, Western music has increasingly emphasized perceptual factors other than pitch and rhythm, until, in the twentieth century, types of music have emerged in which pitch and rhythm no longer predominate. The evolution of style is currently expressed in a wide diversity of kinds of music without a common practice. Also radically dissimilar are the acoustical and organizational properties in the music of contemporary composers. Hence, a theory of contemporary Western music would need to be unusually comprehensive.

ORIGINS AND HISTORY OF WESTERN EUROPEAN MUSIC THEORY

The origins of western European music lie in the music of the medieval Roman Catholic Church. The liturgical plainchant adopted by the Roman Church was codified by Pope Gregory I in the sixth century and was based upon a system of seven-tone modes (scale formations) handed down in Greek tradition from Pythagoras. The tuning of these modes was based, like traditional Chinese music, on relationships of the numbers 2 and 3, symbols of the worldly and the divine. Gregorian chant was monophonic (a single melodic line without accompaniment) until near the end of the first millennium AD, when a polyphonic practice (i.e., combining several voice parts simultaneously), called *organum,* was introduced. From this early counterpoint, at first almost entirely a matter of parallel motion in fourths (e.g., F above C), fifths (e.g., G above C), and octaves, the unique polyphonic tradition of western European music gradually evolved.

The Roman scholar and philosopher Boethius, writing in the fifth century, distinguished three kinds of "music," *musica mundana, musica humana,* and *musica instrumentalis.* Of these, only the last refers to sounded music, the first two indicating, respectively, the arithmetically expressed harmony of the universe (a Pythagorean idea) and the harmony of the soul. By the correspondence between these harmonies, music was believed to symbolize man's place in the universe, and the potent psychological impact of music was to some extent explained. This conception survived for a long time, especially in the tabulation of intervals (distances between notes) in terms of their relative consonance and dissonance, measured as fractions of string length on a monochord needed to produce the intervals. Considerations of this kind were especially crucial in polyphonic music, as were also the methods of rhythmic integration. Thus, medieval and Renaissance treatises usually concerned problems of consonance and dissonance, techniques for integrating polyphonic voices, and methods of notating pitch and rhythm. The most important of these for the subsequent development of music was the fourteenth-century treatise of a French musical theorist, Philippe de Vitry, *Ars Nova,* which provided a new rhythmic notation liberating music from the rigidity of earlier methods. During the thirteenth and fourteenth centuries, the tuning system shifted gradually away from the Pythagorean toward a triadic system later called "just intonation," as intervals of a third (e.g., C–E) and a sixth (C–A) came to be recognized as consonances.

At the end of the Renaissance, as instrumental and operatic music began to replace choral music, the practice of accompanying instruments and voices with an improvised keyboard part, called a "figured bass," led to the organization of compositions around harmonic progressions. This practice had two important effects: to simplify the traditional system of modes into major and minor tonality and to make urgent the need to temper the tuning of the scale so as to provide a wide scope for modulation (change of key within a work) with a limited gamut of pitches.

RAMEAU AND OTHERS

The French composer and theorist Jean-Philippe Rameau went far to establish tonality as a distinct technique of composition. He conceived each triad (a chord formed by two superimposed thirds, such as C–E and E–G) as representing the acoustic proportion 4:5:6 and considered a given triad to keep its identity regardless of the distribution of its three notes. Each triad thereby has a "root" position, a "first inversion," and a "second inversion," depending upon which of its tones is in the bass. Thus the triad C–E–G can assume the forms E–G–C and G–C–E.

Another aspect of theory that gradually acquired importance during the eighteenth and nineteenth centuries was the codification of stylistic and compositional techniques. Such was *Gradus ad Parnassum* (1725), a treatise on counterpoint by the Austrian theorist Johann Joseph Fux, which had a longstanding effect upon pedagogy.

In the nineteenth century the emphasis in this area shifted to techniques for musical analysis. The theories of phrasing and functional harmony of the German musicologist Hugo Riemann gave tonal and rhythmic practices of the "common practice period" increased coherence.

Then an Austrian theorist, Heinrich Schenker, gave the process of tonality its most thoroughgoing formulation. In Schenker's view, pitch (the location of sound in the tonal scale), as both melody and harmony, is the controlling factor in tonal music. Rhythm and dynamics function secondarily to articulate the structures created by pitch design. All tonal compositions can be reduced to a melody, a bass line, and a harmonic progression. In Schenker's view, all modulation should be regarded as "tonicization" of various subordinate progressions within one overall key. Schenker's ideas, designed to apply to common-practice-period music, have been applied to earlier and more recent music with notable success, allowing for some generalizations of his basic concepts.

MODERN THEORISTS

Some twentieth-century theorists have devoted themselves to the codification and teaching of compositional or theoretical techniques. A small number have provided bases in theory for the music of their times.

Arnold Schoenberg's twelve-tone serial theory provides an alternative method of pitch organization to tonality, in which the traditional rules of tonality and harmony are replaced by new rules and principles. This system has been used widely by many twentieth-century composers. Serial techniques have been applied to factors other than pitch, notably among the "post-Webern school" of composers (Anton Webern was a pupil of Schoenberg).

The theoretic work of the German composer Paul Hindemith was directed toward the continuation of the tradition of tonality into post-triadic music. Using the concept of consonance–dissonance as expounded by a nineteenth-century German acoustician, Hermann von Helmholtz, Hindemith provided a method of classifying harmonies by computing the frequencies of vibration interferences produced by their constituent frequencies. His most original contribution was his use of consonance–dissonance as a controlling factor in phrase design.

The most influential of the concepts of the German composer Karlheinz Stockhausen is the breaking down of the field of musical perception into controlling and dependent factors. Beginning with the concept of total organization of all parameters by the composer (e.g., pitch, rhythm, dynamics, tone color, stress, and all other facets of sound), Stockhausen proceeded to a fluid concept of musical control, allowing for much indeterminacy.

The theories of the U.S. composer John Cage are largely aesthetic, with philosophical and religious (specifically, Zen Buddhist) overtones. Insisting that all sounds and also silence itself are materials for music, he developed a theory that places duration at the center of musical organization. This theory was followed by an interest in chance and indeterminacy as valid modes of composition.

The theories of the Greek composer Iannis Xenakis concern the use of probability theory and statistical distribution in composition. His interest in applying mathematical models led him to use computers extensively.

APPLICATION OF MATHEMATICS TO MUSIC

By far the oldest and most widespread application of mathematics to music is the derivation of pitch scales and rhythmic proportions by means of whole-number fractions referring either to frequency or to tempo ratios. The Chinese, the Indian, the Islamic, and the ancient Greek pitch systems were derived in this way. The medieval western European pitch system was similarly based upon modes derived from Pythagorean traditions. Only with the introduction of temperament (the system of tuning in which the intervals deviate from the "pure") in Europe during the Baroque era was this kind of system abandoned. Equal temperament was proposed at about the same time in China but was rejected. In spite of the adoption of equal temperament in the West in the eighteenth century, it was not until the twentieth century that compositional techniques of pitch organization, such as serialism, which are not based on proportional tuning, made their appearance. Not only pitch scales but also laws of harmony, in particular the classification of intervals in terms of consonance and dissonance, derive from proportional tuning. Furthermore, the modern metrical system of rhythmic notation, from its inception in the fourteenth century, is based upon the same mathematical procedure.

TRIADIC TUNING

The lists of intervals in their order of consonance, given by most medieval and Renaissance theorists after the ninth-century French monk-musician Hucbald, reflect the kind of tuning system favored by the musicians of the time. The shift from Pythagorean to triadic tuning is reflected in the greater consonance allowed to thirds and sixths by later theorists. That the acceptance of new consonances was accompanied by a shift in methods of tuning can be verified by the monochord experiments detailed by theorists. From these it is clear, for instance, that the precise size and, hence, tuning of the major third dealt with by earlier theorists differed from that which later came to be preferred. Early medieval theorists, following the Pythagorean system, derived the proper tuning of the third (as well as that of the entire diatonic scale) by tuning a series of fifths: as C–G, G–D, D–A, A–E, the resulting notes C and E then forming a major third. This process yielded a frequency ratio of 81/64 as the relation of top to bottom pitch. Later theorists adopted a major third with the simpler frequency ratio of 5/4, a proportion found in the harmonic series or component vibration pattern of vibrating strings and air columns. For its relation to the natural harmonic series, this later third was known as a *just* third. It differed in size only minutely from the earlier third, by a ratio of 81/80 (5/4 = 80/64; cf. 81/64 for the Pythagorean third), but its sound was generally regarded as more consonant. Although 5/4 involves a higher prime number (81 is factorable into 3 x 3 x 3 x 3) than previously allowed in a consonance, the ear superseded previous theory (but was given legitimacy by invoking the physics of vibrating strings).

This example may shed some light upon how one musical system succeeds another. The simplest pentatonic scale, one used the world over, is obtained by tuning four successive fifths. If, in the interest of filling in the two largest intervals of this scale, two more fifths are added to the succession, the result is a seven-tone diatonic scale, i.e., one consisting of five whole and two half steps. The Pythagorean thirds and sixths of this scale are dissonant. If, in order to obtain smoother thirds and sixths, the system of just intonation is adopted, an alternative tuning of the seven-tone scale becomes available. These scales received letter or syllable names in India and in Europe.

Although two chromatic inflection symbols (♯ and ♭) were introduced to take care of additional fifths or thirds added to the scale, as in forming the twelve-tone chromatic scale from a combination of the major and minor seven-tone diatonic scales, no such pair of symbols was introduced to distinguish in notation between Pythagorean and just thirds and sixths. Such a pair of symbols (+ and -) would refer to the syntonic comma (81/80, or about one-tenth of a tone), an interval too small to be easily perceptible in general usage, while ♯ and ♭ refer to a much larger interval (about a half tone).

MODERN PRACTICE

While the common practice period took for granted the permanence of both the tuning system of twelve-tone equal temperament and the harmonic and melodic tradition of triadic tonality, the twentieth century has called both of these practices into question. The condition of harmonic practice at the end of the nineteenth century resembled, in some ways, the condition of polyphony in the thirteenth century, when the use of thirds and sixths began to become widespread. During the last half of the nineteenth century, extended tertian chords (i.e., derived by the superimposition of thirds) such as sevenths, ninths, elevenths, and thirteenths (comprising three, four, five, and six superimposed thirds) became increasingly prevalent. In both cases, dissonances resulting from combinations of consonances became so prevalent as to demand acceptance as consonances. In the earlier case, a simpler tuning system was replaced by a more complex one; in the recent one, many composers abandoned harmonic organization according to the principle of consonance–dissonance. This abandonment coincided with a rejection of the tradition of tonality. In order to provide an alternative system of ordering pitch in atonal music, Schoenberg, the first to grapple with this problem, developed the tradition of thematic unity into an all-pervasive, twelve-tone serialism. Serialism proved useful not only for pitch but for almost any materials capable of manipulation by the composer. As John Cage pointed out, the ultimate application of atonal thinking is the abandonment of tone as a controlling factor.

At the same time, there have been efforts to devise a new pitch system in place of the old one. The most prevalent of these new systems have been those based upon tempered subdivisions of the twelve-tone equal-tempered scale. In other cases, a new pitch system has been based upon some kind of just intonation. The best-known such system is that of a U.S. composer, Harry Partch, whose forty-three-tone scale is based upon sound frequency ratios expressible as fractions utilizing the prime numbers 2, 3, 5, 7, and 11. A less complex system than Partch's is that devised by the Dutch theorist Adriaan Fokker, associated with a thirty-one-tone tempered scale.

Much music since 1950 has dealt principally with schemes of organization based on less precise kinds of design. For this reason, the period since 1950 has seen extensive experiment with notational methods designed to communicate these less specific modes of order. Such problems as the use of chance and indeterminacy in composition and performance or the use of statistical ordering procedures raise basic questions regarding the kind and degree of the order in music. It is because of the widespread concern about these and related matters that aspects of communications theory such as information theory and systems analysis are finding a role in mid-twentieth-century music theory.

As the world's cultures become aware of each other's traditions through improved communications, the need increases for theoretical tools and concepts sufficiently versatile and nonrestrictive to show the relationship between very diverse kinds of thinking. The exploration of the nature of human intelligence affords one of the most fruitful sources for concepts useful in this endeavor. For this reason, many aesthetic theorists have sought to express their concepts mathematically, in the form of algorithms capable of producing or recognizing specific kinds of systematic order via computers. (An algorithm is a procedure by which one class of problems can be solved and in which the initial state is connected with the final state by an uninterrupted succession of intermediate states, each of which is generated by its predecessor.) The necessity to be absolutely specific about every detail of a computer program is an excellent way of discovering in any discipline exactly what assumptions have been made besides those that are explicitly recognized. Aesthetic behavior is an especially revealing facet of human activity, connecting as it does sensorimotor, intellectual, and emotional modes of behavior. Music especially involves activities organized by means as various as improvisation and mathematics.

BIBLIOGRAPHY

J. Murray Barbour, *Tuning and Temperament: A Historical Survey* (1951), a comprehensive historical survey of systems of tuning in Europe from Greek antiquity onward with emphasis on Renaissance and Baroque periods; Herbert Brün, *Über Musik und zum Computer* (1971), on the development of a conceptual framework wherein the composition of music and the programming of computers appear to be compatible activities satisfying analogous requirements; and "From Musical Ideas to Computers and Back," in Harry B. Lincoln, ed., *The Computer and Music* (1970), 23–36, about the conditions under which systems of digital and analog computers would assist a composer in creating and generating music of contemporary relevance and significance; John Cage, *Silence: Lectures and Writings* (1961), *A Year from Monday: New Lectures and Writings* (1967), and *Notations* (1969), publications of one of the most influential twentieth-century composers; Alain Daniélou, *An Introduction to the Study of Musical Scales* (1943), deals with the problem of scales and modes on an intercultural basis, particularly in relating those of India to those of ancient Greece; Hermann von Helmholtz, *Die Lehre von den Tonempfindungen als physiologische Grundlage für die Theorie der Musik,* 3rd ed. (1870; Eng. trans., *On the Sensations of Tone as a Physiological Basis for the Theory of Music,* 1875), still an indispensable treatise for one interested in the acoustics, and to some extent, the physical aspects of music; Paul Hindemith, *Unterweisung im Tonsatz,* 2 vols. (1937–39; Eng. trans., *The Craft of Musical Composition,* 2 vols., 1941–42; 4th ed. reprinted 1970), presents the composer's personal approach to writing and analyzing music, and contains analyses of a number of twentieth-century compositions; Leonard B. Meyer, *Emotion and Meaning in Music* (1956), an investigation of the nature of emotional and intellectual meaning in music, the responses to musical stimuli, and the social and psychological conditions under which communication takes place in a musical experience; Abraham Moles, *Théorie de l'information et perception esthétique* (1958; Eng. trans., *Information Theory and Esthetic Perception,* 1966), the earliest and most thorough attempt to apply to sequences of musical events the mathematical theories of information developed by Shannon, Weaver, and others for linguistic codes; Harry Partch, *Genesis of a Music* (1949), a personal exposition of one of the twentieth century's most individualistic aesthetics, as remarkable for its philosophy as for its detailed theories of tuning and instrumentation; Leon Plantinga, "Philippe de Vitry's *Ars Nova:* A Translation," *Journal of Music Theory* 5 (1961), 204–23, an epochal treatise of the early fourteenth century that presents a notation capable of expressing more precisely a greater variety of rhythmic relationships than theretofore possible in writing; George Perle, *Serial Composition and Atonality: An Introduction to the Music of Schoenberg, Berg, and Webern,* 2nd ed. rev. (1968), a lucid introduction to early twelve-tone practice that emphasizes motivic manipulation and the atonal origins of serialism (many examples and analyses are included); Hugo Riemann, *System der Musikalischen Rhythmik und Metrik* (1903); and *Die Natur der Harmonik* (1882; Eng. trans., *The Nature of Harmony,* 1886), views all music from the point of view of Riemann's own musical and intellectual heritage—nineteenth-century Germany; Heinrich Schenker, *Neue Musikalische Theorien und Phantasien,* vol. 1 (1906; Eng. trans., *Harmony,* 1954), one of the most influential theoretical treatises of the first half of the twentieth century that involves reducing harmony and melody to their skeletal and functional frameworks; Arnold Schoenberg, *Style and Idea* (1950), a collection of essays on various aspects of music that gives insights into the author's thinking about music, both technically and emotionally; Karlheinz Stockhausen, "How Time Passes," *Die Reihe,* no. 3 (1959), pp. 10–40, an attempt to apply serial concepts to the notation of time and to take time and its ordering to be the basis for composition (difficult and occasionally obscure, but influential and controversial); Oliver Strunk, ed., *Source Readings in Music History from Classical Antiquity through the Romantic Era* (1950), contains basic readings, in English translation, of many relevant areas of music theory, especially of medieval and Renaissance theory.

RATIONAL STRUCTURE IN MUSIC

1976

"Over the whole of the historical period of instrumental music, Western music has based itself upon an acoustical lie. In our time this lie—that the normal musical ear hears twelve equal intervals within the span of an octave—has led to the impoverishment of pitch usage in our music."[1]

We lie especially when we pretend to ourselves that vertical combinations of these pitches constitute harmony. We do not avoid the lie if we abandon harmony in music, so long as we retain a tempered scale.

Feeling that the harmonic mode of pitch perception is far too important a resource of human capability for it to be allowed to fall into disuse, I have set about to reestablish ratio scale usage in pitch organization. This has entailed a number of radical means (large numbers of microtones, for instance, entailing new performing techniques, especially for wind players), some strongly conservative practices such as the resumption of a sharp awareness of degrees of consonance and dissonance as a major musical parameter (which amounts to revoking Schoenberg's much-touted "emancipation of the dissonance"), and even some radical reactionary attitudes, for example, the rejection of the idea that noise, "randomness," and ultracomplex pitch are the primary frontiers for avant-garde exploration.

I have been concerned to reopen doors closed by the acceptance of the twelve-tone equal-tempered scale as the norm of pitch usage. My focus is upon complexity arrived at as perceptible order rather than as seeming disorder. I am especially interested in the role played by proportional order in the domains of rhythm, harmony, and melody. Since as a culture we have developed not only a tolerance but also a taste for a high level of complexity in many areas of experience, this effort necessarily involves a very highly developed proportional ordering system in order to cope with such levels of complexity in pitch and rhythm. We must learn to differentiate sharply between complexity due to large numbers and complexity which delineates subtleties of relationship.

If one purifies Western pitch usage of late adulterations traceable to the adoption of equal temperament, the two most complex examples of systems of proportional relations in existence are the harmonic and metrical systems of Western art music. Rhythm requires no corrective, only the long-since-achieved abolition of the tyranny of the bar line and the fixed repetitive metrical schemes proper to common-practice-period music.

Extrapolating the basic logic from the harmonic practice of traditional Western music is only a first step. A much more challenging and interesting follow-up is the generalization of this logic so that it becomes applicable to unfamiliar pitch materials. Once this has been achieved, the door closed by the acceptance of equal temperament is reopened.

In measurable physical terms, there are only two parameters of sound, duration and energy (measurable as the amount of displacement of molecular particles in a vibrating medium). These are interpreted phenomenologically as a great variety of parameters, a differentiation assisted enormously by our facility in perceiving gestalt phenomena on various scales of time.

On an ordinary scale of time (countable time), the patterning, due always to vibratory events, is intelligible as rhythm. As we move up into larger amounts of time, our ability to count diminishes and the role played by memory greatly increases. Macrorhythmic events, characterizing longer durations, enable us to acquire a sense of the overall shape of music or sound compositions. We also perceive patterning on a scale of time much too rapid to count, but clearly we have nevertheless a marvelously precise ability to measure the duration patterns involved in these microrhythmic events.

Since air or any other vibrating medium can respond to the periodicities of diverse sound sources simultaneously, these different rates of vibration are constantly interacting with one another. If the pattern of interaction is relatively simple, the sound complex exhibits a type of blend traditionally called *consonant* (as defined in, for instance, Helmholtz's *On the Sensations of Tone*). This kind of consonance, though not independent of context and function in a melodic or harmonic pattern, does exhibit, simply in its blend, a greater simplicity than the concomitant kind of dissonance, in the same way that superimposed rhythmic groupings such as 3:2 and 4:3 are clearly easier to perform and to analyze by ear than, say, 9:5 or 15:8.

We also identify such combinations by their relative "size," as measured for instance in half steps or in cents. Because of this double classification of musical intervals (relative consonance and relative size), an interesting situation occurs when there is little difference in size between two intervals, yet a markedly audible difference in consonance. A small increase in the rate of vibrations of the upper frequency of a just major third (the kind found between the fourth and fifth partials of the overtone series: ratio 5/4)—enough to increase the number of vibrations of the upper frequency from 80 per 64 of the lower frequency to 81 per 64—will produce a marked difference in roughness of blend. Since 81/64 = 3/2 x 3/4 x 3/2 x 3/4, this interval can be arrived at by tuning a frequency a perfect fifth (3/2) up from the lower frequency, then another a perfect fourth (4/3) down from that one, and then repeating this pair of tunings. Such tuning sequences abound in traditional musical practice, so the 81/64 major third, called a Pythagorean ditone, is actually a relation used in much untempered music.

Our habit of detuning all the intervals of our scale except the octaves in order to render it an equal interval scale makes us less sensitive to such differences, an insensitivity which we compel ourselves to accept as a constant norm. Because we have selected an "average" size for all intervals near the size of a major third, we use neither the simplest vibration ratio near this size (5/4), nor any of the more complex dissonant ones which are the result of whole-number relations (e.g., 9/7, 32/25, 11/9, 14/11, 81/64). Instead we use the cube root of 2 for the tempered major third, which renders its harmonic meaning (its potential consonant or dissonant relation to other interval combinations in the context, which is expressible in terms of rational fractions) entirely ambiguous. For purposes of systematic harmony we would desire an unequal interval scale were it not for our habitual desensitization. This is in conflict with the natural desire not to have to cope, melodically, with, for instance, several sizes of whole steps and of half steps, a problem that arises in performing chromatic passages in Baroque music.

One of the results of this state of affairs has been, after about a century of such a norm of pitch usage, the loss of harmonic (simultaneous) pitch relations as an effective organizing device in much of the serious art music of our culture. A less obvious but, I think, more serious result is that what had been an open, evolving pitch system (developing within notated musical history in Europe from a harmonic norm of perfect fifths and fourths to a norm of major and minor triads) became a closed system capable of being exhausted of fresh, permutational possibilities of its available interval combinations. As a result, on the level of small-scale rhythmic context, possible new configurations are eventually used up entirely, creating a predictability of vertical (and "diagonal") combinations. This predictability is unrelieved, in contrast to the case of predominantly triadic music, by any larger rational system of harmony which provides a sense of movement and change within an ampler context. Efforts to create such a harmonic system on the basis of serial order have not met with widespread listener understanding.

It seems therefore that a primary effect of the celebrated "emancipation of the dissonance" has been to deprive music of one of its most effective means for organizing longer spans of time. This has been a process long in the making. It began innocently enough with a simple neglect: music notation did not attempt to incorporate into its symbols pitch differences of a syntonic comma (ca. 21.5 cents, or ca. 1/5 of a semitone) resulting in performance practice from a shift, in compositional practice during the fourteenth century AD, from the consonances of organum to those of major and minor triads; and in response to the challenges posed by the emergence of an independent repertory and practice of instrumental music, it culminated in the acceptance of keyboard temperaments in the sixteenth and seventeenth centuries. This last process impoverished the logic of harmony and tonality by weakening the perceptibility of consonance and dissonance. This impoverishment, right from the outset of tonal tradition, resulted in loss of the support which contextual functional relations can gain from a perceptible mathematical logic reflecting the hierarchy of the system of harmony and tonality.

The frequently cited gain in ambiguity and flexibility hardly seems comparable to this loss. It was, in fact, not this aspect of temperament which first recommended its adoption, but the practical solution to the problem of tuning keyboard, fretted, and other fixed-pitch instruments for a music that implied a wide harmonic range. Once equal temperament with twelve tones—the optimum compromise for modulatory triadic music—was adopted, it took only a little over a century for the exhaustion of the fresh possibilities of the system to become a major aesthetic problem.

It has been useful in acquiring mastery of this complex problem to seek, in collaboration with Edward Kobrin and Peter Rumbold, two computer programmers who are also skilled composers, a single algorithm which would enable a computer to derive both the Pythagorean scale system and the triadic scale system known as just intonation. Each scale system is infinitely expandable, to scales with greater and greater numbers of notes per octave. Thus not only the rules for deriving pitches were needed, but also rules for determining when a collection of pitches constitutes an acceptable ratio scale. Interesting differences between the two scale systems had to be explicable as solely the effect of greater and less numerical complexity in their constituent intervals (ratios). Lastly, the algorithm thus derived has to be applied to unfamiliar numerical combinations, to produce as-yet-unexplored scale systems, and these systems tested out as the basis of musical compositions.

This work is at present far advanced, and it is possible now to present scale systems involving not only prime numbers 2 and 3 (Pythagorean), or 2, 3, and 5 (triadic just intonation), but all combinations of prime numbers no larger than 11.

The first presentation of any of this material, an article in *Source* 7, "Phase 1–a," by Edward Kobrin and me, gave only "one-dimensional" scales and accompanying matrices (that is, scales derived from using 2 and one other prime number). The program, in Fortran IV, was also published.

Later, in volume 6 of *Proceedings of the American Society of University Composers,* I published the derivation of the triadic just intonation scale system, this time without a computer program, in an article called "Tonality Regained." This scale system, involving two prime numbers (3 and 5) greater than 2, is a two-dimensional scale system. I had already, in my *String Quartet no. 2* and the orchestral work *Quintet for Groups,* used microtonal ultrachromatic scales from this tuning system.

In 1971 I began a series of compositions using unfamiliar tuning systems but not requiring unusual instruments or electronic means. The choral works *Rose* and *Mass* use "diatonic scales" from systems based upon 2, 3, and 7, and 2, 3, 5, and 7. My *String Quartet no. 4,* commissioned by the Fine Arts Quartet, progresses from Pythagorean (2, 3) tuning through just intonation (2, 3, 5) to a tuning based on 2, 3, 5, 7. It goes as far as a twenty-two-tone chromatic scale in this system.[2] One of the insights this experience has brought me is that precision in just tuning is the more crucial the more notes per octave one uses. This is above all because more than ever, the harmonic and melodic structural functions need the underpinning that greater clarity of differentiation in tuning provides.

The success of these works has greatly encouraged me to continue my research. Parallel to this research has been an application of its findings in the field of metrical rhythm. The most highly developed examples are my *Knocking Piece* for two percussionists and piano interior, *Quintet for Groups, Sonata for Microtonal Piano* (also in ultrachromatic triadic just intonation), and my *String Quartet no. 4.*

While the works involving extended triadic just intonation emphasized new and sometimes startling pitch relations, those involving unfamiliar tuning systems up to now emphasize "normal" and "logical-sounding" pitch combinations. Part of the explanation for this lies in the wisdom of walking before trying to learn to run; but an equally important consideration has been the wish to recapture the beauty of intelligibility and simplicity in an unfamiliar guise.[3]

The most rudimentary mode of perceiving a very complex sound gestalt merely tags it as unique. It is identifiable as itself, should it recur, and can be differentiated from other gestalts.

As soon as we want to compare similar events, we must single out qualities in terms of which to make such comparisons, and we are involved with various perceptual parameters. So long as our measurement of a parameter consists only of determination of greater or less on some gradual scale between perceptually linked pairs of opposites (such as high and low, loud and soft) we are dealing with rough contours merely.

For more precise comparisons or descriptions, we must quantize these parameters and try to assign positions on an imaginary linear scale to given perceptual values. It is here that, for instance, melodic perception of pitch contours becomes meaningful. It is also here that serial organization has meaning.

When simultaneous periodic phenomena such as frequencies (or on an ordinary time scale, tempos) are considered, a further ability emerges: the quantitative comparison of amounts of time, yielding a precise sense of proportion. On the scale of ordinary time, this perception gives us metrical organization. In microtime, the comparison of rates of vibration gives us harmony, a subjective reaction possible because of our unconscious but precise measurement of ratios between frequencies. For this mode of perception, the equal-interval scales adequate for melodic perception are not at all precise enough.

All musical pitch scales are compromises between these two perceptual modes of processing sound, the melodic and the harmonic. For melodic purposes, we need to know which of two pitches is higher, and how much higher. It is convenient to measure such distances additively, as if they were ranged on a linear scale measured in equal increments.

The minute we ask what increments we will use, we are plunged into another perceptual mode, the harmonic or proportional one. Ubiquitously, human cultures divide up the pitch continuum into octaves. An octave is defined physically as the frequency ratio 2/1. And as soon as we want to know not only if a given pitch interval is greater in linear size than another, but also if its blend, its consonance, in Helmholtz's use of the term, is smoother or rougher, we are similarly involved in harmonic listening.

Harmonic relations are not conveniently thought of additively, but rather multiplicatively. What we think of melodically as adding two intervals is, from the standpoint of their pitch ratios, multiplying them. "A major third plus a minor sixth equals an octave" translates to "5/4 multiplied by 8/5 equals 2/1, or $5/4 \times 8/5 = 2/1$."

In using a ratio scale, both melodic and harmonic considerations enter. For this reason, two arrangements of ratios (or their equivalent note names) are useful: the *n*-dimensional lattice and its linear projection into a scale arranging the pitches in order from lowest to highest, within the span of a single octave.

The lattice demonstrates harmonic neighbors (that is, ratios in near proximity are consonant, those farther away being more dissonant). The linear scale demonstrates melodic neighborhoods, a concept already familiar from common use.

The lattice shows not only that two ratios are dissonant or even how dissonant they are in comparison to others, but by what chain of relationships their dissonance is "explained." To "explain" a dissonance in this manner *justifies* it to the ear; it is heard as a natural and inevitable result of a constellation of less complex ratios.

The linear scale not only provides a model for scalar melodic passages, but also a schematic for nonadjacent design elements which form nevertheless a scalar armature for melodic lines (as in Schenker's *Urlinien*). Patterns or "paths" in the lattice may be used to give a sense of harmonic direction even to passages that lack entirely any conventional tonal or harmonic "logic."

Scale derivation is thus not simply a theorist's justification ex post facto of a particular way of conceiving music. It is also not merely a device for generating new arbitrary "systems" for experimenters to play with. Rather it is an effective aid in designing melodic and harmonic audible structure even with unfamiliar pitch materials. Such structure is not serial in type, though serial patterning does indeed result in the interval sequences which comprise the adjacency relationships of the linear ratio scales in all systems of the type described. One may speak of *tonality,* but only if the term is generalized in such a way that it is clear that triadic tonality (whether diatonic or chromatic or ultrachromatic) is only one of many possible types of harmonic (ratio scale) logic. Similarly, *modality* recedes in importance to become only a particular way of using the materials of a given tonal system, just as is modulatory harmony.

A great advantage which ratio scales have over all systems of temperament is that most of the latter are mutually exclusive, and the permutations of available intervals of each are finite and exhaustible, whereas all ratio scales are subsets of larger sets and are infinitely relatable and expandable.

There is in this situation something of the embarrassment of riches. At first it may appear that "if all is possible, all is meaningless." But in fact it is not at all true that an infinite system renders all possibilities either available or equal in significance. Also, even a cursory consideration of method will render clear that one is always necessarily dealing at any time only with a subset or some subsets of the infinite set.

It may be objected that a ratio system is hierarchical and thus philosophically inferior to a system in which there is a total democracy of elements (even assuming that such a system is actually possible). I will counter that an organism is also hierarchically ordered, and that any success in reducing the interrelations between its parts to a total or even approximate democracy will result in its death. We do, in other words, deal necessarily with hierarchical order, which is appropriate and necessary to certain important kinds of functioning. Whether aesthetic order is of such a kind in all cases, or in all successful cases, is a point I do not wish to argue. Suffice it to say merely that hierarchical order is at least one viable kind of aesthetic order.[4]

❧ ❧ ❧

To generate a ratio lattice, one establishes axes around a zero point, which is the ratio 1/1. On each axis the ratios are formed by comparing powers of any given prime number with powers of 2 (Figures 23, 24, and 25). The number of prime numbers greater than 2 determines the number of axes in the system, and thus its number of "dimensions." Each axis divides into symmetrical halves at the zero point, each term of either half being the reciprocal of the corresponding term in the other half. Thus on one half the powers of 2 are in the denominator, and on the other, in the numerator. Each step on any axis raises or lowers the power of the prime number associated with that axis by 1. To allow the musical principle of octave equivalence expression in

A♭+	C+	E+	G♯+	B♯+	$\frac{81}{50}$	$\frac{81}{80}$	$\frac{81}{64}$	$\frac{405}{256}$	$\frac{2025}{1024}$
D♭	F+	A+	C♯+	E♯+	$\frac{27}{25}$	$\frac{27}{20}$	$\frac{27}{16}$	$\frac{135}{128}$	$\frac{675}{572}$
G♭	B♭	D	F♯+	A♯+	$\frac{36}{25}$	$\frac{9}{5}$	$\frac{9}{8}$	$\frac{45}{32}$	$\frac{225}{128}$
C♭	E♭	G	B	D♯	$\frac{48}{25}$	$\frac{6}{5}$	$\frac{3}{2}$	$\frac{15}{8}$	$\frac{75}{64}$
F♭	A♭	C	E	G♯	$\frac{32}{25}$	$\frac{8}{5}$	$\frac{1}{1}$	$\frac{5}{4}$	$\frac{25}{16}$
B♭♭-	D♭-	F	A	C♯	$\frac{128}{75}$	$\frac{16}{15}$	$\frac{4}{3}$	$\frac{5}{3}$	$\frac{25}{24}$
E♭♭-	G♭-	B♭-	D-	F♯	$\frac{256}{225}$	$\frac{64}{45}$	$\frac{16}{9}$	$\frac{10}{9}$	$\frac{25}{18}$
A♭♭-	C♭-	E♭-	G-	B-	$\frac{1024}{675}$	$\frac{256}{135}$	$\frac{32}{27}$	$\frac{40}{27}$	$\frac{50}{27}$
D♭♭--	F♭-	A♭-	C-	E-	$\frac{2048}{2025}$	$\frac{512}{405}$	$\frac{128}{81}$	$\frac{160}{81}$	$\frac{100}{81}$

FIGURE 23. The 2, 3, 5 pitch lattice (the 3 and 5 axes only are shown, the 3–axis vertical, the 5–axis horizontal).

the mathematical model, either numerator or denominator of any ratio may be multiplied or divided by any power of 2 without changing the musical meaning of the expression. By custom, all ratios are "octaved" in this manner to bring their value between 1/1 and 2/1. This has the practical effect of transposing all ratios by octave into the span of a single octave, bounded by 1/1 and 2/1. Thus all ratios are customarily expressed as improper fractions smaller than 2/1. This greatly simplifies the formation of linear scales, since the only further step is to sort out the ratios into ascending order of magnitude. The magnitude is measured by a logarithmic quantity, typically the cent (1,200 per octave). Other measurements may be used, for instance the savart (301 per octave). A simpler way to compare relative sizes of ratios is to convert them into decimals.

In constructing a ratio lattice, it is convenient to lay out the axes first and then, using the same technique used in matrix formation, to fill in the intermediate points coordinating all points on all axes. The lattice will comprise a plane, a solid, or a hypersolid, depending upon the number of axes used.

G♯L	F	E+	G7+	C77++	81/49	81/56	81/64	567/512	3469/2048
D♯L	BL	A+	G7+	F77++	54/49	27/14	27/16	189/128	1323/1024
G♯L	EL	D	C7+	B7♭7+	72/49	9/7	9/8	63/32	441/256
BLL-	AL	G	F7+	E7♭7+	96/49	12/7	3/2	21/16	147/128
ELL-	DL-	C	B7♭	A7♭7+	64/49	8/7	1/1	7/4	49/32
ALL-	GL-	F	E7♭	D7♭7	256/147	32/21	4/3	7/6	49/48
DLL--	CL-	B♭-	A7♭	G7♭7	512/441	64/63	16/9	14/9	49/36
GLL--	FL-	E♭-	D7♭-	C7♭7	2048/1323	256/189	32/27	28/27	49/27
CLL--	BL♭	A♭-	G7♭-	F7♭7	4096/3969	1024/567	128/81	112/81	98/81

FIGURE 24. The 2, 3, 7 lattice (the 3 and 7 axes only are shown, the 3–axis vertical, the 7–axis horizontal).

Any scale system with more than one prime number greater than 2, in order to be of the same type as the diatonic–chromatic–ultrachromatic system of triadic just intonation scales (which uses 2, 3, and 5), will have less numerous parallel "major" and "minor" scales which are then combined and filled out to make chromatic and ultrachromatic scales that are more numerous (Figures 26, 27, and 28). The difference between diatonic and chromatic scales is created by a special restriction on diatonic (major and minor) scales. In these scales, all ratios are chosen from a set of columns parallel to the axis associated with the smallest prime (called the *tonal* axis) and one step in either a "positive" or a "negative" direction on each of the other axes (the *modal* axes). The "positive" direction generates major scales; the "negative," minor scales. The formation of these two sets of scales is exactly analogous and parallel. The minor is the inverse of the major, the symmetry being organized around a pair of ratios adjacent on the tonal axis, the center, 1/1 (zero point), and the ratio one step in a positive direction on the tonal axis. The point at which diatonic major and minor scales are combined to form

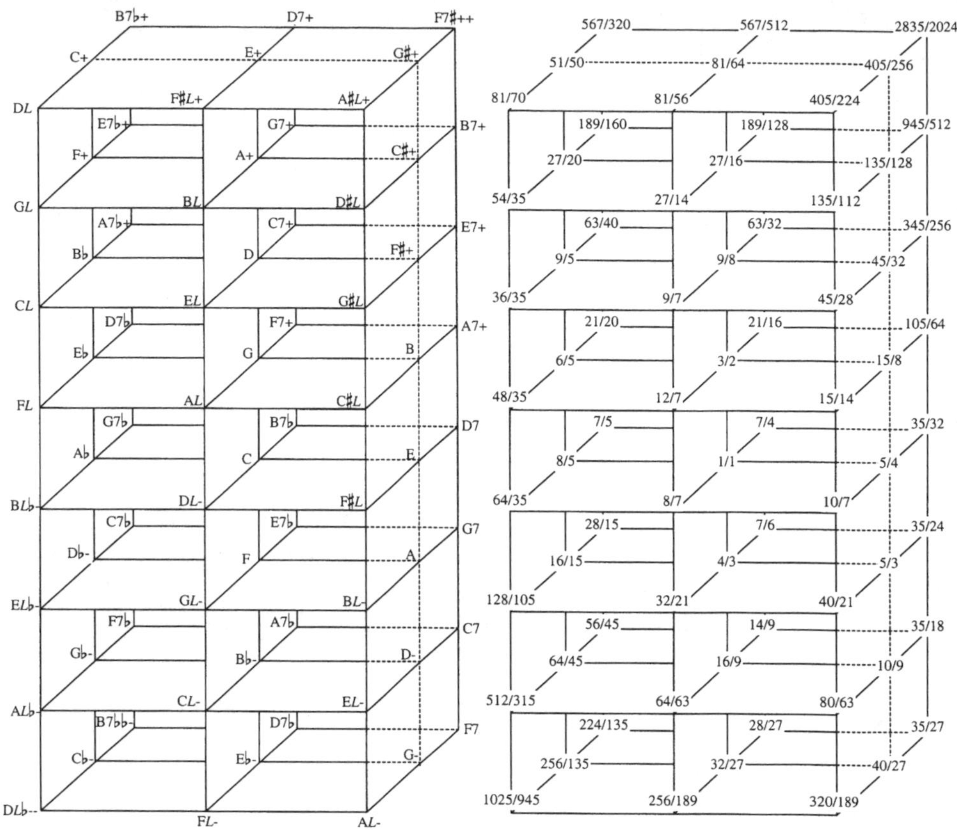

FIGURE 25. The 2, 3, 5, 7 lattice (the 3, 5, and 7 axes are shown, all at right angles to each other).

the chromatic scale is arbitrary. I have set it as the first point when the largest linear scale adjacency ratio is smaller than 250 cents (in the case of a two-dimensional lattice), than 125 cents (in the case of a three-dimensional lattice), than 62.5 cents (in the case of a four-dimensional lattice), etc. In chromatic and ultrachromatic scales, the ratios are drawn from all directions in the lattice.

An acceptable ratio scale must have as few different intervals between its adjacent notes as possible—no more than the quantity of prime numbers in use (including 2). Each scale derivation begins with the "basic chord of the system," either major or minor. This consists of the zero point and one adjacent ratio on each of the axes, in either a positive (major) or negative

1/1 6/5 3/2 2/1
C E♭ G C
--- 6/5 --- 5/4 --- 4/3 ---
1/1 6/5 3/2 9/5 2/1
C E♭ G B♭ C
--- 6/5 --- 5/4 --- 6/5 --- 10/9 ---
1/1 6/5 4/3 3/2 9/5 2/1
C E♭ F G B♭ C
--- 6/5 --- 10/9 --- 9/8 --- 6/5 --- 10/9 ---
1/1 9/8 6/5 4/3 3/2 8/5 9/5 2/1
C D E♭ F G A♭ B♭ C
--- 9/8 --- 16/15 --- 10/9 --- 9/8 --- 16/15 --- 9/8 --- 10/9 ---

1/1 5/4 3/2 2/1
C E G C
--- 5/4 --- 6/5 --- 4/3 ---
1/1 5/4 3/2 5/3 2/1
C E G A C
--- 5/4 --- 6/5 --- 10/9 --- 6/5 ---
1/1 9/8 5/4 3/2 5/3 2/1
C D E G A C
--- 9/8 --- 10/9 --- 6/5 --- 10/9 --- 6/5 ---
1/1 9/8 5/4 4/3 3/2 5/3 15/8 2/1
C D E F G A B C
--- 9/8 --- 10/9 --- 16/15 --- 9/8 --- 10/9 --- 9/8 --- 10/9 ---

1/1 9/8 6/5 5/4 4/3 3/2 8/5 5/3 9/5 15/8 2/1
C D E♭ E F G A♭ A B♭ B C
--- 9/8 --- 16/15 --- 25/24 --- 16/15 --- 9/8 --- 16/15 --- 25/24 --- 27/25 --- 25/24 --- 16/15 ---

1/1 25/24 9/8 6/5 5/4 4/3 36/25 3/2 8/5 5/3 9/5 15/8 2/1
C C♯ D E♭ E F G♭ G A♭ A B♭ B C
--- 25/24 --- 27/25 --- 16/15 --- 25/24 --- 16/15 --- 27/25 --- 25/24 --- 16/15 --- 25/24 --- 27/25 --- 25/24 --- 16/15 ---

FIGURE 26. Scales derived from the 2, 3, 5 lattice, the last being one of the several possible chromatic scales in just intonation.

(minor) direction. Each time a ratio is tested to be added to the scale, it must satisfy various conditions. It must be adjacent in the lattice to a ratio already in the scale. It must divide in two the largest adjacency ratio in the scale already selected. If there are other adjacency ratios in the scale the same size as the one to be divided, each must be divided analogously or in exactly the inverse manner. One of the new adjacency ratios obtained by this division must be identical to one already present between neighboring scale ratios. If there is a choice of ratios which satisfy these conditions, the one that divides the largest adjacency ratio most nearly evenly (as measured in cents or some other logarithmic quantity) is chosen. If there is a choice of such ratios, one selects the one nearest the zero point or nearest the ratio one step in a "posi-

1/1		3/2		7/4		2/1
C		G		B7♭		C
	3/2		7/6		8/7	

1/1		7/6		3/2		7/4		2/1
C		E7♭		G		B7♭		C
	7/6		9/7		7/6		8/7	

1/1		7/6		4/3		3/2		9/5		2/1
C		E7♭		F		G		B7♭		C
	7/6		8/7		9/8		7/6		8/7	

1/1		9/8		7/6		4/3		3/2		14/9		7/4		2/1
C		D		E7♭		F		G		A7♭		B7♭		C
	9/8		28/27		28/27		9/8		28/27		9/8		8/7	

1/1		3/2		12/7		2/1
C		G		A*L*		C
	3/2		8/7		7/6	

1/1		9/7		3/2		12/7		2/1
C		E*L*		G		A*L*		C
	9/7		7/6		8/7		7/6	

1/1		9/8		9/7		3/2		12/7		2/1
C		D		E*L*		G		A*L*		C
	9/8		8/7		7/6		8/7		7/6	

1/1		9/8		9/7		4/3		3/2		12/7		27/14		2/1
C		D		E*L*		F		G		A*L*		B*L*		C
	9/8		8/7		28/27		9/8		8/7		9/8		28/27	

1/1		9/8		7/6		9/7		4/3		3/2		14/9		12/7		7/4		27/14		2/1
C		D		E7♭		E*L*		F		G		A7♭		A*L*		B7♭		B*L*		C
	9/8		28/27		54/49		28/27		9/8		28/27		54/49		49/48		54/49		28/27	

1/1		49/48		9/8		7/6		9/7		4/3		72/49		3/2		14/9		12/7		7/4		27/14		2/1
C		D7♭		D		E7♭		E*L*		F		F♯*LL*		G		A7♭		A*L*		B7♭		B*L*		C
	49/48		54/49		28/27		54/49		28/27		54/49		49/48		28/27		54/49		49/48		54/49		28/27	

FIGURE 27. Scales derived from the 2, 3, 7 lattice, the last being a chromatic scale very different from that in Figure 26.

tive" direction on the tonal axis. This distance is measured in steps along or parallel to one of the axes. If two usable ratios are equidistant, a ratio on an axis associated with a smaller prime is preferred. A ratio in a sector where more factors cancel out when the axis coordinates are multiplied is preferred over one in which fewer factors cancel. If the largest adjacency ratio cannot be acceptably divided by any of the available ratios, the next largest should be considered.

As long as the scale is still diatonic, only ratios may be used which lie on the tonal axis or in the columns adjacent to it one step in either a positive direction (for major) or a negative one (for minor).

When the major and the minor diatonic scales are combined to obtain the

1/1 5/4 3/2 7/4 2/1
C E G B7♭ C
5/4 — 6/5 — 7/6 — 8/7

1/1 7/6 5/4 3/2 7/4 2/1
C E7♭ E G B7♭ C
7/6 — 15/14 — 6/5 — 7/6 — 8/7

1/1 7/6 5/4 21/16 3/2 7/4 2/1
C E7♭ E F7+ G B7♭ C
7/6 — 15/14 — 21/20 — 8/7 — 7/6 — 8/7

1/1 10/9 7/6 5/4 21/16 3/2 5/3 7/4 2/1
C D- E7♭ E F7+ G A B7♭ C
10/9 — 21/20 — 15/14 — 21/20 — 8/7 — 10/9 — 21/20 — 8/7

1/1 10/9 7/6 5/4 21/16 45/32 3/2 5/3 7/4 15/8 2/1
C D- E7♭ E F7+ F♯+ G A B7♭ B C
10/9 — 21/20 — 15/14 — 21/20 — 15/14 — 16/15 — 10/9 — 21/20 — 15/14 — 16/15

1/1 28/27 10/9 7/6 5/4 21/16 45/32 3/2 14/9 5/3 7/4 15/8 2/1
C D7♭- D- E7♭ E F7+ F♯+ G A7♭ A B7♭ B C
28/27 — 15/14 — 21/20 — 15/14 — 21/20 — 15/14 — 16/15 — 28/27 — 15/14 — 21/20 — 15/14 — 16/15

1/1 6/5 3/2 12/7 2/1
C E♭ G AL C
6/5 — 5/4 — 8/7 — 7/6

1/1 6/5 9/7 3/2 12/7 2/1
C E♭ EL G AL C
6/5 — 15/14 — 7/6 — 8/7 — 7/6

1/1 8/7 6/5 9/7 3/2 12/7 2/1
C DL- E♭ EL G AL C
8/7 — 21/20 — 15/14 — 7/6 — 8/7 — 7/6

1/1 8/7 6/5 9/7 27/20 3/2 12/7 9/5 2/1
C DL- E♭ EL F+ G AL B♭ C
8/7 — 21/20 — 15/14 — 21/20 — 10/9 — 8/7 — 21/20 — 10/9

1/1 16/15 8/7 6/5 9/7 27/20 3/2 8/5 12/7 9/5 2/1
C D♭- DL- E♭ EL F+ G A♭ AL B♭ C
16/15 — 15/14 — 21/20 — 15/14 — 21/20 — 10/9 — 16/15 — 15/14 — 21/20 — 10/9

1/1 16/15 8/7 6/5 9/7 27/20 81/56 3/2 8/5 12/7 9/5 27/14 2/1
C D♭- DL- E♭ EL F+ F♯L+ G A♭ AL B♭ BL C
16/15 — 15/14 — 21/20 — 15/14 — 21/20 — 15/14 — 28/27 — 16/15 — 15/14 — 21/20 — 15/14 — 28/27

1/1 28/27 16/15 10/9 8/7 7/6 6/5 5/4 9/7 21/16 27/20 45/32 81/56 3/2 14/9 8/5 5/3 12/7 7/4 9/5 15/8 27/14 2/1
C D7♭- D♭- D- DL- E7♭ E♭ E EL F7+ F+ F♯+ F♯L+ G A7♭ A♭ A AL B7♭ B♭ B BL C
28/27 36/35 25/24 36/35 49/48 36/35 25/24 36/35 49/48 36/35 25/24 36/35 28/27 28/27 36/35 25/24 36/35 49/48 36/35 25/24 36/35 28/27

FIGURE 28. Scales derived from the 2, 3, 5, 7 lattice, the last being a twenty-two-note chromatic scale.

chromatic, all identical adjacency ratios which are divided must be so either in the same or in an inverse manner in all cases. If in two or more cases such an adjacency ratio is divided differently, all cases must utilize simultaneously all such divisions, resulting in two or more interpolated ratios. If, when these conditions are satisfied, the scale still has too many different adjacency ratios, a ratio or ratios must be found which divide any adjacency interval (starting with the largest, as preference) in such a way as to introduce two new adjacency ratios both of which are already present between scale ratios. If after this effort the scale still has too many adjacency ratios, all the possible divisions of all adjacency ratios must be examined to find cases where common occurrences of new adjacency ratios make it possible to reduce the total of adjacency ratios to the minimum level. In some cases this necessitates a large number of scale ratios for the smallest acceptable chromatic scale in a given scale system.

It will be obvious that this process is easier to carry out with the assistance of a computer. Nonetheless, in the process of generating the program to facilitate finding these scales, it was necessary for me to derive all the scales which were to be made available by means of the program before it existed in order to be sure of covering all eventualities. It may seem, therefore, that producing the program achieved nothing. This is assuredly not so, since it was the pressure of having to be so extremely specific and inclusive that made possible my solution to these theoretical problems. I needed the program not mainly for derivation, but in order to make possible the study of reasoning processes necessary to translate an intellectual process which is at least partly holistic in character entirely into a binary language.

NOTES

[Ed.: "Rational Structure in Music" was first presented as a lecture for the American Society of University Composers in 1976 and delivered again on several occasions thereafter, including in Bonn and in Paris in 1981. In the lecture Johnston used occasional taped examples, played on a Motorola Scalatron organ, of intervals and chords in just intonation. It has not seemed useful to reproduce these examples here in notated form.]

1. Quoted from the composer's remarks in Abram Loft's notes to the Fine Arts Quartet's second performance (Chicago, April 28, 1974) of *String Quartet no. 4*.

2. Cf. Randall Shinn, "Ben Johnston's Fourth String Quartet," in *Perspectives of New Music* 15 no. 2 (Spring–Summer 1977).

3. [Ed.: At this point in the original lecture, Johnston incorporated a taped performance of his choral work *Rose* performed by the University of Illinois Summer School Chorus, conductor Neely Bruce.]

4. [Ed.: At this point in the original lecture, Johnston incorporated a taped performance of his *String Quartet no. 4* by the Fine Arts Quartet, recorded at Wilmette, Illinois, April 29, 1974, by radio station WFMT, Chicago.]

A NOTATION SYSTEM FOR EXTENDED JUST INTONATION

2003

Extended just intonation is a kind of ratio-scale tuning based upon pure intervals—i.e., those analogous to the pitch relationships of the harmonic series. To handle the complex ratio relations necessary to achieve a truly accurate just tuning of modulatory triadic music, plus its many harmonic extensions beyond simple triads, a basic notation as close as possible to familiar, widely used Western music notation is desirable. As long as certain fundamental differences in what the symbols refer to are clearly understood, there is no ambiguity in such a procedure.

This notation is not tied to any particular diapason (such as A = 440 Hz, A = 435 Hz, or even a C-based or G-based tuning system). What remains constant are the ratio relations between pitches. The pitch reference of notes without any accidentals is not the tempered scale commonly presumed to be the basis of Western music, but rather a tuning of the seven-tone major scale resulting from tuning the three primary major triads (tonic, dominant, and subdominant) in the ratio 4:5:6. For this reason the note names are subordinated to C, since the key signature of C major has no sharps or flats. The ratio relationship to C of the scale notes is 1/1 (C), 9/8 (D), 5/4 (E), 4/3 (F), 3/2 (G), 5/3 (A), 15/8 (B), 2/1 (C). The sequence of adjacent-pitch ratios is 9/8, 10/9, 16/15, 9/8, 10/9, 9/8, 16/15 (Figure 29).

This results in a scale in which there are two sizes of whole step (9/8, 10/9) and one size of half step (16/15). The interval of difference between the two kinds of whole step is 81/80, the comma of Didymus. This interval is represented in notation by the accidentals + (raise) and - (lower). To turn the interval C, D into a 10/9, it must be notated C, D- or C+, D. To turn the interval D, E into a 9/8, it must be notated D, E+ or D-, E (Figure 30).

In examining this just major scale for its further triadic possibilities, let us keep in mind that a just minor triad is the exact inversion of a just major triad. To add intervals (e.g., C, E plus E, G equals C, G) you must multiply ratios (correspondingly, 5/4 multiplied by 6/5 equals 3/2). Dealing with a

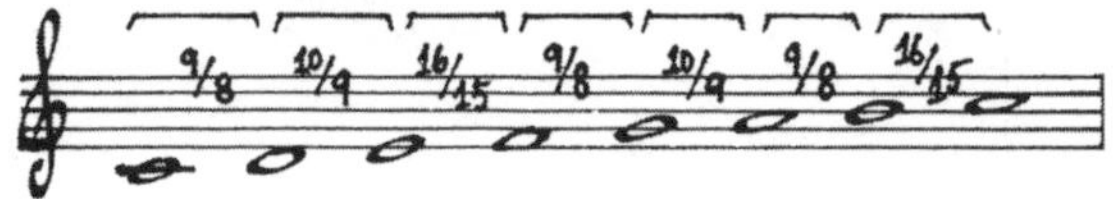

FIGURE 29. Uninflected notational symbols, referring to triadic just intonation (2, 3, 5 tuning) of the diatonic major scale of C: in ratio terms the pitches are 1/1–9/8–5/4–4/3–3/2–5/3–15/8–2/1.

minor triad, begin with its top note (its fifth) and work downward, using the same pair of ratios: 5/4 for the (upper) major third and 6/5 for the (lower) minor third. If you attempt to do this with the D-minor triad (supertonic triad), you discover that although the major third (F, A) is in the ratio 5/4, the minor third (D, F) is not in the ratio 6/5, but 32/27. The pure tuning of the supertonic triad is thus D-, F, A (10/9–4/3–5/3). A further example: the intervals B, D and D, F are in ratio terms 6/5 and 32/27. For the resulting triad to become a just minor triad, not only would F have to become F♯, but an additional + would be necessary: F♯+ (in ratios, 15/8–9/8–45/32). It is in this way that the syntonic comma (comma of Didymus) is used to keep both kinds of triads in just consonant (simple ratio) tuning.

When triadic polychords are formed by piling up triads, as was increasingly the case in nineteenth-century European concert music, leading eventually to early twentieth-century polytonality, the intention to create a just tuned version of such a style leads to complex tuning and often involves deliberate use of just such dissonant versions of thirds as those replaced by consonant versions (as described above). Jazz harmonies of the big-band era, from the 1920s through the 1940s, are an especially rich area for such

FIGURE 30. Examples of the use of the syntonic comma symbols + and -, symbolizing respectively the raising and lowering of a pitch by 81/80. Taking C as 1/1, the four intervals are 1/1–10/9; 81/80–9/8; 9/8–81/64; 10/9–5/4.

tuning, even without the inclusion of the "natural" seventh, so evocative of blues tuning. Take, for example this chord: F, C, E♭, G, B♭, D, F. If tuned so that all the interlocked triads are just, the high F must be F+, which means that between the low F and the high one there is an interval of a double octave, sharp by one syntonic comma (Figure 31).

The way the simple consonant ratios in just tuned triadic music relate to each other can most easily be seen by studying the layout of pitches in the 2, 3, 5 lattice presented in my article "Rational Structure in Music."[1] (See Figure 23.)

Many string quartets use an electronic tuner to achieve accuracy in microtonal inflections. Since such tuners are designed to show deviations from a twelve-tone equal-tempered scale, this can easily result in distortions when applied to extended just intonation unless this process is altered so as to allow that the notes without accidentals in the notated C-major scale *do not* refer to equal-tempered tuning but rather to the tuning described above. The tuning of the open strings which extended just intonation uses is exactly the same as that tuning used by virtually all string quartets: four notes each a just perfect fifth (3/2, or 702 cents) apart. Since A is the traditional tuning note, A and E require no accidentals. But in the just C-major scale used in extended just intonation, the fifth between D and A is one syntonic comma too small, and so the D needs to be tuned as D-. This means also that the interval G, D must be notated as G-, D- (Figure 32). If the comma inflections are applied to tempered pitches, a distorted tuning results. It is important to remember that this is identical to normal tuning: it merely looks unfamiliar. In a just tuned C-major triad involving open G strings (on the violins) and

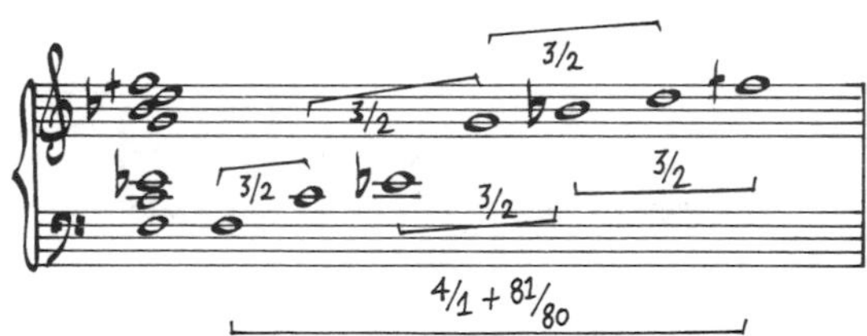

FIGURE 31. An example of the syntonic comma in practice: in this chord all the interlocked triads are just, resulting in a syntonic comma discrepancy between the low F and the high F.

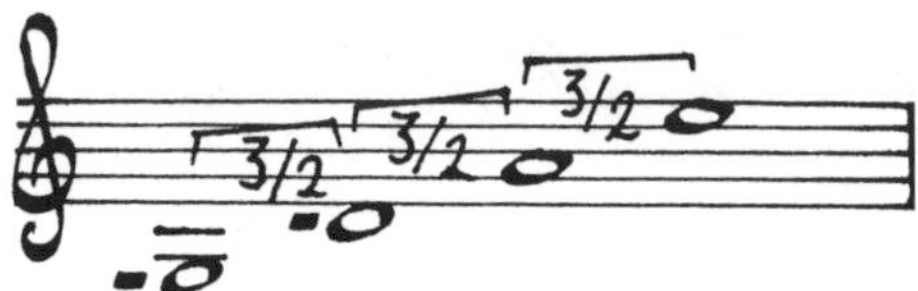

FIGURE 32. The notation of the open strings of a violin in Johnston's system. Because an uninflected A on the staff represents the ratio 5/3 (to C 1/1) and an uninflected D the ratio 9/8, the D needs the syntonic comma symbol (the minus) to bring it down to 10/9, a pure fifth below the 5/3; likewise, the G needs the same symbol to make it the ratio 40/27, a pure fifth below the 10/9.

open C and G strings (on viola and cello), the open E strings of the violins will not be in tune with the just major third of the chord: they are one syntonic comma too high. This shows in the notation: the names of the notes in the C-major triad will be C-, E-, and G- because the open C string and G string are being used as root and fifth of the triad.

What characterizes mainstream Western concert music since the time of *Ars Nova* (the fourteenth century) more than any other aspects is, first, its rhythmic freedom from repetitive patterns; second, its organization into contrapuntal phrases punctuated by recognizable cadences; and, third, its gradual but definite tendency toward triadic consonant harmonies, growing out of the common practice for handling consonant and dissonant intervals between all pairs of contrapuntal parts. As long as vocal music predominated over instrumental, the question of compromise tunings (various kinds of temperaments) did not loom large. The pitch notation of Renaissance music allowed for ♯ and ♭ inflections, gradually emerging from the performance practice of *musica ficta,* but no symbol was provided for the syntonic comma, doubtless because its microtonal size (less than a tempered eighth tone) made it unusable as a melodic interval, and its extreme dissonance (reflected in its complex ratio 81/80) made it unusable even as a nonharmonic dissonance. Its importance as an adjustment to keep triadic harmonic combinations purely in tune emerged only as harmonic progressions began to play a conscious and deliberate part in the design of compositions. This coincided with the increasing use of instrumental accompaniment or even instrumental compositions independent of vocal music.

The use of consonant major and minor thirds (5/4 and 6/5, respectively) began to predominate in Baroque music even over the traditionally inviolable consonances of the perfect fifth and the perfect fourth (3/2 and 4/3), leading to various forms of meantone temperament. Insisting upon both kinds of consonances would have made the conscious, deliberate use of adjustments by syntonic comma unavoidable. It was—above any other consideration—the increasing use of keyboard instruments, not merely for rehearsal but in performance ensembles, that made the search for ever more complex kinds of temperament inevitable as a wider and wider range of modulatory harmonic progression became a goal. During this transitional period and the gradually emerging Classical era, the tuning of keyboard instruments was still in the hands of the performer. With the introduction of the pianoforte, the tuning of the instrument passed to specialist tuners, removing the task of keeping music in tune from the pianist's responsibilities. It is this transition into Romantic music that brought the complex tuning of twelve-tone equal temperament finally into use.

If one wants to reconceive the music of these stylistic eras in terms of extended just intonation, it is first necessary to make limited and very specifically prescribed use of nonretunable instruments, and second to consider what adjustments are really possible for other instruments and whether performers of those instruments will be able, willing, and motivated to make these changes in performance practice. The easiest adjustments are those of bowed string instruments, but the orchestral practice of having large numbers of string players performing in unison works powerfully against this, as does the ubiquitous use of vibrato by string players.[2]

While it is possible theoretically to conceive of piling up powers of prime numbers greater than 5, as a truly functional additional lattice dimension makes possible, the practical usefulness of this is actually quite limited.[3] Piled-up perfect fifths (or more commonly perfect fourths) and progressions based upon chord root movement up or down by perfect fifth or fourth are, of course, commonly used in Western music. Piled-up major thirds are commonly used only in pairs (the augmented triad), but root movement by major thirds or by minor thirds is much more common, leading rather quickly in both cases to what in extended just intonation can only be called enharmonic nonequivalents. C, E, G♯, B♯ is the simplest of such progressions. C, E♭, G♭, B𝄫, D𝄫 is almost as simple. Both these progressions, in their much tamer twelve-tone equal-tempered versions, are standard fare in nineteenth-century Romantic music, notably in much music by Liszt or Wagner. An earlier use of such progressions is in the secular choral music of the High

Renaissance, notably in music by Gesualdo. It is hard to imagine using the prime number 7 in an analogous way, let alone 11 or 13 or even higher primes. (Not that it has not been done: cf. Toby Twining's *Chrysalid Requiem.*) By far the commonest earlier use suggesting such intervals is in complex chords approximating overtone combinations in the music of Debussy and other Impressionist composers. Again the effect of temperament is not only to distort the tuning of such "overtones" but to tame down the expressive impact they have. Call to mind the discussion above of the use of such harmonies in big-band jazz. The performance practice of jazz presumes the inflection by ear of such chords, at least in ensembles capable of such flexibility.

For notation purposes, each higher prime number entails the introduction of a pair of symbols indicating the interval difference between the overtone indicated by the new prime number and the just tuned note in the 2, 3, 5 system nearest in pitch to it which has a simple notation. (This specification will be explained below.) When practical, the number itself is used for the sign belonging to the overtones, for instance 7. The retrograde inversion of this symbol, ㄥ in this case, is used for the sign belonging to the inverted series (analogous to "undertones"). In C major this chord is C, E, G, B7♭, because B♭ (9/5) is the nearest simply notated pitch in the 2, 3, 5 system. B♭- (16/9) is nearer in pitch, but its accidental involves an extra symbol (-). When the symbol 7 is used with a ♭, the stem of the ♭ is used as the vertical of the 7 and a composite of the two symbols results: 7♭. In E major the notation is simpler: E, G♯, B, D7. In E minor (remember, the inversion puts B at its top) the notes are B, G, E, C♯ㄥ. When the symbol ㄥ is used with a ♯, the right vertical of the ♯ is used as the vertical of the ㄥ, and a composite symbol again results: ♯ㄥ. In C minor (remember, the inversion puts G at its top) the notation is simpler: G, E♭, C, Aㄥ. If the symbol 7 is combined with a ♯, the left vertical of the ♯ is used as the vertical of the 7, and a composite symbol results: 7♯. If the symbol ㄥ is combined with a ♭, the vertical of the ♭ is used as the vertical of the ㄥ, and a composite symbol results: ♭ㄥ.

In moving around in the harmonic space generated by a multidimensional tonal lattice, many relationships not easily understood from a single overtone series can be observed to have an easy intelligibility to the ear even though they may seem complex when described intellectually. An easy way to understand this is to consider just tuning the C-major and C-minor triads. Then add the seventh partial (B7♭) to the major and the sub-seventh partial (Aㄥ) to the minor. If one makes a progression from one of these chords to the other, the C and G are common tones. The thirds, E and E♭, are a chromatic half step (25/24) apart. (5/4 divided by 6/5 is 25/24.) The interval between the two sevenths (B7♭ and A∠ refer respectively to 7/4 and 12/7) is 49/48 (7/4 divided by 12/7 is 49/48). Since, in the overtone series, 25/24 in the next octave of partials is 50/48, we can observe that the chromatic half step is split, in the overtone series, by the 49/48 interval. In the overtone series of C, 25 is the major third of the major third, and 49 is the natural seventh of the natural seventh. (Imagine the chord C, E, G, B7♭, D7, F7+, A77♭+, or the same chord in the overtone series of A: A, C♯, E, G7, B7, D7, F77+. This is a complex chord and would be difficult to hear with accuracy. But in the case of moving from C major with its natural seventh to C minor with its natural sub-seventh, both of these relationships are present and are not difficult to tune by ear.) This is an example of chromaticism in extended just intonation. We are dealing here with a progression which is an example of what Lou Harrison called "free style" composing: composing not restricted to a single overtone series nor to a predetermined choice of notes to be used (as with the use of a mode or a raga).

In the case of the number 11, using the Arabic numeral is not practical. The eleventh partial of the overtone series is often used by piano tuners needing to tune two pianos a quartertone apart, because it is quite close to halfway between the perfect fourth and the tritone. This points up a characteristic of intervals involving 11: they have an ambivalence (e.g., 11/9 sounds like a neutral third, neither major nor minor). This ambivalence suggested using the arrow, which has sometimes been used in twentieth-century music to indicate inflection by quartertone. Up-arrow raises; down-arrow lowers. The arrow is used to alter the perfect fourth, rather than one of the several just tritones, the notation for any one of which involves at least two symbols. In the overtone series of C, the 11th partial is F↑. In the undertone series beginning on C (F minor) the sub-eleventh (16/11) is G↓. The neutral third, prominent in some folk musics, can be represented in just tuning by the 11/9 ratio. In a neutral A triad derived from A major, the neutral third would be notated as C↑- (since A is the 9/8 above G-), the ratio 55/54. Alternatively, this neutral triad could be derived from A minor, in which case (since E is a 9/8 below F♯+) the neutral third would be notated as C♯↓+. This latter is a much more difficult tuning to achieve by ear.

As an example, consider the opening statement of the folk hymn "Lonesome Valley" in my *String Quartet no. 5*. The hymn tune, traditionally in a pentatonic scale, is here tuned so that the minor thirds in the pentatonic scale are neutral thirds (Figure 33). It was the major mode derivation that was used in this passage. Here the aim was not to create a neutral triadic harmony but

FIGURE 33. The opening statement of the folk tune "Lonesome Valley" in *String Quartet no. 5,* and the pentatonic scale on which it is based. With F- considered to be 1/1, the third and fifth degrees of the scale are eleventh-partial relationships, respectively 27/22 and 18/11. Copyright by Smith Publications, 2617 Gwynndale Ave., Baltimore, Maryland, USA. Used by permission.

to present thirds that defy identification as major or minor. In the course of this quartet, a number of different tunings of this hymn tune are presented, in a meditation on its many possible emotional meanings (Figures 34 and 35).

The interval made between the third octave of the fundamental of an overtone series and its thirteenth partial, the ratio 13/8, is approximately 27 cents larger than the just minor sixth. Because the resulting interval is much closer in size to a minor sixth than to a major sixth and the minor sixth is seldom used as an "added sixth" in common Western musical practice, the 13/8 interval is much more likely to occur as an "under-third" (a 16/13) placed below the root of the chord. In C major this chord will be A13♭, C, E, G. In this case the numeral itself is used as the accidental. In C minor the equivalent

FIGURE 34. Transformation of the "Lonesome Valley" melody in *String Quartet no. 5,* employing a 7–limit scale. Copyright by Smith Publications, 2617 Gwynndale Ave., Baltimore, Maryland, USA. Used by permission.

FIGURE 35. Further transformations of "Lonesome Valley" from *String Quartet no. 5;* the scales used successively in this viola passage are a 13–limit and an 11–limit one. Copyright by Smith Publications, 2617 Gwynndale Ave., Baltimore, Maryland, USA. Used by permission.

chord would be C, E♭, G, BƐɩ. (The last symbol here is meant to represent a 13 rotated laterally 180 degrees. This added "major seventh" is verbalized "B sub-thirteen.") The scale made by the eighth through the sixteenth partials of an overtone series (in C: C, D, E, F↑, G, A13♭, B7♭, B, C) can be used as an eight-tone mode, or as a tone cluster, or as a widely voiced chord in the manner of big-band jazz harmonies. Any of these manners of use are not difficult to learn how to tune by ear. It is hard to imagine how the thirteenth of the thirteenth could be made musically meaningful, so very limited use of a complete 13–limit matrix would be practicable.

The sizes of the successive ratios in the overtone octave between the eighth and the sixteenth partials gradually decrease from a whole tone (9/8) to a half tone (16/15). In the next overtone octave, between the sixteenth and thirty-second partials, the sizes of the successive intervals gradually decrease from a different form of half tone (17/16) which, at 105 cents, is very close in size to a tempered half step, to a quartertone (32/31) which is very close in size to a tempered quarter step. The ratio 19/16 (298 cents) is easily regarded as like an equal-tempered minor third. The prime number ratio 23/16 is slightly sharper than an equal-tempered tritone. The prime number ratio 29/16 is slightly sharper (by 6 cents) than an equal-tempered minor seventh.

The new prime-numbered partials in the overtone series between the sixteenth and the thirty-second are not easy to tune by ear harmonically, especially in a musical context of just tuned intervals clearly based upon intervals formed from lower prime number relationships. But a melodic use of these intervals is a learnable pattern, the performer approximating the size distance in cents which they make as a melodic scale. In my *String Quartet no. 9*, the fourth and final movement makes extensive use of this scale and the inversion of it. At the time of the quartet's premiere performance, the Stanford Quartet learned these patterns entirely by experimenting by ear without any electronic model to use as a guide. (In passages where some of the unfamiliar prime-numbered intervals were used experimentally, the performers were much less secure about their accuracy.)

The seventeenth partial is regarded in the notation as an altered chromatic half tone (25/24). Thus the symbol 17 raises the notated pitch by the ratio 51/50 (34 cents or about a sixth tone). The ratio 17/16 is thus notated as C♯17. Since the 17th partial is commonly used as a minor ninth added to a just tuned dominant seventh chord, this notation is an unfamiliar one and may seem arbitrary in that usage, but the complication of symbols involved in using D♭- (the diatonic half-tone) argued against using it, and the distance in cents from D♭ plus the fact that D♭ is used far less often in just tuned equivalents of familiar progressions argued against using it. The inversion of this symbol is.ㄥɪ

The nineteenth partial is regarded in the notation as an altered minor third. It lowers the pitch by 17 cents. The ratio 19/16 is thus notated as E♭61. Its inversion, which raises the pitch by the same amount, is symbolized by 19. To avoid the impression that this first symbol is the number sixty-one, the 9 of the 19 should be written with a diagonal straight line (as in many people's script writing of this numeral), so that when its retrograde inversion is used it does not look like the numeral six.

To notate the ratio 23/16, it is the augmented fourth 45/32 (F♯+, a major third above the supertonic 9/8) which is altered by the symbol 23. The left side of the bottom of the 3 (in the 23 symbol) is attached to the upper end of the left vertical of the ♯. To notate the inversion of this interval, the ratio 32/23, the note altered is the diminished fifth 64/45 (a major third below the minor seventh 16/9). In the key of F minor (figuring down from C) this is the G♭- which is a major third below B♭-. The retrograde inversion of the symbol 23 is easily drawn by hand. It looks like an E rounded to resemble a cursive script capital E followed by a 2 rotated up 180 degrees so that the horizontal straight line is on the top. The end of the curve of the rotated 2 is attached to the vertical of the ♭ symbol: Ɛᘔ♭.

To notate the ratio 29/16, it is the minor seventh 9/5 (a minor third above a perfect fifth) which is altered by the symbol 29. As with the symbol 19, the

9 is not drawn to look like an inverted 6, but with a diagonal straight line. In the overtone series of C this interval is notated B♭ with the diagonal of the 9 (of the symbol 29) attached to the vertical of the ♭. To notate the inversion of this interval, the ratio 32/29, the note altered is the major second 10/9 (a syntonic comma smaller than the major second 9/8). In the key of F minor (figuring down from C), this note is D-, a minor third below F. The retrograde inversion of the symbol, 6ᘔ, is easily drawn by hand. It looks like the inverted 9 (6) drawn as described above, followed by the rotated numeral 2 (already described above). The end of the curve of the inverted 2 is attached as before (see above).

To notate the ratio 31/16, it is the major seventh 15/8 which is altered (a major third above a perfect fifth) which is altered by the symbol 31. In the overtone series of C this interval is notated B31. To notate the inversion of this interval (32/31), the ratio altered is 16/15 (a major third below the perfect fourth). In the key of F minor (figuring down from C), this note is D♭-, a minor third below F. The retrograde inversion of this symbol is Iℇ with the ℇ notated like the cursive capital E (rounded like the numeral 3).

The notation symbols may be combined into composite symbols to save space in notating accidentals, except that the syntonic comma (+ and -) is never combined with any other symbol and always comes next to the note itself.

The systematic shown in Figure 36 can be expanded or contracted to include

raise	lower	ratio	cents	amount by which...	exceeds
♯	♭	25/24	71	5/4	6/5
+	–	81/80	22	9/8	10/9
ㄥ	7	36/35	49	9/5	7/4
↑	↓	33/32	53	11/8	4/3
13	ƐI	65/64	27	13/8	8/5
17	ㄥI	51/50	34	17/16	25/24
6I	19	96/95	18	6/5	19/16
23	Ɛᘔ	46/45	38	23/16	45/32
29	6ᘔ	145/144	12	29/16	9/5
31	IƐ	31/30	57	31/16	15/8

FIGURE 36. Notational symbols devised by Johnston for just intervals through the 31–limit, showing their ratio value, their size in cents, and their derivation.

any combination of prime numbers, and it is not necessary to have reference to tonal lattices or even to ratios, once the intrinsic meaning of the symbols used and their degree of modification of the pitches they precede is understood. If it is understood not only in theory but by ear, the free invention of a modulatory music in just intonation extended to any degree becomes a practical undertaking. It is not the mathematics that makes music sound in tune: it is the performers following leads from composers who themselves understand how to design the music so that this clarity of vibration relations results.

NOTES

1. Cf. "Rational Structure in Music." The notes near to each other on the lattice are more easily tunable by ear than those which lie farther apart. Remember, in studying the lattice, that notes diagonally adjacent are not harmonic neighbors but can be reached only by using straight verticals or horizontals and right-angle changes of direction. The way to make dissonant intervals intelligible to the ear is to connect them by a path of easily tuned consonances on the lattice as the F and F+ were connected in the example given above.

2. Even very commonly used progressions in music, such as I, vi, ii, V, I, have hidden problems of intonation. Look at this progression in C major. Chord I is C, E, G; with common tones C and E it moves to A, C, E; with common tone A this moves to D, F, A, but the interval D, A in the extended just C-major scale is not a true perfect fifth, needing to become D-, A; with common tone D- this moves to G-, B-, D-, and with common tone G-, moves on to C-, E-, G-. The entire progression has not moved in a circle, returning to C, but in a spiral, flatting in pitch by a syntonic comma (about 21.5 cents). This amounts to movement on the 2, 3, 5 tuning lattice to a new location (and a new notation) for C. (Cf. my description of lattices in "Rational Structure in Music.") Since there is a contradictory tradition (in the majority of Western concert music) of returning at the end of a composition to the same tonic note as at its beginning, the progressions of a composition have to be very carefully designed to make a "round trip" on the lattice, and the movement the musical progressions make on the lattice needs very conscious planning.

3. Each axis on the lattices presented in "Rational Structure in Music" represents the ratio relation of each prime number and successive powers of it to the number 2 and powers of it. Rather than 0 at the center and 1, 2, 3, 4, 5, etc., mirrored by -1, -2, -3, -4, -5, etc., as is the case in a familiar graph, these integers are instead exponents. So we have, on the 3–axis, in the center, 3 to the 0 power and 3 to the successive powers 1, 2, 3, 4, 5, etc., mirrored by 3 to the successive powers -1, -2, -3, -4, -5, etc. This process applies similarly to each successive prime number. It should be immediately apparent that this leads to a multidimensional system impossible to represent adequately on the two-dimensional surface of a page.

PART II

ON MUSICAL AESTHETICS AND CULTURE

MUSICAL INTELLIGIBILITY: WHERE ARE WE?

1963

Music is first of all for the ear. Well-designed music alerts memory, integrates a span of time. Its event patterns evoke symbolic insight.

In a time of rapid change it is hard to achieve this. Our tradition is branching again. We need a larger cultural context.

Vocal polyphony originated during the same period when the Gothic cathedrals were being built. After the Renaissance, instrumental music asserted independence. Since then a series of historical transformations has cast us into the single but unintegrated world of the twentieth century. We can no longer be provincial but our new wholeness has to be built.

The branching is multiple. It is too soon to say which shoots will survive, but growth depends upon a strong inner connection with the roots.

What is the root conception behind vocal polyphony? The clue is in how it is performed. The familiar dispute whether unaccompanied part-singing was or was not the custom somewhere some time is not in point here. To sing a motet you have to adjust your pitches to the other parts by listening to get the intervals in tune. This is done by ear, not by analysis; but the music must be designed to make it possible.

Medieval music theory, derived from archaic oriental traditions and passed on through ancient Greece, knew this and provided a method. The philosophical lineage passes through Pythagoras, who had the teaching from Eastern sources. At Samos music was a means of psychological understanding. There is ample evidence in Plato to support this.[1] But in the music of the Western Christian Church this influence lost its identity.

During the Gothic period some of the methods, perhaps even the original conception, came to life again. The bearers of the seed were the theorists. It took root and flourished but afterward again lost touch with its origins.

In the Renaissance, faced with practices in composition and performance more germane to secularized art, and with the new possibles and impossibles of instrumental music, the central tradition went underground again.

Still another grouping of possibles and impossibles faces us today in synthesized, performerless music. It is wise to return to basics. The point is not whether music is sung or played or synthesized electronically. The point is first *why* and only then *how* we make music.

The growing end of Western musical tradition shows today a cluster of opposing trends. Electronic music with no performer exists side by side with totally improvised pieces with (almost) no composer. Some compositions have mathematically designed schemes of organization, while others almost indistinguishable from these to the listener are made by methods of random choice. There are sound compositions in which pitch serves only as a color element, in sharp contrast to others in which pitch relations are organized and refined to an unprecedented degree. Effective reconciliation of these opposites will take decades of serious artistic effort. We can expect opposing *isms* for some time. But there is a common problem, the solution of which could eventually integrate musical styles on a new basis.

This problem is *musical intelligibility.* Without alert reception by ear, music can mean nothing. Attention must be engaged. A failure on this level is catastrophic but all too common.

Good composition is good mnemonics. A listener needs to discover order in music. He will even impose order upon it if his interest is intense enough.

The greatest interest is aroused by an impression of emotional significance. Music may seem symbolic of personal experience or of something greater than that. The time-shape its sounds make may awake the profoundest symbolic images a man can conceive, far outweighing in interest any merely personal experience.

Exploring symbolic content is an emotional discipline. The rich meanings of a symbol hang together by common emotional content. Music makes a particularly strong impression on emotions and so can be a valuable symbolic tool. We are back at Samos: music can be knowledge, a knowledge not merely of the intellect. Whatever may be the sociological role of a piece of music, it is the possible psychological value it may have which makes it art.

Relations between composer, performer, and listener have changed profoundly in much recent music. Merely to record a performance changes everything for the listener. Live performance has an excitement born of unpredictability. Recorded performance has a fixed perfection. It is like the difference between stage and film acting.

Push fixed perfection and precision to an extreme and you replace the performer with a machine. In studio-made music the horizon of sound expands breathtakingly. In theory anything audible is useable. It is not so easy, however. Between the conception and the realization falls the electronic studio. Not only technical limitations pose problems. In eliminating the performer, the composer has lost his collaborator. He has to do the whole job himself. The newness of the sound materials, the tedious process necessary to try things out by ear, the need to make, once and for all, the "definitive performance": all this makes synthetic composition a tough job.

Is it surprising that so many composers are tempted to pin their faith on mathematical *arrières pensées* "guaranteed" to structure the sounds? Or that others abandon control and preconception in favor of chance and "experiment"? Is it even surprising that both these procedures lead alike, from a listener's vantage point, to maximum unpredictability: either of unintelligible ordering procedures or else of no ordering procedures at all? But at least these methods help to counteract the eventual total predictability of any recorded or performerless piece of music.

Unpredictability turns out to be as important an aesthetic need as inevitability ever was. The use in performance of improvisation and other indeterminate elements is another reaction against the mechanization of performers. It is to be expected that most performers will turn away from music that makes inordinate technical demands and at the same time leaves them less creative contribution than ever.

Perhaps even more basic are the changes in the relation of the composer to his materials. Research into new sound materials proceeds in two directions: inclusion in music of the whole range of audible sounds and expansion of the timbre and pitch resources of ordinary musical sounds.

So long as we are dealing with musical instruments, the trial-and-error method suffices for experimentation. But electronic means actually offer a composer the complete sound world, both by recording and by electronic synthesis: the only boundaries are the perceptual limitations of human beings. The method of trial and error is too clumsy a means for exploring this world.

Perceptual limits are neither simple nor obvious from ordinary experience. Up to the present nearly all psychoacoustical experiments involving music, with the conclusions based upon them and presented in books as scientific fact, only mislead. Experiments by Milton Babbitt at the Electronic Music Center of Columbia-Princeton, using the RCA Synthesizer, show for the first time how thoroughly contextual and interrelated are these limits.[2]

To state anything meaningful about any one parameter of sound perception, specifications must be made at once in all parameters. What is more, to isolate these sound events from a context of music, in which all kinds of sound cues are present, already falsifies considerably any conclusions that can be made about what is or is not perceptible.

As an example of this, some common assertions about loudness perception turn out to be false. We cannot distinguish proportions in loudness. The dynamic degrees from *pianissimo* to *fortissimo* are not even an equal-interval scale. Knowing greater and less is the limit of our ability to make loudness distinctions. Loudness is the most thoroughly contextual of all musical parameters. Its function in composition is a passive one. Serialization of loudness levels (for instance) is an imaginary refinement.

The problems of psychoacoustical limits offer a stiff challenge to the keenest musical minds. The testing of musically uneducated subjects on the ground that "unprejudiced" reactions will thus be obtained is exactly like asking the man-in-the-street to pass judgment on the validity of scientific data on the ground that his lack of scientific education renders his judgments unprejudiced.

In an analogous way, effort is constantly wasted upon organizational devices as imperceptible to a listener as "sounds" outside human perceptual limits. For example, many devices of organization in totally serialized music are knowable only from a study of the score, preferably with footnotes. New technical means bring complex total organization of all musical elements within reach, but they cannot enlarge our perceptions, our attention, our memory, nor our ability to discover order and pattern in temporal events. If we want to organize intelligibly, we must learn our capabilities and keep within them.

❧ ❧ ❧

One of the most noticeable effects of the expansion of musical materials has been the development of nontonal organization.

Ordinary musical sounds treated atonally begin to affect us like nontonal sounds. It is no coincidence that serial techniques find so wide an adoption among composers of electronically made music. Serialism is inherently better suited to nontonal sounds than to tones since it ignores most ramifications of the cyclicity of pitch. Composers of "organized sound" (to borrow Edgard Varèse's term) for a time used either serial ordering techniques or "concrete" composition, in which associative reminders of the "real" world of sound are so prominent. In recent years there has been more and more a departure from either of these means. The result has been called a "new impressionism."

The term is apt. This new offshoot has a thoroughly respectable line of tradition. Instrumental style itself was already a step in this direction. The adoption of temperament was necessitated by problems of instrumental design and performance. It severed the intonational distinctions preserved in our notation system and in traditional rules and disciplines of composition from the actual sound distinctions our instruments can make. With expanding instrumental and soloistic possibilities, music became more and more coloristic and externally complicated. Notational discriminations and traditional rules meant less and less.

With the music of Claude Debussy, color became a primary compositional element. Arnold Schoenberg made harmony itself a color element, so that it functioned as a structural element in a thematic rather than in a tonal sense. Schoenberg's twelve-tone technique, the first system of musical organization to be based intrinsically upon equal temperament, achieved actually the break implicit in the adoption of temperament. Percussion music, concrete music, and electronic sound compositions are only a short step beyond this break.

In organized sound compositions, the basic image projected by music is changed. Music is no longer an ensemble of "voices" carrying inevitably with it the image of performing human beings. It is an aggregate of sounds from different sources, approximating abstractly our experience of the sound environment itself. Thus "melody" and "counterpoint" become conceptions as inappropriate as "harmony" has become. Instead of phrases we have "constellations" or "sound-objects." In George Rochberg's phrase, music is *spatialized.*[3]

Spatialization of sound can tempt a composer into forgetting his own experience of listening. He may apply principles of organization valid enough in visual use of space, where the whole can be seen all at once, to temporal events which can be experienced as a whole only retrospectively or vicariously (through looking at the score).

For example, with total serialism the question is not primarily whether the basic serial sets really impress themselves upon the memory sufficiently for their permutations and variations to produce a perceptible ordering of the design. Rather it is whether large-scale designs generated by devices of permutation and combination of basic sets are sufficient to integrate longer compositions. Unquestionably such design elements can contribute to musical intelligibility, but do they successfully replace all other organizing principles? I do not believe that they do.

Some parameters of music should not be serialized because we cannot perceive the ordering even if it is accurately realized. Other parameters can use a more subtle organizing principle capable of establishing perceptible part-to-whole relationships even though the whole is never there all at once to perception.

Time is notoriously impermanent to perception. If it is to be grasped in an aspect of permanence, directly perceptible connections must be found between the fleeting moment and the potential total experience of a duration. This element must be sought in a *dynamic* perception of events which yet has the organizing force to relate durations to each other as they are being experienced. The element in question is *rhythm.*

Rhythm is *proportion.* Sounds make (and are themselves) patterns of duration and loudness.

Ordinary rhythmic patterns are on the same scale of duration as voluntary human movements. Pitch and timbre are rhythmic patterns on a duration scale approximately one thousand times more rapid. Phrases, sections, movements (or analogous formal divisions used in music) are rhythmic patterns on a much slower scale.

Loudness is spatial. It is the movement which is patterned in duration. Loudness shapes and differentiates musical events on all scales of duration, creating accents of greater and less prominence.

Tempo, on any time scale, is the *average rate of change* of rhythmic events.[4] The successive events (whether beats, phrases, or vibrations) need not be similar either in duration or in internal pattern. When the durations forming a succession or the tempi of different successions approximate simple numerical proportions in their relationship, form is more easily intelligible. But it is a mistake to consider strictness of proportions either a norm or an ideal. Organic shapes and events always exhibit variation and approximation within a proportional scheme.

Musical meter is a silent fiction with which to measure audible proportions. To imagine all rhythmic proportions reducible to a succession of equal durations is to mechanize rhythm. Equality is only one of many proportions. A succession of events is only exceptionally periodic. Similarly, a recurrence of precisely the same event is a special case. Organic rhythm consists of successions of events on various time-scales, mutually dividing up each other. Its proportionality is approximate, though often distinctly perceptible.

We perceive rhythmic events on the time-scale of pitch as though from a great distance. We cannot become aware of individual vibrations and complexes of vibrations, only of statistical averages of these.

The longer durations of musical phrases and sections exhibit their internal shapes more readily than their interrelations. It is as if we are observing something very large at close range. We do not perceive such durations as "simultaneous" wholes except with the aid of memory. The most difficult and most important problem of musical composition is how to approximate this "simultaneous" perception. To assume such an ability in any listener is naive. It would be literally a superhuman effort voluntarily to extend the musical present moment up to large-scale durations. To achieve maximum attentiveness and alertness of memory a listener needs all the help he can get.

The musical present exists on the scale of ordinary rhythm. On this scale we are as if at a comfortable distance from the events we are observing. This is the level of notes, beats, measures, motives.

The more complex, the more random; the simpler, the more predictable. As complexity approaches randomness, formal properties diminish in clarity. From proportionality there is a drop first to equal-interval ordering. A further drop in intelligibility means we can merely discriminate greater and less in terms of qualities. Finally only like and unlike can be distinguished. In extreme randomness (as of white noise) we can no longer even single out individual events.[5]

In harmonic thinking we are comparing pitches as proportional systems of rates of vibration. To think of pitch scales and melodies as patterns made up of selections from equally spaced intervals is a rough, though useful approximation. A succession of pitches is actually a fluctuation of very rapid tempi. In thinking melodically, however, we presume selection from an equal-interval scale rather than to emphasize proportional relationships. Melodic and harmonic thinking are not in practice separable. We need both in making pitch designs.

When we find no average tempo on a pitch level we hear noise, color, texture. Sufficiently complex pitch relations approximate noise.

The orderly ratios of pitches or the rapidly changing random proportions of noise can be imitated on the time-scale of ordinary rhythm or on the still larger scale of formal proportions. Translation of techniques of rhythmic organization from one time-scale to another is characteristic of contemporary composition. Nearly all the musical innovations of our time depend upon this research.

To extend musical order further into the unintelligible jungle of randomness, and without simply eliminating that jungle—this is perhaps the fundamental aim of contemporary composition. Synthesized music, improvised music, totally organized music, music by chance, noise music, and music with extended pitch resources all tend either toward mere randomness or toward the extension of organizing techniques into more complex sound situations.

Proportionality aids memory greatly besides providing strong part-to-whole relationships. To base the organization of complex compositions solely upon serial techniques, which depend mainly upon interval-scale ordering, is to use an inadequate mnemonic tool. A composer must settle for undigested randomness or else he must take great care to stimulate memory and proportional awareness on all time-scales.

Research is being conducted with information theory and electronic computers which is pertinent to this problem. In particular the work of Abraham Moles in France and that of L. A. Hiller at the University of Illinois should be cited.[6] It is too soon to evaluate the ultimate effects of such research, but it has already provided useful intellectual tools for the study of musical intelligibility.

❧ ❧ ❧

Even a casual glance at contemporary music reveals the dethronement of conventional tonality, metricality, and traditional form. These devices of organization are simply inadequate to make intelligible the complexities of contemporary musical materials.

Twentieth-century composers have refused to rule out the new world of sound in favor of the safe ground of tradition. Debussy abandoned the traditional logic of harmonic progressions. Schoenberg proclaimed the "emancipation of the dissonance." Edgard Varèse concerned himself directly with noise composition. John Cage abandoned control in favor of chance and indeterminacy.[7]

Schoenberg is especially important because while greatly expanding the sound vocabulary of music he also tried to provide new means for organizing new complexities. But in the long run a conception like "atonality" is, like Cage's "no-continuity," an abandonment of the problem of rendering complexity intelligible. Serial technique, Schoenberg's solution to the problem of organization, is applicable even to noises. Yet in an important and basic way serialism is, as I have suggested, a *less* sophisticated technique than tonal organization.

It is clearly necessary to generalize the concept of tonality if it is not to be abandoned altogether. The solution should have the characteristic of including traditional tonal methods within it, as special, limited cases. Serialism does not provide such a connection between tonal and nontonal sound patterns. It is an elaborate development of thematicism, not incompatible with tonality but not a fully satisfactory substitute for it. Tonality is based upon ratio organization, whereas serialism is based upon ordinal and interval ordering. A ratio scale does not, like an interval scale, provide equal sizes in all adjacent intervals. Its special virtue is that it expresses each term as a relation to a single point of reference. This is precisely what is characteristic of tonality.

Tonality can be defined as the organization of pitches by ratios. Pitch is tempo; thus tonality is *a system of proportional tempi.* This can exist on any time scale, not only on that of pitch. Ordinary metrical rhythm is a simple application. The "symmetrical" phrase rhetoric of classical European tradition is another. The generalization of the concept of tonality can accurately be called *proportionality.* In contemporary music, simple proportionality is replaced on all levels of organization by complex proportions. These are expressible in our rhythmic notation without extensive innovations. But a similar extension of proportionality in the domain of pitch entails a reexamination of our musical scale.

We have for so long been accustomed to take our musical scale for granted that we have forgotten the function of a scale. Scales are precompositional devices in a far more basic sense than are serial sets. In most cases a scale is the basis of instrumental design. This is why temperament and tuning was such an issue during the seventeenth and eighteenth centuries, when instrumental music was gaining ascendancy. With unaccompanied vocal music or with electronic synthesis, the choice of scale is flexible. With instrumental music it must be decided first, in nearly every case.

The problem of temperament is not so much that it is out of tune. Except for instruments on which the performer cannot control the pitch, intonation is adjusted by ear. Tempered intervals are only a theoretical point of departure much of the time. For the rest the ear accepts approximation willingly enough. But temperament has led to an unquestioning acceptance of the twelve-tone division of the octave as an equal-interval scale. The origin of this very scale from pitch ratios is largely forgotten today. Even composers who have explored new scale possibilities have usually based these upon equal temperament of arbitrary numbers of notes to the octave.

In actual performance the precise pitch of each tone is determined by ear from its context. To play harmonic relations in tune we need a variable pitch region for each scale tone. The intellectual expression of this process is a ratio scale. Pitch ratios, arranged in order of ascending pitch, form approximately equal-interval scales at several stages of their derivation. The twelve-tone scale is one of these stages. The fifty-three-tone scale is another. Both these stages of scale derivation approximate equal-interval scales whether the ratios employed are generated by prime numbers 1, 2, and 3, or by prime numbers, 1, 2, 3, and 5. The former derivation is that of Pythagoras, also of ancient China. The latter is that of Ptolemy's intense diatonic scale, also of ancient India. The Pythagorean scale provides perfect fifths and fourths. The Ptolemaic provides in addition *just* thirds, smoother and more easily tuned than Pythagorean thirds.

Tonality and harmonic thinking imply microtonal pitch distinctions. Actually to realize these implications in conventional music serves to clarify and purify its texture. But to base compositions upon untempered microtones is a recent development in Western music. It brings us back into contact with an ancient Asiatic musical tradition, the same that so interested Pythagoras.

This direction, within our own tradition, was rediscovered by Harry Partch, who invented a whole new orchestra of instruments to achieve new pitch relations. Partch's instruments, largely percussion and plectrum types, and his aesthetic bent, which leads him into theater, do not emphasize the microtonal pitch organization upon which his music is based. But the design of the instruments is intricately related to the ordering of the tones, so that in writing idiomatically for the instruments he is at the same time basing his compositions on a microtonal harmonic structure. Partch's scale is derived from prime numbers 1, 2, 3, 5, 7, and 11. He employs very few secondary ratios (multiples and dividends of simple ones, providing chains of analogous relationships). Whatever may be the present or future critical verdict on his contribution to musical composition, Partch's example in the field of precomposition is of great value.

Karlheinz Stockhausen's *Electronische Studie I* is based upon untempered interval ratios treated serially. It suffers from insufficient intervallic variety, partly because his application of serial techniques restricts tonal variety too much.

Varèse has said that pitch in organized sound compositions has no relationship to the tempered scale.[8] He has also affirmed the supremacy of the ear in all musical judgments. Although he has pointedly declined to present a rationale for his music, in striking contrast to the advocates of serial technique, his remarks indicate clearly his aesthetic position.

Cage once remarked that the only way to go really beyond the style of Anton Webern is to explore microtones or noise. If Webern did not actually achieve the exhaustion of the musical possibilities of the twelve-tone scale, he certainly has come to symbolize that effort. "Post-Webernism" has led directly into a dense jungle of complexity and randomness.

Although all these examples point to our need to find our way in a world of unprecedented complexity, they offer little more than hints at what might be a reliable guide. Great complexity in the materials of art calls for a compositional technique with maximum organizing power. To establish connection between the known and rational and familiar on the one hand and the unknown and irrational and unpredictable on the other requires subjecting them to the same measure. *Proportionality is such a common measure,* if we bear in mind the modifying principles of variation and approximation. It is not incompatible with other modes of organization such as serial ordering. It applies with equal effectiveness to formal, rhythmic, and pitch organization. It can be realized best by ear, in the case of pitch; by kinesthetic perception, in the case of rhythm; by intuitive timing, in the case of formal divisions. Yet it is capable of intellectual formulation and manipulation.

Art is not only a symbol of life; it is also a symptom of it. If contemporary music produces in our hearts and minds and bodies images of tension and anxiety (and worse states), we cannot deny it is holding up a mirror. The danger is clear. We have a choice of weapons. We may sharpen our understanding in order to cut through the complexity, or we may cultivate acceptance of anything and everything. The active and the passive attitude. Undoubtedly we need something of both. Perhaps our solution will point beyond itself.

NOTES

1. Cf. especially Plato's *Republic* and *Timaeus.* The application (in the latter) of Pythagorean harmonic ratios in a discussion of psychology (the human soul) is especially suggestive.

2. Milton Babbitt, in lecture series "Problems in Electronic Music," Second Princeton Seminar in Advanced Musical Studies, Princeton University, August 1960.

3. George Rochberg, lecture at Illinois Wesleyan Symposium on Contemporary Music, Bloomington, Illinois, March 1962.

4. The following discussion of tempo and meter owes much to a lecture, "Time Relations," by Robert Erickson at the 1962 Illinois Wesleyan Symposium.

5. Cf. S. S. Stevens, "On the Theory of Scales of Measurement."

6. Abraham Moles, *Théorie de l'Information et Perception Esthetique;* L. A. Hiller Jr. and L. M. Isaacson, *Experimental Music.*

7. John Cage, *Silence.*

8. Varèse, in a lecture to Vladimir Ussachevsky's class in electronic musical techniques, Columbia University, January 1960.

A TALK ON CONTEMPORARY MUSIC

1963

Let me begin by asking some awkward questions about the place of music in our lives, because for many people contemporary art music seems baffling. They are tempted to accuse it of unnecessary ugliness.

The first question is: What is music for? Why do we bother with it? The question is embarrassing because it should be so easy to answer, and it is not. In the first place we do not have a music; we have a number of them, answering numerous real and imaginary needs. But all these varieties satisfy, with more or less success, two kinds of needs: sociological ones and psychological ones.

At the moment we are here in the midst of a large-scale sociological occasion for art: a festival. Festivals and special concert series are today the principal occasions for contemporary art music. Music in a contemporary idiom predominates markedly in most other musical occasions than musical concerts (for instance, radio, television, movies, theatrical productions, and popular music). Very little of this flood of music is good art, and much of it has no artistic aims at all. But in musical events where the music *is* seriously intended, both as art and as the main focus of attention, the conventional audience wants and gets comfortable, familiar music, even at the cost of boredom, because it has not learned the excitement of a truly pertinent aesthetic experience.

A festival, as an occasion for listening to music, has limitations similar to those of an art museum as a place to see paintings and sculptures. Even assuming infallible good taste and imagination on the part of the planners, there is too much to take in. It is remarkable if the works of art do not cancel each other out aesthetically by too-close proximity and by contradictory intentions. The public has to choose between sampling and savoring selectively or ordering the whole menu, which takes a very good digestion.

Most serious composers and performers of contemporary music retreat from the problem of an audience almost altogether. They are each other's audience most of the time, and not a very large nor a very sympathetic one. In a festival or special concert series their works are brought before a much larger audience, even if under somewhat artificial circumstances.

For those occasions where music has a real and clearly defined supporting function to perform (such as music for movies, TV, radio), it is easier to see how well it lives up to the responsibility of its role. Although such music is seldom more than very lightweight art, one can sometimes see it become more than that, to the extent that musicians rise to the occasion and to the extent that artificial limiting requirements are removed.

While it is true that such functions seriously limit music, in a sense they give it clear aims. But not only theatrical and popular music is meaningful. Could anyone, with a clear conscience, cut away all abstract music as useless? Surely such music has a significance beyond the prestige of being high culture.

Then what is wrong? Why does contemporary music succeed so well in a background role and so equivocally in most concerts? Why do conventional concert audiences accept serious artistic content in outdated styles and reject such content in contemporary styles?

I believe there are two evasions responsible for this state of affairs. One is a failure of listeners; the other, a failure of musicians, particularly of composers.

The fault with listeners is in wanting all art to be pleasant entertainment. Music affects as well as reflects our psychological makeup. If some contemporary music produces in our hearts and minds and bodies images of tension and anxiety (and worse states), we cannot deny it is holding up a mirror. Most of us prefer not to look. Music of other times mostly lacks this disturbing quality. It presents us with an image which is not ours. True and beautiful it may be, but not ours.

But the pertinence of *our* music to life in our times is not enough by itself. The fault with most serious composers today, when they undertake to present listeners with an honest view of the tension and complexity of contemporary life, is that much too often they leave it at that. A habitual psychological state of high tension such as contemporary life tends to produce is not merely a status quo to be taken for granted, but a serious problem. It is a problem art can help to solve, by bringing to recognition, analyzing, and making intelligible the complex patterns of these tensions. Music which evades the issues of complexity and tension or which simply reflects these aspects of life is not accepting its psychological responsibility. The truly significant task for contemporary music is to make this complexity intelligible.

The importance of an occasion such as this festival is that it brings the music of present-day composers before a wider audience than in-group concerts are ever likely to command. This music is potentially valuable. If audiences realize what they *can* get—so much more than they usually ask for *or* receive—then they will insist upon a genuinely alert, exciting, urgently pertinent experience at concerts. A listener who *seeks* a lively aesthetic experience has every right to demand expert help. The more this insistence is felt, the more enthusiastic will musicians be in responding. Contemporary art music will cease to be a hothouse plant and will become a staple of our cultural diet.

Today's music shows a number of opposing trends. Electronic music with no performer shares programs with totally improvised pieces which have (almost) no composer. Some compositions are mathematically designed, while others, at times almost indistinguishable to the listener, are made by methods of chance. There are sound compositions where pitch is only a color element, in sharp contrast to others based upon elaborately expanded pitch relations. Effective reconciliation of these opposites will take years. We can expect opposing *isms* for some time to come.

Twentieth-century composers have chosen to explore a greatly expanded world of sound at the cost of abandoning the safe ground of tradition. Traditional techniques of composition are simply inadequate to make intelligible the complexities of the new musical materials.

As early as 1900, with the music of Claude Debussy, harmonic and instrumental color became *primary* compositional elements, making the first big step toward the emergence of a new musical rhetoric. The new music is no longer an ensemble of instrumental "voices" carrying inevitably with it the image of performing human beings. It is a combination of sounds from different sources, approximating in abstraction our experience of our sound environment itself.

In the development of this new tradition during the first half of our century, Arnold Schoenberg was especially important, because, while greatly expanding the sound vocabulary of music he also tried to provide new means for organizing new complexities. In logical extension of Debussy he proclaimed "the emancipation of the dissonance" and simultaneously abandoned the traditional method of organizing tones. Serial technique, Schoenberg's solution to the problem of musical organization, has been both expanded and refined in the works of his disciples, notably Anton Webern, who pioneered in the development of new musical forms and textures appropriate to serially composed music.

Serial technique is applicable even to noises, but it remained for other composers not principally interested in this technique, such as Edgard Varèse, John Cage, and the French *musique concrète* school to concern themselves directly with noise composition.

The post-Webern school, following Webern's lead after World War II, pushed serial composition to such lengths that its results are extremely similar to compositions of Cage and others which are based instead upon chance and indeterminacy.

Cage once remarked that the only way to go really beyond the style of Anton Webern is to explore the minute shadings of pitch called *microtones*, or to explore noise. He suggested that perhaps an expanded pitch scale, such as one finds in various oriental musics or, to take a Western example, the music of Harry Partch, is the only lively alternative to noise music. If Webern did not actually exhaust the possibilities or the traditional occidental twelve-tone scale, he has certainly come to symbolize that effort. Post-Webernism led directly into a jungle of complexity and randomness.

Relations between composer, performer, and listener have changed profoundly in much recent music. As in our lives, one of the biggest change bringers is automation. Especially with computers our possibilities grow shockingly and unpredictably. Automation, through recording as well as through synthetic, performerless music, changes everything for the listener. In synthetic music, the horizon of sound expands breathtakingly. In theory anything audible is usable. Live performance, on the other hand, has an excitement born of unpredictability, which can be heightened by the introduction of improvisation or of variable elements which cause a composition to change radically with each performance.

In the face of these dizzying developments, is it surprising that so many composers are tempted to make music a branch of applied mathematics? Or that others abandon choice in favor of total permissiveness? What are the means to include the whole world of sound or any fraction of it which we may prefer, and cohesive enough to integrate, into a single whole, diverse elements of style, technique, and acoustics?

To extend musical order further into the jungle of randomness and complexity, and without simply eliminating that jungle—this is perhaps the fundamental aim of contemporary serious music. Complex, unintelligible music reflects complex, unintelligible living. If in art this complexity can be made understandable, perhaps it can induce a similar change in our lives.

FESTIVALS AND NEW MUSIC

1965

A musical event is, most frequently, a transaction among three participants, a composer, a performer, a listener. Music exists for the listener. If it is art, however, it does not aim simply to gratify the most comfortable of his tastes. Rather art music leads him into aesthetic experiences which have been judged valuable. The performer exists to project these experiences powerfully to the listener. The composer tries to discover for himself "timeless" aspects of experience, and to restate them in a context which is unmistakably of his own day. He is not, any more than the performer, expressing merely himself.

We live in an age when most of the available audience expects pandering to its most commercialized tastes, when most performers see little need for new music which does not paraphrase the old, when "serious" composers band together in cliques in defiance of both performers and listeners.

Furthermore, we live in a country where as yet the government does not widely subsidize the arts. Foundations, universities, and private individuals must do most of this. Americans have been slow to realize that art is more than amusement, and cannot be expected to compete for a mass audience.

Thus festivals and subsidized concert series are highly necessary and significant phenomena. All such series of events bring at least performers and audiences into lively interaction. The contemporary festival or series brings composers actively into relationship as well. It is thus an event with greater potential significance than any other kind of concert series.

When such a festival or series begins its activity, it has to take the aesthetic initiative, first with the audience, then with its performers, and finally with composers. The best festivals encourage and bring about not only performance but also creation of new and significant music. A listener's curiosity can grow into an active search for fresh meaning and artistic challenge. The ambitions of a performer can mature until he becomes a guide in this search.

When composers come into fruitful interaction with such audiences and performers, really vital artistic activity results.

A tradition which aims merely to repeat the past is dead. A fashion which is *de rigueur* is a trap. The programs of this festival represent a number of trends, from conservative to avant-garde. The aim has been to avoid anachronism in conservative styles and avant-garde conformism in radical styles. The planners hope that a lively series of events has resulted from this policy.

THREE ATTACKS ON A PROBLEM

1967

THROUGH PHILOSOPHY

Schoenberg's solution to the impasse of music in his day was a heroic but temporary expedient. The sickness he diagnosed was real; the therapy he devised was more than adequate for him and for his time, since he enjoyed great creative vitality. Between his right and left hand, no collusion: his practice did not restrict itself to his theory.

A great composer and an independent thinker, Schoenberg would have deplored the academy which has been erected upon the very part of his technique which he refused to teach to his students (regarding it, no doubt, as his own peculiar solution to composing). Schoenberg did not wish to break with the past. He wanted very much to bridge the abyss he saw before him, not simply to leap it and start life all over again.

At the onset of this century, the grand European tradition of music was sick with a mechanical overripeness. Its very means for creating the primary aesthetic illusion of that organic unity were creaky. In an effort to conceal its wobbly wheels, the whole mechanism had been clothed more and more magnificently. So that finally the term *nineteenth century* came to mean "pretentious."

Music, even if viewed purely as an experience of sensation, is an exercise in attention. It attracts and keeps attention; it arouses interest. If it is to do this, it cannot forever reiterate the same sounds, the same patterns.

As an expression of man's inner life of feelings, music cannot afford to seek again and again the same responses, because these responses will deteriorate not only in intensity but also in significance. At first bringing challenge and discovery, a significant musical composition eventually breeds a contempt that masquerades as comfort and acceptance.

A musical system is a set of logical symbolic relations. As any such system becomes thoroughly known, it gradually bankrupts itself of information, to the point of exhaustion. To the point of contempt, one might say. We become contemptuous: of cliché, of platitude, of perfunctoriness, of insincerity. The *symbols* become exhausted: of meaning.

It was this depletion which Schoenberg faced courageously. Music's pitch usages he found badly outworn. Schoenberg's solution, based upon an extension and refinement of thematicism, largely replaced tonal devices in his music as a means to create an impression of organic unity. This technique later proved to be as applicable to any other measurable aspects of music as to pitch. A not altogether unpredictable result of this broader applicability has been that many composers, tired of tonal clichés, have either abandoned pitch or, more accurately, have organized it as if it were noise.

In an article addressed to the general public (in *Saturday Review of Literature*), Aaron Copland describes the nearly exclusive preoccupation of a whole younger generation of composers with neglected parameters of sound and performance. "They have changed the rules on us," he comments wryly. Well, why not? Who made the rules? Who, for that matter, made the game?

What is *really* behind the development to which Copland refers is the bankruptcy of overused parameters, notably of *pitch* and *metrics.* And the problem of these aspects of music is not being solved, but evaded. The currently fashionable means for organizing sound—serial, aleatoric, statistical—are not *more* productive of musical order than earlier systems, but less so.

However, these trends are definitely moves in a constructive direction, since they represent new parts of a larger complete system than earlier musicians used. The main organizational techniques of the past also fall within this larger system.

Elsewhere I have discussed this system, a hierarchy of kinds of aesthetic order, based upon a theory of scales of measurement devised by the Harvard psychophysicist S. S. Stevens. The kind of scalar order of which tonality and metricality are special cases *is* mathematically the most sophisticated of the kinds possible within this system, which also provides a number of less intricate modes of order. Other special cases of this most versatile of scalar order types include the pitch systems of classical Chinese music, of classical Islamic music, of classical Indian music.

Schoenberg replaced a tired system with a less subtle but more vigorous one. Alternatively, others have tried to replace tonality with parallel alternative systems such as the Asiatic ones just mentioned. But when your own tradition outgrows its childhood, it is not a workable next step to abandon your own line of development for a parallel one. Nor can you permanently abandon overworked sides of your development to concentrate on potentially healthier ones.

Unfortunately, in tacitly accepting as an arbitrary "given" the twelve-tone equal-tempered scale, Schoenberg committed music to the task of exhausting the remaining possibilities in a closed pitch system.

There are people who cannot stand to be confined in no matter how large an enclosure. They find the walls and are made miserable by them. They don't care how many bars you put in the cage—twelve, twenty-four, forty-eight, nineteen, twenty-two, thirty-one, fifty-three—they will hurt themselves on them. Or break them down.

When you reach a philosophical impasse, you need to get to a more basic idea. You need to raise your assumptions about your field to a higher level of abstraction. If you do this successfully, what used to be basics will turn out to be special cases of more general principles. Einstein's physics does not invalidate Newton's. It simply reveals Newton's laws to be special cases of more general ones. The discovery of DNA, a substance which controls the intracellular synthesis of proteins and is thus basic to life itself, does not knock out all of biochemistry up to that breakthrough, but rather forces a reevaluation of many of its assumptions.

So let us revivify the problem of pitch as some composers have begun to revivify the problem of metrics. There is no need to rule out chance, statistics, serialism. But let us also pursue, still more subtly, the techniques of rational proportion, which are capable of vastly more than has hitherto been asked of them. What can be grasped with equal alacrity by ear, by mathematics, and by intuitive feeling is the best material for art. And this intelligibility is not a mere matter of conditioning: some relations are *naturally* more easily understood than others. This makes them on the one hand primary, and on the other hand obvious. I am interested in a spectrum from the most obvious to the most subtle.

THROUGH THEORY

The term *just intonation* connotes to most people either a very specialized concern with Renaissance and medieval choral music or an equally specialized concern with pre-piano keyboard music. To performers with uncommon erudition it may connote (if somewhat foggily) an ideal of playing in tune by ear in a way that necessitates careful and minute adjustments of pitch not taken care of by the design and the manual performing techniques of their instruments. This ideal also brings out a bias against keyboard and other fixed-pitch instruments which make these tuning adjustments impossible. But often the "in-tune" playing defended in the name of just intonation is quite as literally irrational as the temperament its defenders profess to deplore. It is not that players cannot hear subtle pitch differences; rather it is that there is great confusion about what they intend when "playing in tune."

It is a rare performer who has any knowledge of tuning and temperament. Available books on the subject confuse the average musician by translating the whole discussion into charts of numbers and other rudimentary but nonetheless mysterious mathematical symbols.

Most composers have little grasp of the subject and almost as little curiosity. This includes the majority of those who find mathematics a convenient and fascinating tool in composition. References to tuning and temperament in writings by composers are almost always parenthetical and generally refer to the problems rather than present them clearly.

Concern with this field by musicologists is usually connected with ancient or medieval music theory, with Asiatic or North African music theory and performance, or with the tuning of early keyboard instruments. This leaves almost only mavericks like Yasser, who are attracted to speculate in what almost amounts to a branch of applied number theory.

Even acoustics, turning resolutely to the fields of hearing and experimental psychology, leaves very much behind such latter-day Pythagoreans as Helmholtz.

In the last distillation of all, there remain a tiny handful of composers who are incurably fascinated with pitch relations, who are intrigued rather than frightened away by all the arithmetic, and who refuse to be bound to twelve-tone equal temperament, which after all was no more than an expedient necessitated by keyboard instruments intended to play tonal music.

This small group fringes off into a wider group of composers who have an occasional interest and concern with alternative tuning systems, but who find no more basic quarrel with twelve-tone equal temperament than that many of them consider it a happenstance of historical tradition.

In any case, anyone who wants to tackle the problem of writing music in a new tuning system must either (1) rely mostly on fixed-pitch instruments or (2) realize the music directly, without the intervention of performers, or (3) reeducate the listening habits of performers.

Most of the earlier gropings in this direction were either entirely theoretical, or involved experiment with keyboard, fretted, and pitched percussion instruments. Undoubtedly the most extensive work of this kind has been done by Harry Partch, who has literally designed and built an orchestra of such instruments for his own use. The training and coaching of performers, the maintenance and carrying about of his instruments, the persuading of people that so unconventional a project is worth so much effort and expense, not to speak of the theoretical research, the design and building of instruments, and the composing itself—all these constitute a monumental life work, mostly carried out, moreover, in conditions of poverty, public indifference, and rejection by his colleagues. Anyone interested in this field owes him not merely a debt, but an apology. Partch was determined to get this kind of music out of the limbo of theorizing, and he did it. Almost no one else has produced more than an occasional oddly tuned keyboard piece, such as Ives's *Quarter-tone Impressions.*

The second alternative, adopted by many electronic composers, can be done either by ear, as Varèse insisted, or by computation and measurement, as Stockhausen made his *Gesang der Jünglinge.* In designing such music by computation, the danger lies precisely in the fact that almost anything conceivable can be executed, with sufficient ingenuity and patience. But since not everyone shares the faith that whatever is mathematically intelligible will be audibly so, this can be a serious problem. In losing the performer, one removes an automatic check: whatever can be played can be understood by ear, but not so, whatever can be synthesized. If you operate as Varèse did you are safe from that pitfall. But is the unaided ear really better than the ear plus the analytical intelligence?

It is the third alternative, retraining the performer's ear, which offers the most fruitful challenge, forbidding as it seems. If a performer can teach his ear to know its way around in a strange pitch system, then a listener can make sense of the result. It is far easier for performers to do this if the new system is based upon one with which they already are intimately familiar.

The earliest attempts to do this inserted additional melodic tones "between the cracks of the keys," providing a "hyperchromatic" melodic scale, and the possibility of "distorted" intervals adjacent to the more familiar ones. Until after the advent of electronic music none of these attempts involved a serial use of pitch. Hába's string quartets use the new pitch relations as a further complication of modulatory chromaticism inherited from the late nineteenth century. Ives's quartertone piano pieces and some of his songs point to a fresher approach to harmony derived from Impressionism.

Impressionist harmony, especially that of Debussy and of later Scriabin, strongly implies a just intonation using higher partials of the overtone series, the very thing later to be developed systematically by Partch. Similarly, much of Ives's harmony (not only in the explicitly quartertone passages) implies an extended just intonation tuning.

This use of harmonic intervals tuned just (by eliminating the roughness of beats) provides a better point of departure than any tempered equivalents. Cyclic patterns (of chains of equal-sized intervals) do not return to octaves of their starting pitch, but instead to displaced octaves, microtonally distant from octave equivalents.

To make a just intonation pitch system, you select a small number of generative intervals which you can tune precisely, by ear. For a triadic system the unison, the octave, the perfect fifth, and the major third will suffice. All other intervals can be obtained by combining these. Such a system yields scales more and more closely approximating equal-interval scales at five notes per octave, at seven, at twelve, at nineteen, at thirty-one, at fifty-three. Partch's system, a *hexadic* one, needs as generative intervals the unison, the octave, the perfect fifth, the major third, the "natural" seventh, and the "natural" eleventh. He linearizes a scale (by choice) at forty-three tones per octave.

Keyboard and other fixed-pitch instruments are by their very design unsuited to just intonation. The best one can do with them is to select any convenient, desired number of tones from the system, and be content to use only these. This more or less drastically restricts movement within the infinite system of pitches provided by just intonation. It is only with instruments of flexible pitch, with performers who adjust the tuning by ear as they play, that one can have full freedom of movement within such a wide-open pitch system. Partch's extensive reliance upon fixed-pitch instruments is mostly due to his introduction of unfamiliar generative intervals, "natural" sevenths and elevenths. In an expanded triadic system no such difficulty exists, since the generative intervals are known to every musician, and precision in tuning them by ear is mostly a matter of clearing up confusion about what to listen for.

THROUGH PRACTICE

I have been warned by just about everyone who knew I was writing this paper not to permit it to become just more words without music. Aesthetic philosophies and theories of music are known by their fruits: by the *music* written and played and heard with their aid. For several years I have been writing music based on the position which I have just presented. I certainly cannot claim that what I have written up to now exploits fully the philosophical and theoretical possibilities which I can already see. I am quite prepared to devote the rest of my creative life to this artistic effort. I would not wish for anyone to adopt my technique. There are as many compositional approaches to the musical problems with which I am concerned as there are composers. In speaking of my own music I am giving the example which I know best.

About *all* words can do to intensify the listening experience is to call attention to sounds which may especially interest us. Words do not usually do this, but lead us away from the experience of hearing sounds.

It is at present most unfashionable to speak about the "meaning" of a piece of music, about the experience of its intuitive, emotional, symbolic content. Almost the only way to do this is to attempt a translation into poetry—and we have had a surfeit of nineteenth-century-style program notes. We have the same difficulty in speaking of any powerful experience. We run a risk of detracting from it, so that many people prefer to say nothing.

With musical meaning, as with listening itself, about all words can do is to hint at the character, the color, the intensity which the experience of a piece of music *may* bring.

In the *telling* it is the remaining side of music, its intellectual machinery, which alone can receive justice. But I prefer to think of all intellection in the process of composing as a nozzle. Once, in answer to a question about technique, I replied that it is what I do with my mind while I am composing. To me this *nozzle,* this focusing mechanism, is of great importance. Without it what comes out is weak and diffuse. I believe that the manner of the focusing should be relevant to and symbolic of the inner meaning of the music. What makes it worth studying, for instance, Beethoven's Piano Sonata op. 109, is the discovery that a structural, intellectual analysis of the work points to and deepens the direct intuition which you get when the sonata is brought to life in performance. It is, I think, dangerous to discuss this aspect of a work when your listeners have not had this intuition of it.

For these reasons, more than from modesty, I shall keep my remarks on my *String Quartet no. 2* brief and suggestive.

I wanted to write a piece in which the players would need to listen to each other carefully and to take much greater care than usual in locating the pitches. It would be a little like mountain climbing: the foothold of each note would be dependent upon making precisely the right connection—the right interval—with some other player's note.

(I actually believe that all music not played on fixed-pitch instruments should be played in this manner: it is keyboards, more than anything else, which create the illusion that "C" is some absolute pitch, that our scale is a fixed ladder of "steps.")

The intervals the players must tune in this way are precisely the consonant ones of triadic music, but the harmonic character of the music is almost never triadic. There are three distinct kinds of interval texture in this piece.

Where I used mostly consonant intervals and that type of dissonance traditionally called "diatonic," I thought of the texture as "diatonic." The second movement is in this idiom. The term *diatonic* in no way implies even an occasional use of so-called functional diatonicism. This music has, on the contrary, a harmonic idiom of rapid chromatic changes and microtonal cross relations, far closer in sound to Gesualdo than to Bach. These microtonal pitch relations describe a strict spiral pattern, ascending one octave of a fifty-three-tone just intonation scale.

A second type of texture results from emphasizing dissonant intervals produced with the aid of simple consonances, but predominating over them. When a large number of these dissonances are what, in traditional harmonic terminology, are called "chromatic intervals" (that is, *augmented* or *diminished* intervals), I thought of the texture as "chromatic." This is the character of the opening movement. I composed this movement entirely of permutations of a single three-note motif, interpreted with a great variety of tunings, and always combined into one of three strict permutations of a twelve-tone set. The starting tone of each successive set-form rises one more pitch in a complete fifty-three-tone octave. In this movement, the rhythmic and durational relations are governed by a proportional system analogous to the just intonation system which govern the pitch relations.

The third kind of pitch texture, which dominates the final movement, is created by melodic and harmonic use of microtonal intervals and microtonal alterations of larger intervals. These intervals also result from combinations of simple consonances, and occur mostly with these. In some places, however, the players are told how to find these microtonal variants by *melodic size.* The middle section of this movement serially treats a thirty-one-note scale. The movement also serializes durations and is a microtonally exact retrograde inversion of itself.

As you listen to the quartet, you become increasingly aware of microtonally altered intervals and of actual microtones. In the first movement these occur only in the widely leaping melodic lines of the instruments and never in the harmony. In the second movement they turn up in the harmony, in sharp contrast to the uncomplicated melodic lines and to the harmonious consonances of the just intonation. In the last movement such intervals are much of the time in the foreground of attention, set off more than ever by the clear consonances they surround. But in the middle section they eclipse all other types of intervals, in a frenzy of contrapuntal activity.

If I may venture a "subjective" adjective or two, I would describe the effect of the first movement as shifting and iridescent; the second, as clear and lyrical; the last, as intensely unsettling and expressionistic.

I hope I have conveyed the conviction I have that music should be heard and not seen. We have set ourselves to talk about it: that is already error enough.

ON CONTEXT

1968

Thinking about music is not nearly so clean-cut and so specialized a problem as some of us university musicians seem to think it is. There is no doubt that the role of music in our lives, the place of art in our values are undergoing profound changes. This ferment is part of a much larger and more pervasive process, a global technological and social revolution.

We are flooding the world with people. Technology is building a kind of ark to get humanity through this crisis. It will take all the ingenuity of avant-garde thinkers to invent for us new ways of living appropriate to the new conditions. And if we are not utterly to lose all civilizational continuity it will take careful selection, uprooting, and transplanting of traditions to maintain anything of the past in our new situation.

In the center of this violent process of change, the United States is struggling to mature culturally. Our role in the larger context of the world is transitional (out of regional identification into global identification). This translation must not be made nationalistically nor exploitatively. It must not be made egotistically.

Insofar as we build imitatively upon our European heritage, we maintain at the root of thought and action a number of dualistic pairs of opposites which have long roots in European cultural history. Chief among these are the individual versus the collective, traditionalism versus experimentation, conscious intellect versus nonverbal intelligence. The parent of these supposed opposites is Aristotelian dualism, so fundamental a philosophic bias in Western culture that recent tendencies to break its monopoly upon our worldview seem to some people to threaten the bases of civilization itself.

Although we act as though the world should learn from us, we in the United States nevertheless, again and again, have exposed our culture to influences from the rest of the world, in a sense few Europeans either understand or will be willing to accept. We are constantly welcoming the very things that irritate us. At present there is widespread interest in oriental thought, and this is breaking down our dualism. Americans have perpetrated some double-thinks by trying to turn "either–or" into "both–and." We cling in many respects to our outmoded isolationism at the same time we feel called upon to teach much of the world how to live. We tend to insist simultaneously upon cultural cooperation and competitiveness.

We often deplore, as if to European parents, our lack of deep traditional roots and the absence of cultural uniqueness which our polyglot population produces. But just these lacks are what can enable us to cut Europe's apron strings and come of age. In the arts, typically the vanguard of civilization, we can see that this has already taken place. What has happened is not the emergence of just another national style, like those of Europe, but an annihilation of boundaries.

The state of the arts in the United States does not presage an era of world domination by North American culture, but rather the end of all such dominations.

All traditions belong to me if I claim them. Equally, none of them belongs to anyone. An intellectual world in which Jesus and the Buddha, Confucius, Moses, and Aristotle, Immanuel Kant and Sri Ramakrishna rub shoulders is proof against Christian, Semitic, and Nazi exclusivities, to name only a few virulent forms of prejudice.

The state of music reflects this situation but, as is typical of the arts, at a further stage in the process than that of the majority of human activities. The musical world in which Machaut, the Beatles, Wagner, Ravi Shankar, Pete Seeger, Bach, and Xenakis meet is only as far from me as my record player. This musical world, too, is proof against takeover by any such exclusive points of view as tonality, serialism, indeterminacy. Attempts to move Vienna to the USA or New York to England are just as seriously in error as the attempt to move the United States into South Vietnam.

There is much we can learn from each other and much help we can give each other, but only if we stop acting like missionaries. It isn't up to anybody as stupid as we are—as *I* am, as *you* are, as any group of men is—to improve the world, to save mankind from destruction, to guarantee the future of music.

In this fluidity the one thing we can be sure of is change. To attempt to keep a thing fixed, rigid, is to doom that thing. Perhaps the earth's needs will not include music or even people, after a point. Perhaps circumstances will slowly alter, into some new single kind, the music (and people) we have around. Leonard Meyer suggests we'll have fifty-seven varieties from now on, while arguing the opposite.

It is alarming how many of us think it really *is* up to us to decide what to do, and knowing without realizing our utter inadequacy in the face of superhuman tasks. We careen between pride in our ideologies and technologies, and desperation in the face of overwhelming problems. It is this which may do us all in. In our anxiety to do things "right," we become hysterically insistent upon our own proposed solutions, losing any sense of humility or even ordinary self-doubt.

Whatever the eventuality, one thing seems clear to me. We have to stop exploiting and plundering nature and each other and start trying to learn how to cooperate. This means learning each other's needs and allowing for them. In the case of nature, it means learning the earth's needs and cooperating with those. It means ceasing to be deadly parasites and taking the strain off our symbiotic relationship with our planet. We have to learn how really to be good neighbors. Recently a colleague was lamenting former days when it seemed clear what was music and what wasn't. To which Sal Martirano replied, "The fence is down."

Clover.

That's why I think it's spring.

The reason for the deluge is ice breaking up. For deluge we have: the beginning of an utter fluidity of living, of making art, of action on all levels. In our winter season we took Blake's advice: "Bring out number, weight and measure in time of dearth." Winter also brought quiescence, a season of anonymity. Now, in the breakup of rigidity, there is enormous energy and confusion. We may measure what we could again by what we clearly may lose. We may lose the idea of perfecting individual lives and works, replacing it by a new community of creative techniques and technicians. It will do us no good to cooperate and band together if there is not excellence and freedom in each of us. A meditation together of Jala-ud-din Rumi and Shams-i-Tabriz is not to be confused with a be-in or with a coven. Avant-garde musicians are exploring ways to live and work in this season of change. In an editorial in issue two of *Source* entitled "Is the Composer Anonymous?" the situation is described:

> [T]he all powerful, all-knowing composer of the fifties—and before—is replaced by the anonymous composer of the early sixties . . . Such self-effacement has its roots in John Cage's admonition that the composer should strive to eliminate himself from his work and simply let the music happen . . . Is the composer still anonymous? In the final years of this decade he is finding a new identity. His music and the performer—for whom and with whom he

> writes—are one. He expresses this through intimate identification with the performer—*not just through the instrument he plays* . . . We have a new understanding of our medium, a new humanism among the creators of today's music. We are not anonymous.[1]

In such music everything depends upon the relatedness—or intentional unrelatedness—of those who make and experience the artwork. Sensitive responsiveness to the unexpected predominates over prescribed and rehearsed ritual. Discipline is not only mastery of one's materials, one's instrument; it consists even more in awareness of existing and possible relationships.

The complexity of today's world makes tyrannical any attempt to legislate relationships in terms of fixed forms and roles. But it is equally destructive to counsel acceptance of anything and everything. Awareness makes free choice possible. Freedom requires responsiveness: responsibility. That is why, as a composer, I am interested in studying the kinds of order and relationships possible in my art and the way in which human beings understand these relations. Cultural and aesthetic traditions teach me much. Science and technology add still more. In the transactions between composer, performer, and listener, the many kinds of order and relationships, once *possibilities,* become *experience.* From all participants art exacts subtlety in understanding, alertness in perception, sensitivity in relationship.

The way I see the present situation is slightly different from this. It is as though we have to cross a chasm. If we are to build a bridge over it, we will have to anchor its ends far in the past and far in the future. Tradition thoroughly assimilated will help us anchor in the past; only a sharp eye for where we are going can help us anchor in the future. Technology will help us build the bridge, which will not impose upon nature but will be possible because we understand how things happen and cooperate rather than interfering. My own search is for philosophic, theoretic, and practical means broad enough to include the whole world of sound or any fraction of it I may prefer, cohesive enough to integrate into a single whole diverse elements of style, technique, and acoustics. But no one composer's holistic solution should be determining: art, like knowledge, results from each person's capability *to do* with the information we accumulate.

NOTES

1. Larry Austin, "Is the Composer Anonymous?" *Source* 1(2): 3.

CONTRIBUTION TO IMC PANEL

1968

I'm going to talk in turn, briefly, about each of three topics: the sounds of things to come; the attitude of the youth; and the composer, the performer, and the changing audience.

I think that the sounds of things to come will be many things to as many people: no one style or idiom, but a plurality of them rubbing shoulders.

In my opinion the single most important revolutionary musical fact of life in the twentieth century is the extension of the acoustical materials of the art to include the whole world of sound. Challenged by this vast horizon, music should not be encouraged to split into an art of sound and a separate art of tone. Pitch and metrics are not outmoded, nor is performing, nor is composing. But all the old customs touching these fundamental matters are under prolonged and justifiably fierce attack, so that at present many new works seem hardly to deal at all with one or several of these traditional aspects of music.

There is no good reason why all compositions or all composers should attempt to integrate a total spectrum of sound from the most complex and unpredictable noise to the purest and most consonant of pitch relations. But I think it is most important that some works attempt to encompass this gamut. Perhaps no one as yet is fully ready for this synthesis. Certainly the majority of compositions illumine only a part of the sound spectrum. Further, a large percent of their composers act from one of several mutually contradictory aesthetic bases. Any one of these viewpoints can become the cornerstone of a claim to exclusive rightness in aesthetic matters. For as long as this is true I favor denying any exclusivity the right to claim absolutism for its point of view.

Almost as important as the revolution in the materials of the art of music is the revolution which is changing the role and the meaning of music in the total environmental context of people's lives, including, of course, musicians', and especially composers'.

There is a wry joke among United States composers concerning the term *young composer.* It seems this term can be applied without stretching to anyone whom the person using it considers able to write whatever he calls "music," provided said composer is under the age of forty.

As a young composer of forty-two (and at my age the term carries with it an implication which is slightly pejorative) I shall seize this loquation to point out the first "attitude of youth" to which I want to call attention. This attitude is one of exasperation at being kept artificially junior for so ridiculously long a time by what many young people, in none too jovial a tone, call "the establishment." This not quite Kafkaesque bureaucracy fills its ranks mostly with those who, having waited out so protracted a "youth," finally have their time in the sun and, in taking it, keep yet others waiting. Really independent thinkers and artists typically aren't given such recognition until they are well on their way to becoming senior citizens.

How did we evolve such a junior-grade, semi-word-of-mouth honorary society? It has come about largely because in the world of conventional concerts the music of our own times constitutes so abnormally small a fraction of the musical fare. At the same time, the number of people writing music is sharply increasing in many parts of the world. This double bind produces a trend: more and more supply, with severely limited demand. Thus even a docile young composer whose fondest dream it would be to write music for conventional solo, chamber, and orchestra concerts is kept waiting for more than half of a long life not only for recognition but for anything more than a few scattered performances.

That is why young composers (and more recently young performers as well) continually organize festivals, concert series, even permanent performing groups which more and more tend to concentrate on *new* works, often kinds of new works which negate the very occasions, attitudes, and behavior patterns which society has established for concerts.

That is why "the establishment," which aims to continue conventional traditions and customs of concert presentation indefinitely into the future, feels the tenor of many young musicians' activities to be not merely nonconformist but actively revolutionary. Such musicians are seeking and finding a new audience, new kinds of social occasions for listening to music, new ways of presenting sound experiences to people. They work with performers so closely that the boundaries between composer, performer, electronic technician, and theatrical director are often all but obliterated.

The kind of composer of which I speak is not at all content with an audience of specialists whose expertise approximates his own. He *cares if you listen,* but he is not about to say what he thinks you wanted to hear. The kind of performer who will give to his work the same respect and meticulous care he regularly gives to Bach is simply not good enough at all. A new challenge has been offered the performer: to participate as actively as the composer in the creation of the work of art, not merely to *interpret* it, certainly not merely to *realize* it. There are too many young performers who meet this challenge enthusiastically, relieved, themselves, to drop the role of museum curator for that of fellow artist.

Many of the new centers of such activity in the United States focus around university music schools. This has come about first because there are in some universities and colleges active groups of performers and composers who are not dependent upon the competitive commercial music world for their livelihood. The phenomenon is, in addition, due to the concentration in universities of young students, especially graduate students forced to return to school for advanced degrees by the same artificially prolonged youthful status I have already mentioned, which keeps them waiting in line for full professional status in an overcrowded field, in this case teaching.

There is, you will hear, an occupational hazard in being a composer-teacher. It is said to isolate a composer from the "real world of music" in an artificial academic milieu. Of course the academic mentality is as prevalent today as it ever was. It produces music which is better seen than heard, no matter what its stylistic idiom. Such a mind is happier teaching than doing most other things. But the really effective teacher today, especially in the university, cannot allow himself to be *academic,* not if he wants the respect of his students. The university *is not* an ivory tower. It is very much a part of the "real world," very much a *central* social phenomenon. As such it tends to generate its own musical life, complete with composers, performers, audiences. The music it produces is frequently less academic than most typical contemporary concert fare in metropolitan centers.

The present stage of the communications revolution means that a young musician anywhere in most countries of the world (and we all know what are the exceptions and why) can be informed accurately and extensively about what his peers are doing the world over. With a little effort he can get tape recordings, articles, programs, not to speak of personal news and gossip. He participates in an artistic community which is by no means provincial. That is why creative musical activity in the United States is decentralizing.

This decentralization happens steadily despite the concentration of musical activity and publicity in major metropolitan centers.

There is an increasingly large number of young musicians who don't want acceptance into "the establishment," nor do they especially care to do battle with it. Its values, musical and cultural, bore them, and not because they are without culture and intelligence. On the contrary, they find conventional and official culture smug and unaware of its own irrelevance and impertinence in the face of the manifest realities of life in the second half of the twentieth century.

In less than a generation, the age group of which I speak will outnumber considerably its seniors. Perhaps it will generate its own "establishment," but that will be of a very different kind from the one that now dominates what is called our "national musical life." The percentage of musicians in the United States who don't think "business as usual" can apply to the arts is already larger than ever before.

HOW TO COOK AN ALBATROSS

1970

The world of "serious music" stubbornly bases itself on a sterile presumption. Since the "standard repertory," in no matter what areas of performance, is historical, it creates a museum situation. While there is nothing wrong with having museums, we should not take their contents to be the principal means to satisfy contemporary needs. Perennially we make just this error.

The proportion of music of our own times now in the repertory of most concert artists and ensembles is smaller today than at any other period in the history of concert giving. When most performing artists, warned that they are not bringing about a repertory for the future, set about to find new works, they seek imitations of the old works, which they believe they "understand." In fact, most of them do not understand the art of the past at all. They do not make the effort to imagine what it was in its own time, taking it instead in the context of today. The role they find repertory music playing in today's society they impose unthinkingly on today's music. Looking back for all "greatness" has become so reflex an action that it is presumed normal. In fact, it is not normal at all: it is an historical anomaly. As Gilbert Chase writes:

> In the eighteenth century it was an asset rather than a liability for a composer to be alive. Not only his music but also his living presence were solicited as a privilege for the public . . . The eighteenth century might indulge in idolatry . . . but it was the distinction of the nineteenth century to develop the cult of musical necrolatry . . . The "Great Repertoire" cannot change, because it involves too many vested interests. Far from being an incentive to the American composer, it is a permanent barrier.[1]

In the United States today a "serious composer" is called "young" up to the age of fifty if he has not been accepted into the musical establishment by then. The composers' wing of the establishment is a bureaucracy, comprising the few who, after waiting out a protracted "youth," finally have a moment's recognition. This privilege they defend for as long as they can, knowing its radical impermanence. Innovators are recognized by the establishment, if at all, only in old age, since independent thinkers are the toughest competition of all.

Most performers and conductors advise composers (if they want performances) to write music (if they must write at all) which does not deviate much from the standard repertory. But a docile composer who wants only to write conventional music for standardized solo, chamber, and orchestra concerts has to struggle for all of his career for more than a few scattered first performances. His work (it is pointed out) is poor competition for the "masterworks." The following arrogant quotation was recently widely reprinted in the press and popular magazines: "I occasionally play works by contemporary composers, and for two reasons. First, to discourage the composer from writing any more. And second, to remind myself how much I appreciate Beethoven" (violinist Jascha Heifetz). To cite Gilbert Chase again:

> The difficulty was that by the end of the nineteenth century admission to the Standard Repertory (the effective vehicle of the Great Tradition) has become increasingly difficult for new composers . . . Not only was the competition keener, but the club was getting crowded. It was approaching the saturation point. Guest memberships were available, but permanent admission was virtually impossible, save for a very select few. To make a place for himself a newcomer had to oust an old member. The Europeans had all the advantages; not only were most of them dead, but those who were living had an inside track on the Great Tradition. No wonder that no American composer has ever really made it.[2]

Conventional concert and opera audiences, led by performers and by writers about music, usually gravitate toward comfortable, familiar music, even at the cost of boredom. They seem to know little about pertinence. The idea that a piece of music could be apt (or inept) at a given time and place for reasons more important than its vogue seems never to have occurred to most concertgoers. A concert may be pleasant, diverting, and "uplifting," but the listening experience it provides rarely has any urgency or potency. At the worst it can even induce sleep by its failure to keep attention.

The public performance of repertory music has become a variety of genteel entertainment. To fulfill this role it confines itself to readily intelligible schemes of order, to familiar and accepted emotional associations, and to conventional musical sounds. For the kind of people who want confirmation that the status quo will not be threatened by changes, such entertainment is a symbol—not to say a ritual—of social and ideological stability. When (and if) most performers and conductors seek new works, their criteria are above all those of the "Great Tradition," which they claim the public demands.

Such demand as there is comes from a small, elite, and largely wealthy public, conditioned to want this traditional music by social custom, by musical education, and by promotional propaganda (which encompasses the vast bulk of music criticism). This conditioning is, moreover, class oriented.

Now that more than a wealthy minority of society faces a leisure problem, we find "the amusements" rushing in to fill the vacuum created by alleviating the hard, competitive struggle for existence. There is widespread alarm among many thinking people at the harm done by a manipulative, irresponsible amusement industry.

Properly understood, art would be a far healthier activity with which to fill leisure time, because it is educational in the classic sense: it can train one's abilities, which can then be applied as one sees fit. Art is our sharpest tool for training sensitivity and responsiveness in action with others, along with keen sensory observation and alert muscular coordination in the performance of precise actions, and with intelligent grasp of the many kinds of order and disorder in phenomena and in behavior. The problems of what to do about leisure time and of what to do about our culture's abysmal failure to educate feeling and sensitivity in people can become one problem. Until and unless "serious" composers and performers serve such a real need as this, and not simply a status-seeking and status-serving one, they will deserve exactly what they are getting: a social function as dubious luxury items.

It is dishonest and self-deceiving to claim that by maintaining the supremacy of the standard repertory we are enabling the public to benefit from the continuance of a precious artistic heritage from the past. It is not true that the public understands Beethoven more easily than Webern, Webern more easily than Cage. The overfamiliar is what people usually understand least. Even the irritation of an audience jolted into listening with unjaded ears shows a much greater degree of understanding than their conditioned response to the classics.

Just as commercial exploiters of popular taste usually claim to be supplying a demand, when in fact they are actively engaged in creating one, so leaders of community musical culture make the same false claim. Actually, little long-range effect upon concert series' policies of program selection results if a majority of their audiences express like or dislike of a particular work, composer, or musical style. If the moneyed few who donate funds to support the concert series disagree, they decide otherwise.

When Eleazar de Carvalho resigned as conductor of the St. Louis Symphony Orchestra in 1967, he stated that this was because the Symphony Board demanded to make up the program content for each season. The board's strongest objection was to de Carvalho's utilization of the available rehearsal time in favor of new works. This had resulted in some rough performances of standard works.

Former critic Peter Yates attended one of these premieres and afterward was quoted to this effect by a St. Louis newspaper. Yates later expressed alarm and resentment at this quote for being taken out of context. A letter he wrote to Barney Childs about the new (American) work on this same concert suggests the proper context of his remark: "The audience divided between applause and booing . . . The enthusiasts kept the applause going until the booers quit. Occasions like this make possible the existence of a native music."

Yet ignoring completely the audience's manifest insistence upon accepting the new work, the press implied repeatedly that this and other new works of the 1965–66 season in St. Louis had received negative reactions from the audience. Ostensibly on this basis the board cracked down. They claimed that attendance at concerts had dropped off, due to de Carvalho's musical policy.[3]

An argument is often advanced to the effect that new works have (in Europe) perennially received hostile treatment at first, and yet have gone on to become repertory. So runs the argument, what are American composers griping about?

Quite simply, they are griping about being forced to choose either to be treated as poor relations of Europeans or to become dropouts. Almost without exception, up to the present generation, to be a dropout from the musical establishment required accepting "amateur" status, either supported by an independent income, like Charles Ives, or not supported except part-time now and then, like Harry Partch.

But today it is possible to drop out and still remain an effective member of the profession. Independent composers and performers more and more often organize festivals, concert series, even permanent performing groups. These increasingly tend to concentrate on works which are new in more than a chronological sense, and to negate explicitly or by implication the very occasions, attitudes, and behavior patterns which society has established for concerts.

That is why the establishment, which aims to continue conventional traditions and customs of concert presentation indefinitely into the future, feels the tenor of many young musicians' activities to be not merely nonconformist, but actively revolutionary. Such musicians are seeking and finding a new audience, new kinds of social occasions for listening to music, new ways of presenting sound experiences to people. They work with performers so closely that the boundaries between composer, performer, electronic technician, and theatrical director are often all but obliterated.

The kind of composer of whom I speak is not at all content with an audience of specialists whose expertise approximates his own. He cares if you listen, but he is not about to say what he thinks you wanted to hear.[4] For his purpose, the kind of performer who will give to a composer's work the same respect and meticulous care he regularly gives to Bach is simply not good enough at all. A new challenge has been offered the performer: to participate as actively as the composer in the creation of music, not merely to interpret it, certainly not merely to realize it. There are many young performers who meet this challenge with enthusiasm, relieved finally to drop the role of museum curator for that of fellow artist.

William Blake observed in *The Marriage of Heaven and Hell* that "One law for the Lion & Ox is Oppression." He might have added that one music for all people is a bore. Popular music has won its revolution. The monopoly of musical trivia for so long forced on everyone by means of commercial promotion has given way. Tin Pan Alley's song lyrics get stiff competition now from real poetry. Today's rock music is a far better equivalent to the folk music of rural cultures than were any intervening varieties of urban popular music. For "serious music" to win an analogous revolution would really give grounds for optimism, because that would indicate that intellectuals were giving up class values in art for more durable values.

I do not know a better formulation of the "rock" point view than Burt Korall's:

> Today, however, the voices of dissent are louder, for cause; we cannot wait any longer for the rapport to develop whereby we can live with one another. It is either pass down an inheritance of absurd reality or change direction . . . it becomes clear that it is no longer possible to separate music and life as it really is. Politics, sexuality, racial pride, deep and true feelings have entered popular music to stay. Our youth is central to this metamorphosis . . . Confusion reigns. Truth and honesty are at a premium. A valid way of life is sought. To this end, the young explorer rolls across a wide spectrum of subject mat-

> ter and musical means and mannerisms. He experiments with ideology and sounds, often shaping answers in the process. But they are always open to change; flexibility is part of the concept . . . Hope is implicit in the negation of past and present mistakes—the hope for an apocalypse which will make the blind see, the intractable feel, the world's fearful face change.[5]

A radical left position outside the context of pop culture has found incisive expression by John Cage: "Twentieth Century arts opened our eyes. Now music's opened our ears. Theatre? Just notice what's around . . . the last thing I'd do would be to tell you how to use your aesthetic faculties . . ."[6] And, even more searchingly, Cage writes:

> How does Music stand with respect to its instruments, . . . pitches, . . . rhythms, . . . degrees of amplitude . . . ? Though the majority go each day to the schools where these matters are taught, they read when time permits of Cape Canaveral, Ghana and Seoul. And they've heard tell of the music synthesizer and magnetic tape. They take for granted the dials on radios and television sets. A tardy art, the art of Music. And why so slow? . . . in our laziness, when we changed over to the twelve-tone system, we just took the pitches of the previous music as though we were moving into a furnished apartment and had no time to even take the pictures off the walls. What excuse?[7]

The first of these two views (the rock musician's) is moral, prescriptive, critical, involved. The second (Cage's) is detached, liberating, critical, involved.

In both cases abstract matters of perennial concern in the tradition of Western music (such as order, structure, form, proportion) either are banished or are assigned subordinate, almost nonessential roles. In both a vital new alternative to the establishment is sought—earnestly, uncompromisingly. In both cases the aim is freedom, artistic and social. The rock movement, however, is a group phenomenon, while Cage very much affirms the primacy of the individual.

If the values and perceptions of our heritage from European art are to be kept alive, they must be discovered afresh by us against a background of vital contemporary art. It is above all the traditions of making art which must be preserved, not intact, but seminal, ready to take root in no matter how different a culture. The art treasures themselves, including musical ones, are a matter for museums. It is only common sense not to throw out our European artistic inheritance, but the way we are maintaining it invites radical opposition. The dominance of an imported art culture has always tended to arrest the development of indigenous art. Compare the effect of the art of ancient

Greece upon that of Rome, or the effect of the art of nineteenth-century western Europe upon that of contemporary Russia. The existence of a free avant-garde in the United States makes possible an escape from such cultural smothering. An imported tradition can be domesticated for local use. It can even serve as a staple of cultural diet, but not if it is treated as a sacred cow.

We are now in the midst of learning the hard lesson that glamorous, neoaristocratic temples of art like Lincoln Center in New York, or the community arts centers in Atlanta and Los Angeles, or the Krannert Center for the Performing Arts in Urbana are alarmingly apt to tend in our culture to officialize the art of the past (as in the USSR) or else to deteriorate into centers for commercial mass entertainment. This results from the most direct of causes: aristocratic art on a big scale is expensive. Someone must pay. If the very wealthy or the government are to pay, the official solution is the only likely one. If the general public is to pay, then exploitation of the public by commercial interests with ready capital is depressingly probable.

In either case, today's vital art (whether mass-directed or aristocratic in its appeal) is concerned with the realities of life in the second half of the twentieth century. It naturally shuns such anachronistic environments, which suggest to audiences that they have entered an island, sheltered from the surrounding world: a safe, comfortable seclusion that is the death of art.

In contrast to this, the last few years have seen increasing support of new centers of contemporary music by foundations, universities, and even in some cases state and national subsidy. A ferment of new activity has grown up wherever such support has been extended to active groups of performers and composers, freeing them from dependence upon the competitive commercial music world for their livelihood. Creative musical activity in the United States is decentralizing steadily, despite the concentration of musical activity and related business and publicity in major metropolitan centers.

This can happen today because the present phase of the communications revolution means that a young musician in almost any country of the world where political power does not suppress exchange of information can be informed accurately and extensively about what his peers are doing the world over. With a little effort he can get tape recordings, articles, programs, not to speak of personal news and gossip. He participates in an artistic community which is by no means provincial.

There are increasing numbers of young musicians who don't want acceptance into the establishment, nor do they especially want to do battle with it. Its values—musical and cultural—bore them, except when they arouse anger, and not because these young people are without culture and intelligence. On the contrary, they find conventional and official culture smug and unaware of its own irrelevance in the face of the manifest realities of life here and today.

In less than a generation, the age group of which I speak will outnumber considerably its seniors. Perhaps it will generate its own "establishment," but that will be of a very different kind from the one that now dominates what is called our "national musical life." The number of musicians in the United States who don't think "business as usual" can apply to the arts is already larger than ever before.

NOTES

1. Gilbert Chase, "The Great Tradition," unpublished lecture.

2. Chase, "The Great Tradition."

3. A news story by Robert K. Sanford that appeared in the *St. Louis Dispatch,* Sunday, May 7, 1967, bore the following headline: "De Carvalho Tells Why He Chose to Leave: Asserts Management Ordered 'Workhorse' Compositions." I quote from the body of this story:

> De Carvalho, who has been conductor and music director of the orchestra since 1963, has presented a number of contemporary musical works in his programs. Eleven compositions were presented here as first performances, nine as first performances in the United States.
>
> But during discussions about programs for the next season he was told that the contemporary works should be avoided, that they were bad business, the conductor said. In recalling a conversation with three persons described as "very high in management," De Carvalho said the restrictions went beyond contemporary works. He said he understood that in selecting a Beethoven symphony, for instance, he should not choose Beethoven's Second, or Fourth, but should choose the Fifth or the Ninth, compositions with which people are familiar.

4. The allusion is to an article by Milton Babbitt, "Who Cares If You Listen?"

5. Burt Korall, "The Music of Protest," *Saturday Review of Literature,* November 16, 1968.

6. John Cage, "Diary: Audience 1966," in *A Year from Monday,* 50ff.

7. John Cage, "Rhythm, etc.," in *A Year from Monday,* 122.

ART AND SURVIVAL

1971

The aims of avant-garde art show themselves in large part destructive: happily so, to be sure, but quite ruthlessly so. It is important that destruction not proceed indiscriminately, as well.

Most musical concerts are, without any need to parody them, a form of anti-art. Nevertheless, if concerts are to be destroyed, what then will be the occasions when we listen to music? On records and tapes only? In concerts which have become theater occasions? Solely in historical museums?

Some music is enhanced by the impersonal formality of conventional concerts, but much of it is stultified by this environment. Always to have such concert customs creates a stifling atmosphere which audiences may accept but which frequently bores them.

Harry Partch's "corporealism" is a protest against the dehumanizing abstraction of the concert occasion. So, in its own time, was Franz Liszt's virtuosity; and so also, in a much different social context, is Nam June Paik's reassertion of sex in concert music.

Formality is not the only trap into which concert giving can fall, however. The utter informality of certain avant-garde concerts, with people constantly entering and exiting, talking out loud, eating food, and rattling paper, can destroy utterly everyone's ability to attend to any music which takes close and active listening. Obviously this custom, too, as an a priori condition for concerts, is severely limiting. The tyranny of the traditional concert could only too easily give way to a new tyranny of opposite aesthetic persuasion. Revolutions are well known to be followed frequently by dictatorships, no matter what the contradiction of explicit revolutionary ideals.

For better or worse, we are in the midst of profound changes in our musical customs. One of the principal causes is technology, which is altering music from the ground up. There is far more electronic music today than any other kind if you include in the term phonograph and tape reproductions. This state of affairs has an adverse effect upon established customs of concertgoing.

In addition, through mass media, the arts now reach millions of people, in sharp contrast to the aristocratic status quo of earlier times. This changes utterly the nature, the aims, the techniques of the arts. In most record companies the pop, rock, and other mass-consumed music support the "serious" music as a kind of prestige item. This has long been the case with music publishers. ASCAP and BMI have to operate on this basis.

The tradition of American public school music education up to now divides itself between a parade- and football-oriented band program and sundry adapted varieties of traditional concert music. Faced with the increasing self-assertion of youth and with the spectacular commercial success of youth music, which far outdoes any of the concert or educational varieties in popularity, some educators are playing with the idea that such music might make a superior basis for public school music programs. Since the performance training provided in public school music programs is a large part of the foundation of almost all advanced musical study in the United States, such a policy would precipitate a major shift in our artistic life.

When you consider also the economic straits in which nearly all United States symphony orchestras and opera companies find themselves today, it is evident that we are approaching a crisis in the musical life of our country.

We are rapidly approaching a time when those who value the artistic traditions of the past must search for a mutation of these which can survive in the changed conditions of contemporary life. Technology is trying to enable *us* to survive, if possible even to thrive in the face of overpopulation and its attendant mass culture. If the arts are to help us to maintain sensitivity and alertness of perception in these circumstances, they will need a great deal of help from all who understand what art is.

It has been pointed out by many philosophers that the arts are potent means for emotional education. No kind of education is more widely or more disastrously neglected today. Meaninglessness, lack of beauty, aimlessness, and boredom are as great causes of suffering as are hunger, disease, and exposure. The role of these and similar emotional factors in causing delinquency and mental illness is basic. The poor have no monopoly upon these ills. It is well known that the incidence of delinquency and mental illness in affluent segments of society is very high.

Much of the thrust of the avant-garde is toward erasing boundaries, whether between stage and audience, between socially proper and socially shocking, between black and white, or between nations and between cultures. Inhibitions and habits are under attack, along with prejudices. A crucial shift has occurred in many avant-garde works: they are no longer about experience, whether concrete or abstract; they are experience.

Paralleling the long-established trend away from representation in painting, twentieth-century music early underwent a disenchantment with emotional expressivity. These trends have by now taken a full spiral turn, to the point that we now have a new kind of naturalism. (Consider, for instance, John Cage's insistence that the sound environment *is* music.) The emphasis in much avant-garde art is not upon intellectual content, nor is it upon emotional meaning: rather it is directly upon sense experience. Emotion itself, rather than emotional meaning, has reentered some of the new art, and for its own sake, not as a symbol of life.

For example, in mixed-media works, with electronic capability to inundate the senses with *power,* we get not only intermodal relations between different senses, but sometimes the Dionysian ecstasy itself. Information overload can produce an emotional intoxication similar to that induced by drugs, and sometimes almost as destructive. Small wonder that the varieties of psychedelia have at least an adjunctive relevance to avant-garde art of this type.

As Marshall McLuhan has observed, it is not only his nervous system which man has "outered" (in the form of an all-pervasive communications network) but also his brain itself. In the absorbing exploration of the workings of artificial intelligence, it did not take artists long to get computers to simulate processes of artistic composition. In particular, Lejaren Hiller's experiments with computer-composed music have led to radical speculations about the nature of artistic creativity. Beside this there is widespread use of computers to synthesize musical performance. Consider especially the experiments of Max Matthews of Bell Laboratories.

Computers can also be used to discover and to exploit hitherto forbidding areas of complexity. Iannis Xenakis's use of the computer to produce a "statistical" music, in which only very large-scale, long-range decisions are made by the composer, is one such use. I am engaged at present with an associate, Edward Kobrin, in an extensive series of experiments to determine the nature of ratio-scale order and to exploit this in computer-composed pieces of music. I am convinced that the problem of order in music (and by extension in all aesthetic perception) can be approached fruitfully through the use of mathematics, provided the mathematics is sufficiently comprehensive and complex. The many failures and near failures of such methodology in the past convince me only of the relatively narrow theoretical scope used by those who have attempted the application.

Since I believe that the fertile idea behind any new or old musical tradition is understandable through application of a kind of scale theory not different from that currently in use in laboratory psychology, I hope to help make possible the rejuvenation of many a tradition by this means. For instance, in most avant-garde music today, the organization of time by means of pitch, metrics, and periodic form is in eclipse. If any further vital ideas generating new movements in musical composition are to spring from these traditional nerve centers of musical practice, a radically new functioning of them is imperative. It is this particular problem to which I am at present addressing myself.

If the older side of the generation gap is in error to believe that things will right themselves if only they can be enabled to continue as usual, the younger side is equally rash to invite a clean break with the past. One of the most difficult problems for music to surmount, once the crisis of which I spoke earlier is hard upon us, will be how to find the new relevance of traditional modes of musical organization. Needless to say, pitch—not only as melody, but as harmony and as tonality—flourishes in such neofolk idioms as rock; but its organizing power is vastly less sophisticated than that of concert music. If we are not to descend as in this case to lesser levels of organization in all our art, we must find ways to make pertinent and interesting radically new approaches to these now almost "outmoded" dimensions of music.

The wide separation between "easy-to-get" survivals of musical tradition and rarified extremes of experimentation is already seeking rapprochement. We find this trend not only in the use in rock music of electronic and other "advanced" techniques, but also in the tendency of much avant-garde music to theater, even to comic theater in the vaudeville tradition. It is as though in the midst of the most recondite scientism, a down-to-earth reminder of music's entertainment function bursts out.

Insofar as any entertainment is of greater human value than "killing time," it *is* art. In what has usually been called art, the emphasis has traditionally been on the "profounder" values of life, expressed symbolically. Art has not always even intended to entertain, but the more it has sought to reach a wider public, the more it has used techniques of entertainment. Today, when the role of entertainment media in reaching and beguiling masses of people is so all pervasive, it behooves artists to assert as strongly as possible their influence to deepen the content as well as the impact of mass-consumed entertainment. It also behooves them to assert the minority rights of exceptional people, for whom much of mass entertainment is boring and trivial. This assertion entails, to some extent, creating occasions for less popular art which are lively and pertinent to life as it *is* being and as it *can be* lived. Near-exclusive concentration on the art of other times and places is not only stifling but also dangerous, in our present circumstances. We may well lose all grasp of the relevance of art to life through our historicism, thus emasculating the very father of artistic creativity.

Whether an artist is a revolutionary or not (and an artist is well suited to that role), he is by nature a nonconformist. That is so fundamental a trait of artists that to insist that art reaffirm the status quo, as do the Russians, is to attack the basic health of art itself. No matter how assiduously an artist may try to conform to norms and standards, he is temperamentally unsuited to do this. He may not be antisocial or pathological, but he is certain to find ready-made adjustments to convention intolerable. It would be well to study carefully apparent exceptions to this, like J. S. Bach (reputedly a bourgeois paterfamilias in good standing with his religion). There can be found in almost all such cases some important area of life in which the artist diverged profoundly from the standards of his times. If there was in truth no such area in Bach's life, it will prove most interesting to study him as an exception.

I think that this applies to *all* lives, except that lack of courage or of clarity of direction in a life may mire it down into conformity. A great artist cannot lack courage or clarity of purpose. So he is set against conformity; and a time like the present, which makes large demands for conformity, renders every artist to some degree an outsider.

Art is not the servant of social solidarity. On the contrary, it is frequently the bringer of change and unrest. But neither is it an excuse for any kind of self-indulgent idiosyncrasy. It is nothing less than a vigorous and seriously responsible denial of society's prerogative to dictate norms.

The revolutionary position of all great religious leaders inexorably silts over with centuries of orthodoxy. The founders of all the world's great religions have in all cases exacted shockingly nonconformist demands as conditions of discipleship, in a self-dedication sharply distinct from the institutional and usually oppressive religions which they challenged. To approach *essential* truth from any sector of existential space demands that one put behind himself all other ambitions. Nothing short of such a commitment avails; and it is useless to imagine that it can be made vicariously, by the intercession of a hierophant or by inclusion in an organization.

Art makes something of the same imperious claim upon its devotees. The muse is well known to be a proud and arbitrary mistress, awarding favors where she will, as heedless of pleas as of cajolements. Not only is she said to be untamable, but also, goddess-like, to be jealous and demanding of unstinting loyalty and service, regardless of returns. The artist does not decide to say something and then draw upon his artistry to express it effectively. He struggles to discover what seeks to be said through him, channeling it as skillfully as he can by his craft into an intelligible experience. If nothing seeks expression through him, then that is his misfortune. He can only be ready for the effort in case he finds it possible.

What a far cry this is from the docile little Gebrauchsmusiker society sometimes claims it wants. But society is fickle, too, and much more apt to woo the difficult and uncouth artist who defies customs and categories.

It is perhaps commoner today to abuse the freedom of being an artist. Once established as a bona-fide artist (and that is no small task!), a dishonest man can indulge eccentricities in the name of artistic freedom. Because a pseudo-artist has little to give, his art gradually grows stale, and his egocentric game comes to an end. Because people are aware of this possibility, it is a slow process for a truly innovative artist to gain recognition. Generally he has to have had a very great effect on many exceptional people before a wider public can know him for what he is.

But in all this we are still speaking of a rather limited public, of a very specialized group of people. If we concern ourselves with really great numbers of people, the problem becomes still more perplexing, the rules of the game still less clear.

In general the wider public has great difficulty in comprehending what art is. They are apt to mistake it for amusement, or for some special kind of status making, or for propaganda. The artist's problem in trying to reach many of these people is extreme. They are suspicious of his nonconformity, and of his enigmatic social role.

Faced as we are today by social and ecological conditions which imperatively require change, we really choose only what kind of change we shall undergo, and this only to the extent that we can wrest control of the situation from relentless processes of development already in motion. People who would cling to a status quo are dangerous dreamers. Not only an artist but every person needs to become a responsible nonconformist. One thing we should emphatically do is to alter habits of the use of art which foster conformist attitudes.

One of the crucial causes of the generation gap is the perception of this crisis by many young people, who can also see clearly how resistant their elders are to such a perception. Their frustration and apprehension at this disastrous blindness lends extreme urgency to their protests and causes.

It is interesting to observe that the character of the Madison Avenue–dubbed "now generation" is not modeled on the scientist or the engineer but on the artist. While technology is admittedly one of the few hopes in an otherwise desperate situation, great numbers of young people turn to the arts and to religion for sustenance. They are, I think, one jump ahead of events. While it is true that the population problem, pollution problems, poverty, and a host of other extremely urgent crises can be solved only by technological virtuosity of the highest order, even with all these matters well under control the best we could hope for would be a worldwide affluent society.

There is more to making the world a beautiful place to live than simply to stop polluting the air and water. And there is more to living a good life than having enough to eat and a decent place to live. The spate of amusement purveyed by mass media offers a poor solution to leisure-time needs, since it is largely aimless and irresponsible. With greater awareness of the need for change and with real artistic standards to replace exploitative commercial ones as a basis for the entertainment industry, we could achieve a vast improvement in public attitude on many fronts.

The so-called radical youth, who are by no means all hippies and yippies, want to bring to confrontation the crisis in human relations which reflects the intolerable living conditions of a majority of people. These conditions are not primarily material, although material conditions afford an obvious place to start in trying to effect a change for the better.

It is here that the tie-in with religion becomes most evident. It is clear that the kind of institutionalism which organized religion offers is not at all satisfactory to many young people. Typical adherents of the leading Western religions rely too much on their congregations as bastions of middle-class convention. They are mostly too little concerned with self-transcendence, not nearly willing enough to take the lead in social reform, to put at rest the consciences of many people, especially young people.

Unfortunately a young person is more likely to find a lively awareness of the self-transcendent in life among drug users than among conventionally religious people. If this omission does not actively capitulate him into drug addiction, neither does it recommend conventional religion to him.

With the exception of minority groups like the Quakers, religious groups have not yet become leaders in pressing for constructive social reforms. More and more the young turn to secular leadership in these matters.

The fact that great numbers of the young today are actively religious and yet are not joiners of churches poses a crisis for conventional religion. In effect the youth are saying to the religions: "Shape up." The more contemplative oriental religions are having a wider appeal than commoner Western religions.

In these connections it is a fact that *Sergeant Pepper's Lonely Hearts Club Band* is more pertinent than Bach's B-Minor Mass or Beethoven's Ninth Symphony. John Cage's total admission of environment noise into music is far more meaningful, in a crowded, information-loaded world, than is the cultivation of the analytical listening habits prerequisite to a sophisticated appreciation of classical sonatas or Baroque fugues. The model of behavior learned in aesthetic situations should carry over into everyday life. Most of us have more use today for the ability to concentrate in the midst of distractions than for the intellectual ability to follow intricate formal patterns. Compositional techniques dealing with great complexity can tell us more about dealing with order and disorder in a complex world than can the relatively simple aesthetic structures of eighteenth-century musical forms.

Some years ago I felt impelled to ask myself searchingly, "Why are you an artist? What good is there in being one? Is it simply in order to make a living doing what you enjoy? If a world crisis of sufficiently overwhelming scope should occur, would you consider the profession of art a nonessential occupation?"

It is in seeking answers to these questions that I have been led to the kinds of speculations I am here making. It seems to me the arts can be, perhaps are on the verge of becoming extraordinarily pertinent and valuable human activities. But on the whole, in their functioning *as art* they are not so; nor are most of the arts thought by most people to be capable of becoming really essential areas of human activity.

Like most people who are deeply committed to and involved in the arts, I experience some of the isolation and the wish for isolation attendant upon being an artist. The experience of sensitivity is painful; the act of creation is as revealing of private surfaces as of depths of common humanity. It is a rare artist who has no problem with vanity, no "temperament." But being at the same time a teacher, I am continually reminded of society's basic requirement of professionals: that they serve humanity objectively, not out of cupidity or vanity. I therefore turn a critical eye to some artists' self-intoxicated poses; but at the same time I contradistinguish and assert the rightness of artists' nonconformism. When society itself is sick, this may take strange forms. It is above all in this nonconforming relation to society that art is "ahead of its time." Many severe protests now widely voiced by young people were vigorously set forth two or three generations ago by avant-garde artists. The destructiveness of avant-garde art is more an appearance than a reality.

An artist is like a sensitive instrument, tuned to respond promptly and perceptively to cultural conditions. It is time our society awoke to the importance of such instruments. The twentieth century is a great period in the history of art, but twentieth-century civilization may well fail to take advantage of this greatness.

Many people believe we are living through a transition in human history at least as great and as fraught with danger as any which has ever occurred. There is, so to speak, an abyss facing us, over which we have somehow to cross. I believe that not only the bridge which will bear our weight but also the bridgehead on the opposite rim of the canyon *cannot* be built without the contributions of artists.

To translate this metaphor into down-to-earth details would be to contribute materially to the solution of the task it symbolizes. It is first of all the task of artists to make this translation.

This is a position of leadership, and one which takes a certain amount of daring, most especially since the artist is not a likely man to whom the general public will turn for such guidance. And if the artist is interpreting his mandate to nonconformity as license to repudiate society's needs, he will fail in his leadership.

What is more likely than that failure is a negative response to society's perennial deaf ear to the artist's perceptions. He could then become a nagging Cassandra, saying "I told you so!" after it's too late.

If it is not to be too late, then we must not fail to close the generation gap and in addition to that the cultural lag between the vanguard of humanity's creative geniuses and the present moment, in which alone we can act. Our artists are not letting us down. Let us hope we do not let ourselves down by not hearing what they say.

ON BRIDGE-BUILDING

1977

In the sixties, I wrote a paper called "On Context," in which I expressed the opinion that we are collectively at a moment of history where a chasm faces us, which we must either bridge or fall into. I sounded an optimistic note, though the paper came just at the darkest point of the decade. (It was read the very day Martin Luther King was assassinated.) I said I felt that for a bridge over the abyss to hold, it must be anchored far in the past and far in the future.

Later, in trying to rise to the challenge of giving an overview of my own work, I discussed several works in relation to this chasm: whether they lay on the past side or on the future side or whether they dealt with the depth themselves. The concept seemed more than ever apt, coming as it did just in the heyday of *The Exorcist* and in the final days of Richard Nixon's agony, events which seemed clearly hell-images.

Whether the "abyss" be understood to be atomic holocaust, ecological disaster, world revolution, apocalypse, or simply a private season in hell, it is very much a phenomenon of our lives today. I began to see that I had been writing most of my works in relation to this experience. Today, when things seem at least temporarily less disaster prone I still feel very much that we are walking the knife edge and that the best prophetic capabilities artists can muster are very much needed by humanity today.

Much of my work relates intimately to various aspects of our musical past and to our global heritage. I think *nostalgia* is a shallow "pop" version of a very apt and real concern for vanishing species. This is not a new awareness. Earlier in this century it motivated neoclassicism and much eclecticism. It is not a false concern, but it does take many false forms.

The falsest of all is the ubiquitous museum mentality of nearly all concert series and impresarios. The practice of constantly recycling old and accepted "masterpieces" as if that serves a cultural need is not only false: it is genuinely pernicious. It blocks reception and production of vital new art that could speak significantly to people about the needs and truths of their own lives. It does not even present them with Beethoven's truths (however dated these might be) when it presents Beethoven's music, because with overfamiliarity the music's meanings have undergone a total sea change, but into something which is neither rich nor strange, but is rather something comfortable and complacent, something which saps all appetite for art while providing very little nutrition.

An appetite for art is an appetite for the mythic symbols which constitute this time's vision of the meaning of existence. We come upon these depth-images when we open ourselves to them, a receptiveness that costs dearly in courage and in tenacity. It also costs in terms of the rejection such meanings meet upon first encounter, since people do not always love truth above comfortable complacency. There are certainly insights which are not at all new, which nevertheless hold for us a compelling immediacy. And these, in finding a right form of expression, generate artistic traditions which can endure as genuine wellsprings of meaning, not at all as idols which we adore more for their power to insulate us from the transforming experience of genuine symbols than for their own intrinsic worth.

One of the undesirable effects of doctrinaire avant-gardism is its tendency to inhibit or to prevent entirely the rediscovery of these perennially valuable mythic themes and modes of expression suitable to them. There is a vast difference between the use of these themes and an aping of the manners of another time and place. If it were not for the persistence and power of symbolic themes, there could be only a spurious value in playing the music of any other time and place than our own. It is, in fact, the alien manner of older music which most seriously obscures our grasp of these meanings. It is ironic that it is precisely the manner of traditional music which creates a cult of "classical music," causing people to reject the manners of their own times, when they encounter them in art. When you add to this the resistance new myths always meet, a serious handicap to art in our culture becomes evident.

The example of Harry Partch awakened me to the need to start all over, to question our entire heritage, and to accept for my own use only those parts of it that symbolize exactly what I want them to mean. The hypocritical relation of twelve-tone equal temperament to tonal music and its clumsiness for atonal music disqualifies it as a practice.

The example of John Cage urged me to seek principles of composition suitable for using the whole sound world as raw material, and basic enough to transcend the myopic limitations of our culture. I am not drawn to chance as a method, and it does not seem to me the only or the best way to escape the ego-limited traditions of European art. Rather it seems to me the most important contribution art can make today is to help make complexity intelligible. And the kind of complexity needed to understand the intricate symbiotic interdependence of organic life on earth seems to me more valuable than the kind which clarifies the statistical behavior of inanimate multitudes, though certainly both are important.

In trying to find a more comprehensive system of order and at the same time to found pitch upon a better basis than the tempered scale, I discovered S. S. Stevens's psychophysical scales of measurement. Ratio scale tuning afforded a promising alternative to the statistically less sophisticated interval scale of equal temperament, while interval scale order did provide a generalized basis for serial procedures. Ordinal scale provided a good theoretical basis for many indeterminate modes of organization, and nominal scale order provided the basis for *objet sonore* perception. This corroborated what I had intuitively grasped much earlier and found reinforced in Partch's work.

In 1952, following an encounter with John Cage, I inquired about applying for a Fulbright Fellowship to go to Paris and work in the Studio des Recherches de la Musique Concrète. Though I succeeded in getting an invitation from Pierre Schaeffer, I gave up the project to gamble on making my then-temporary appointment at the University of Illinois a permanent one. I did not then work with tape music, and even when Lejaren Hiller founded the Experimental Music Studio at the School of Music in the late '50s, I was only a supportive bystander.

I had come to UIUC in 1951 fresh from work with Harry Partch in 1950 at Gualala, California, with only a brief period with Darius Milhaud at Mills College between. I did not then follow up on my Partch interest, except to maneuver to get Partch to Urbana, which happened in the middle '50s. When in 1958 I decided I had to act on my convictions about the morass modern tuning practices had generated, I applied for and got a Guggenheim Fellowship to investigate making untempered pitch compositions electronically. I went to the studio at Columbia-Princeton during 1959–60 and tried to get into the solution of the problem of extended just intonation through tape music. The effort was a failure. It was, however, in the years immediately following that stimulating if unproductive year that I made my first efforts to tackle the problem in instrumental terms.

Unlike Partch, I wanted to use ordinary, familiar instruments and techniques. Also unlike Partch, I wanted to transform European traditions rather than to search out other ethnic heritages. My first such pieces were the song cycle *Five Fragments* from Thoreau and the song *A Sea Dirge,* from whose precompositional ratio sequence I later made *Knocking Piece;* I began work on my *Sonata for Microtonal Piano,* which took me five years to complete, and before finishing that wrote my *String Quartet no. 2,* which was later recorded for Nonesuch by the Composers Quartet. In 1966, I wrote *Ci-Gît Satie* for the Swingle Singers and *Quintet for Groups* for Eleazar de Carvalho and the St. Louis Symphony. Following that I composed *String Quartet no. 3*. All these pieces except *Ci-Gît Satie* were concerned in one way or another with reconciling twelve-tone serial pitch usage with extended just intonation. From about 1970 on, I addressed myself instead to the problem of reconciling large extensions of the pitch domain with immediate intelligibility and clarity in communication. Especially in *Carmilla,* a rock opera which is in no way microtonal, I wanted to use vernacular idioms to enhance communication. *Rose* and *Mass* set about in addition to be easily performable. In *String Quartet no. 4* I added to these intentions a further exploration of elaborate proportional rhythm. Although not an easy piece, it has been attractive to a number of quartets.

There have been only three brief detours from this path. In the late '60s I wrote three concrete tape pieces and some indeterminate pieces. In the early '70s I wrote *Carmilla,* and recently I joined the New Verbal Workshop to do *Visions and Spels,* a realization of *Vigil.* While *Visions and Spels* is improvised entirely "by ear," it is rather elaborately microtonal at times and represents the closest approach to Partch's vocal writing in any of my work, so much so that I incorporated a taped performance of the work into my *In Memory, Harry Partch, 1975.* I am at present at work on a *Suite* for retuned piano, and on my fifth string quartet. Both works deal with microtonal just intonation.

The systematics of ratio scale order involve some relatively simple applied mathematics: group theory (the rational numbers constitute an infinite Abelian group), topology (neighborhoods in a multidimensional ratio lattice and neighborhoods in linear projections of segments of it), and simple arithmetic involving complex fractions. A limited amount of ratio theory is obtainable from older sources. Gerhardus Mercator, Leonard Euler, and Christian Huygens all broke ground in this area in the sixteenth and seventeenth centuries. Much of this (and much else) is summarized in Hermann Helmholtz's *On the Sensations of Tone.* The Chinese, the Indians, the ancient Greeks, and the medieval Arabs all made contributions to this development. Alain Daniélou's *An Introduction to the Theory of Musical Scales* gives a cursory summary of many of these developments with more emphasis on Indian music. Daniélou covers the same ground more thoroughly in *Traité de Musicologie Comparée.* Harry Partch's *Genesis of a Music* is one of the best books for this purpose. The work of Adriaan Fokker in the Netherlands is also of considerable value. A good summary of some of these and additional sources is in Joel Mandelbaum's dissertation, "Multiple Pitch Choice and 19–tone Equal Temperament."

For further information I must point to my own articles, especially "Scalar Order as a Compositional Resource" and "Proportionality and Expanded Pitch Resources" (which appeared in *Perspectives of New Music*); "Three Attacks on a Problem," "Tonality Regained," and "Rational Structure in Music" (which appeared in *Proceedings of the American Society of University Composers*); and two articles about my music: "Ben Johnston's *Quintet for Groups*" by Barney Childs, and "Proportionality in Ben Johnston's *Fourth String Quartet,*" by Randall Shinn (both of which appeared in *Perspectives of New Music*). Shinn's analysis in particular is meticulous and detailed, getting at the essence of the technique I call "proportionality."

Let me summarize that technique. The three levels of time perception: ordinary rhythm (countable time), macrorhythm (longer durations from phrase lengths up to complete compositions), and microrhythm (vibrations per second and phenomena on that time scale) are all subjected to organization by ratio quantities. This entails microtonal just intonation, metrical modulation and simultaneous use of proportional tempi, and proportional duration plans for longer amounts of time. All of these processes are controlled by ratio scale lattices and linear projections from these (scales). The technique consists basically of setting up proportions in small whole numbers between vibration rates, tempos and durations, and also patterns of neighboring quantities which lie next to each other in scales selected from the lattices made up of these proportions. This amounts (when applied to pitches) to harmonic and melodic design. But a far greater refinement is possible than in traditional harmony or melody.

Since most of the parameters emphasized in music after about 1950 stress scalar order of the nominal, ordinal, or interval type, this amounts to a radical departure from today's common practice. And since these kinds of order have less statistical predictability than ratio scale order, the potential of this music to stimulate memory, the attempt to predict what will happen, and thus interest is more powerful. By reinstating some of the most potent organizational devices music has ever devised and by opening the door to an indefinitely expanding horizon of intelligible complexity, I believe I have found a strong basis for future musical developments. One has no need to give up any of the other organizational techniques to use proportionality. But it adds a strong bulwark against unintelligibility and the resulting semantic isolationism. Perhaps this is that needed bridge over the chasm.

SEVENTEEN ITEMS

1980

1. Since 1960 my music has concentrated mainly upon microtonal just intonation, though I have done a variety of other kinds of works as well. I am concerned not to compose all works in a single, predictable style. I aim to show the applicability and value of microtonal just intonation to a great variety of kinds of music and a wide range of styles.

2. The first composer to interest me seriously was Claude Debussy. Of my teachers, Harry Partch was the most influential. Among contemporary composers György Ligeti, Iannis Xenakis, and Toru Takemitsu interest me particularly. The ideas of John Cage, more than his music, interest me very much. I like classical north and south Indian music and Japanese Gagaku music very much. Charles Ives is a very important influence.

3. I am not interested much in those contemporary composers who still retain most of the values and aims of nineteenth-century European music. I do not like composers whose work can be described as cerebral. This includes many twelve-tone composers, though I have benefited from this technique very much. I am not impressed with music in the service of ideology or commercialism.

4. I would like to think my music helps people to get in touch with that part of themselves which is capable of mythic thinking. Music should appeal to the senses, the emotions, the intellect, all in the service of important mythic ideas and potential experience of the human being.

5. I regard this as the inner purpose of my music. It may have many outer purposes, depending upon who wanted it and for what function.

6. I feel that I can get beyond exoticism in my appreciation of Indian music, Indonesian music, and Japanese music. I value this ability highly.

7. I would like my works to be valuable to posterity, but I do not know if they will be. I do think that my approach to composing is of great potential value in a world music context.

8. I am interested in the ideas of C. G. Jung. I am much interested in

philosophies that bridge the gap between Asiatic and European-American thought and in synthetic as distinct from analytic thought.

9. The ideas of "mythic" thought mentioned above derive from writings of Joseph Campbell. I feel that nearly all my works attempt to connect levels of thought in myself and so perhaps in others.

10. I have been at some pains to learn Western and to a much lesser extent Eastern traditions for the deepening of the roots of my creative work. I do not want to leave tradition behind but rather to revivify it.

11. I do not think sex is a main determinant in art. Certainly there are male "specializations" and I doubtlessly reflect these. I believe we all have characteristics of both sexes, but to different degrees. If we fail to develop all these sides of ourselves we are only partly realized.

12. My formative musical years were the '50s and '60s. I owe much to serial music, to Cage, to emerging "world music" attitudes. I cannot separate myself from these trends, but I have found my own path, which is no longer typical of any of these.

13. I am particularly interested in mathematical proportion as applied to rhythm, pitch, and form. It is the basis of microtonal just intonation, my main concern.

14. I am a leader in Western microtonal music. In other words, a tiny fraction of a tiny fraction of present-day music. Classifications are slowly eroding away but still have some power to govern taste and behavior.

15. I am very much interested in the impact of technology. What I am doing implies new instruments, new concepts in all areas of music.

16. Silence is a basic aspect of music. It is of enormous value and power.

17. I particularly like the sounds of nature, and resonant phenomena. Resonance has much to do with my music.

ART AND RELIGION

1981

Properly understood, art and religion have the same aims. Only we do not commonly understand either art *or* religion.

Is religion superstition, a primitive, childish worldview? Is a religion a group of ideas manipulating groups of people? Is religion an institution dedicated to good works, elevated morals, and the worship of the Creator? Or is it each man's search inward: an effort to bring each surface life into meaningful relation with its most personal, least egocentric level of self?

Are the arts diversions which entertain and amuse? Do the arts make their most important contribution to culture, to status, to traditions, to national or racial pride? Is art personal expression, private therapy, individual communication? Is art an especially subtle and powerful form of propaganda? Or is it an effort to contact the deepest strata of human understanding?

In this context a person does not speak from his small, daily self. Practical, political, economic, pleasure-seeking values drop away, leaving—what? Something words are all but useless to convey, something the complex symbolism of art, its combined appeal to feeling, thought, and sense perception, still wrestles to express.

It was this understanding of art which nineteenth-century Quakers reached, leaving behind an earlier Quaker view of art as a worldly frivolity. They learned to see art as a "window on the soul," a window to let in the inner light, not simply a window opening on the world. Aesthetic perception reminds us, as the profoundest psychological experiences do, that we do not live by bread alone.

But this does not mean that art is to express only the attributes of God and the climate of Heaven. The quest for inner peace is seldom if ever a peaceful quest. To turn away from violence does *not* insure against suffering and struggle.

When you look inside yourself, the first things you see are things that are wrong with you. This vision is profoundly unsettling. Many people stop the search right there. Still more people deny what they have seen and will not look again. Some persevere and break through to a more peaceful experience.

To be an artist is like that; only you *may* see the inner turmoil as not your own, and so never reap the psychological gain of that confrontation. What you cannot escape is the conviction that the turmoil, the beauty, the suffering, the peace are every man's. So it seems worth it to try to capture some of this in art, even if you never manage to live up to it in your life.

When artists give the world a harsh and violent image of life, they are holding up a mirror. It is more than a pity if they cannot get beyond this image; but even *that* is still far better than if they evade it. To attack artists because you do not like what they express is very much like getting angry with a thermometer because you don't like what it says. The complex, tense, violent contemporary world is not only outside of us. It is also inside each of us. There is no honest evasion of it. There can be an honest transcendence of it, if there is first acceptance of the problem.

In *The Poor Man of God,* the Greek writer Kazantzakis has St. Francis say,

> The Lord condescended to save me, to save me the sinner Francis of Assisi in the following manner: While I was still wallowing in sin, I felt an unconquerable aversion to lepers. God cried out, therefore, and tossed me in among them, commanding me to hug them, to kiss them, to undress them and cleanse their wounds. And when I had hugged them, kissed them, and cleansed their wounds, the world seemed to change. What had formerly appeared so bitter to me was transformed; it became sweet, like honey. Not long after that I left the world, left this vain world and all its goods in order to dedicate myself heart and soul to God.

What we fear we reject. We do not fear what we understand, or what we have conquered without violence.

The last thing we can ask of art *or* religion is *escape* from life. We cannot even ask escape from the harsh, the ugly, the evil. We can only ask for *greater truth,* transcending evil.

Theology today is throwing at us a barrage of extreme and difficult perceptions and points of view. Art today points to at least equally disturbing problems.

Do we accept the challenge?

EXTENDED JUST INTONATION: A POSITION PAPER

1986

In 1962 and 1963, when I was writing "Scalar Order as a Compositional Resource" for *Perspectives of New Music,* I sent several versions to the editors before we agreed on one for publication. The story of the second revision is instructive. I had been trying to meet what I felt was *Perspectives*'s rather thorny prose style and was at the same time insisting to myself that the article be readable by other than specialists. In the midst of this effort I gave the manuscript to a teacher of technical prose writing who offered to critique it. I got a scathing criticism and a very intense short course on how to get rid of jargon and related problems. I dutifully rewrote the entire article in short, terse sentences with a deliberately well-known vocabulary and in brief, well-disciplined paragraphs. Finally, I sent it on to the editors.

They scarcely recognized it and in haste urged me to restore it to its former acceptable scholarly style. The rest of the story is not very interesting, concerning, as it does, a compromise of style if not content, and certainly a curtailment of possible readers. Since then the editorship of *Perspectives* has undergone a transforming evolution, and this situation could not arise today. But it gave me a lot to think about and after about a decade bore some surprising fruit.

In the early seventies I grew dissatisfied with the musical style I had been using since beginning in 1960 to compose in extended just intonation. It was a style rooted in serial music, which was what had interested me most just before that. But I was tired of composing music which interested few listeners beyond other composers and participating in specialized concerts which attracted mainly that audience. I was convinced that composers were at least partly to blame for the ignoring of new music by most performers and audiences. In a spirit of defiance against my own prejudices, I began a series of works which thoroughly concealed their complexity and which addressed themselves to a far less specialized audience. The response was immediate and dramatic. People came up to me after concerts and thanked me for writing what they had just heard. Performers I had never dreamed would be interested contacted me about new works. Even critics, though some with much suspicion, were markedly more positive in their evaluation of my compositions.

They could not have been more suspicious than I. I gave myself a thorough and searching self-criticism to make sure that I had not simply begun saying only what people already wanted to hear: falling into the trap Herbert Brün calls "plausibility." I was assured by nearly everyone I confided in that this was definitely not the case. The seemingly parallel course of writing music in styles and idioms used in earlier music produces an acceptance based too much upon a nostalgia for the past of music and a misperception of the way in which the arts can illuminate the way we live. I wanted at all costs to avoid that. If music of the twentieth century does not reflect the degree to which life today is greatly different from life in the nineteenth or the eighteenth century (to select two periods whose music meets with ready acceptance by contemporary audiences), then it is in an important sense escapist, as is the conventional programming of the music of the past. I am not speaking only of the ugly or negative aspects of contemporary life, but of the climate of it—the feel of being part of it, the typical emotions and patterns of living it entails. Being contemporary is not a matter of following trends and fashions; it is much more a matter of turning one's attention and actions to bear upon life as we live it rather than to escape by living vicariously in the art products of another time and place.

The concern with just intonation saved me from some of the errors I might otherwise have committed. The differences in structure due to composing with an open, infinite field of pitches rather than a closed, finite system, such as twelve-tone equal temperament, guaranteed new shapes and even a new ambience of sound. The constant heightening of contrast between the simple and the complex by the use of simple arithmetic ratios, the intensification of emotional affective reaction, the inevitable inclusion of microtonally small pitch distinctions, all contributed to protecting my music from a too-familiar impression. I became interested in such questions as: How would late Romantic chromaticism have developed if untempered extended just intonation had been used rather than twelve-tone equal temperament? Would the atonal movement have occurred? What if one treats a just tuned scale with atonal techniques? What would a big-band jazz style sound like in extended just intonation? And most important of all, how can the extreme complexity of contemporary life be reconciled with the simplifying and clarifying influences of systems of order based upon ratio scales?

This change of aesthetic intention coincided with my decision to begin to employ relationships based upon overtones higher than the sixth partial, rather than to remain within the triadically generated system I had been using. I became interested in the morphological analogy between structures, such as scales based upon triadically generated bases and the much more complex ones generated by using higher overtone relationships. This led to a type of complexity which, in spite of microtones and large numbers of pitches, was organized by principles similar to those of diatonic triadic music. This gave me the possibility of being complex but nevertheless immediately intelligible. The fact that ratio scale ordering facilitates remembering patterns by ear to a far greater extent than interval scale ordering (of which serial ordering is a familiar example) greatly enhanced this intelligibility.

I have said in other contexts that I was concerned to continue what I considered great traditions of Western music but to purify them of adulterations introduced by the use of temperaments. This remains a central concern. My whole compositional output since I began to use extended just intonation may be considered a demonstration of the enormously varied technical and stylistic procedures which are clarified and subtilized by the use of extended just intonation. This body of works may also be seen as a gradual initiation into the new demands upon the ear, and upon instrumental and vocal techniques which this systematic entails.

To date, the best analytical study of my work is Randall Shinn's "Ben Johnston's Fourth String Quartet" (*Perspectives of New Music* 15, no. 2 [Spring–Summer 1977], 145–73). This, with my article "Rational Structure in Music," gives a rather good introduction to compositional techniques I have used. A book by Heidi Von Gunden on my music was published this year (1986) by Scarecrow Press. It would certainly be redundant for me to anticipate its survey of my work up to 1985. In any case, I believe that nothing can better state my case as a composer than my compositions.

A.S.U.C. KEYNOTE ADDRESS

1987

Being here reminds me pointedly of the American Society of University Composers meeting in St. Louis in 1967 when the membership rejected the narrower focus of many of its founding members and set itself to represent the actual state of American music as reflected in colleges and universities. I remember in particular the aggressive stand of Peter Yates, who very strongly pushed for a broad and representative society. It was especially memorable for me because Peter was chairing a panel on microtonality, which was the first time I had publicly spoken about the then-recent change in my work which set me upon the path I have followed ever since. I suppose what I have in mind is to reassert something of that moment for us here. But all any of us can do is to state where he individually is, at any given moment. I cannot presume to sound a keynote for American music in general, or even for this society in particular. What I must do is to make my own position as clear as I can, and hope that this will resonate in other minds.

My principal compositional technique, extended just intonation, has its roots in the radical departures of Claude Debussy, whose harmonic language approximates, as well as can be in equal temperament, a movement from overtone series to overtone series, with an emphasis upon higher partials. There is some mixing of series polychordally and some evidence of the use of a principle of inversion, which generates a system of Otonality/Utonality analogous to Harry Partch's. In contrast, Arnold Schoenberg, both in his atonality and in his serial pitch usage, seemed to be intent upon exploiting the unused portions of a closed system of pitches. His work is, as I have pointed out elsewhere, the first example of a compositional technique which takes the twelve-tone tempered scale for exactly what it is. In all earlier music it represents an acoustical compromise to facilitate instrumental design while still making possible extensive modulatory flexibility. Schoenberg is an example of a radical thinker motivated strongly by a claustrophobic sense of nearly exhausted resources. Debussy, in sharp contrast, seems motivated by an expansion of harmonic resources and a greatly widened horizon. But for Debussy's revolution to have been achieved fully, the tempered scale would have had to go, in favor of extended just intonation, so that the overtone structures would have been unambiguously recognizable as such. The sense of brilliant colors provocatively mixed which generated the comparison to Impressionist painting would have been enormously heightened.

It is well known that Debussy himself did not welcome the designation "Impressionist" but would rather have preferred "Symbolist" in recognition of his great debt to Stéphane Mallarmé. In *Un Coup de Dés Jamais N'Abolira le Hasard,* Mallarmé pushes toward a new syntax and format: almost a new language, like that other famous symbolist James Joyce, who goes substantially further than Mallarmé, particularly in *Finnegans Wake.* The profound influence of Mallarmé upon Pierre Boulez has been acknowledged; that of Joyce upon Luciano Berio less explicitly. In his twentieth-century history, Geoffrey Barraclough has described Symbolism as the last great European literary movement to achieve worldwide dominance. After it, third world and Marxist influences displace western European on the world stage. Symbolism, as the word implies, has an almost mystical dimension. Mallarmé and even Marcel Proust have been described as secular mystics, and Joyce, while scarcely a mystic, devoted enormous effort to replacing Christian myth with a much wider cross-cultural mythology. Evelyn Underhill, in her study *Mysticism,* observes that mystics surface almost always in the final cultural phases of civilizations, when the breakup of one culture begins to be accelerated by the birth of a new one. It is obvious that the early twentieth century was such a time, and on a worldwide scale. Barraclough's observation about Symbolism gains focus and intensity from such a context. It is interesting that Partch, the first exponent of extended just intonation, was aggressively anti-European and anti-Christian, acknowledging many more Asian and African influences than European ones.

Before a new culture can fully replace an old one, there must be actively disintegrative forces to clear away the old ways. It seems to me that the indeterminate movement in American music of the sixties was such a force. It is epitomized by the work of John Cage, whose very philosophy and theory of composition undermine traditional attitudes and procedures. Cage's philosophical basis is primarily Asian in origin, blended with Dada, itself also a consciously disintegrative movement. Marcel Duchamp, in fact, has been called a destroyer, an anti-artist. It is interesting to note Cage's preoccupation with *Finnegans Wake* beginning in the late sixties. There remains only one ingredient in the transition: an adaptation of traditions of the outgoing culture to become useful to the new one. It is important to connect Debussy and Partch, to complete the revolution and connect it with a redefinition of older values. In my article "Beyond Harry Partch" I have delineated this need.[1]

∞ ∞ ∞

It has been unclear just what the direction of American composition in the seventies and eighties has been, if one consults the critics. One prediction seems to have been accurate: Leonard Meyer's pluralism, which reflects a great deal about our culture both good and bad. There is no doubt it has been a conservative period, in contrast with the sixties, but while some critics have been trying out new labels, like *neoromanticism,* none of them seems particularly apt. Two relations to the sixties can be discerned: a reaction away from their experimentation, and a gradual consolidation of many of the experimental innovations of that period. Another major change has been the failure of Europe to come up with anything paralleling the ferment of the fifties and sixties there. The use of computers in music has come into its own, and much technological change is taking place. However, this has not generated a genuinely new style or movement in composition.

It has been for me a period of humanizing my music and of reaching out to wider audiences. It has been the time in which I extended my just intonation to include all that Partch did and more. It has been a time in which I have seen the risk I took in 1960, when I began to use just intonation, begin to bear fruit.

In the early sixties, when Elliott Carter was a guest professor of composition at the University of Illinois, he spoke of his earlier decision to abandon his neoclassic style in favor of a much more complex style involving in particular a high degree of rhythmic complexity. As he saw it, the gamble was that it would either establish him as a unique and important composer or it would result in a massive neglect of his works. It is clear for a long time now that he won the gamble. It is not always fatal to challenge performers and audiences vigorously.

I feel now much as John Cage said he did in 1968 when he was readying *HPSCHD* for performance. He said he thought the compositions he was writing after his current one were works that really should be written by others. It was almost as if he was expressing a degree of guilt for moving in on others' territory. That was actually not the case, but it is the feeling which is significant. I think what was actually happening was a realization that his time of radical innovation was ending. His works since *HPSCHD* do not break new ground but rather build upon his earlier work in a most solid and impressive way. They have a maturity and a clarity which give them great strength and meaning. It is in this period that his fascination with *Finnegans Wake* came to fruition. I am now three years older than he was then, and I have a similar feeling. It does not take the form of feeling that I am treading on ground which should belong to others, but I do have a sense of having achieved what I set out to do.

What remains is to carry extended just intonation into other performing areas and to recommend as strongly as possible that it opens the way to further musical growth as no other alternative does. That cannot be done by me alone, and I have quite intentionally not encouraged my students to become disciples. A few have undertaken in their own ways the kind of intonation I am using, but not because I urged them to. I have taught extended just intonation when asked to do so, but not in exclusion of other ways of composition. I have simply been providing a reconnaissance. My method as a teacher has always been to try to understand just where a student is as an artist, and to enable him or her to see that more clearly and if possible to achieve that individuality more effectively. I have relied upon example and nonverbal personal influence to effect any directional changes in artistic activity in others. I think it is proper for me to continue to function in this way as I approach you here. It is difficult to do this in a speech.

Perhaps the best way is to imagine that I am addressing the culture as a whole. As a preliminary observation I would like to say what I think art does in human life and why I think it is important. In his multivolume work *The Masks of God,* Joseph Campbell sets out first to explain that in an animal with a conscious, verbal intelligence, the instincts which rule the interior and exterior lives of other animals do not disappear but take the form of archetypes (in Carl Jung's sense of the word). These thought forms exist more as potentialities which can be activated by us or simply by life circumstances to become dreams or ritual or art. In the view of Jungian psychologists, dreams have a compensatory function in the psyche, suggesting what aspects of one's life need attention and change. The activation of archetypes by art and religion is like this, calling into play themes of existence which, when relevant, stimulate action. Tribal ceremonies are intended to activate these atavistic memories or, more accurately, built-in possibilities of psychic and physical action, and in most societies of the past, religion has served this function. But religion in modern societies has undergone a drastic change, which renders it both less effective and less available for most people. In contemporary society the arts perform this function more effectively than anything else. This is the real reason why governments subsidize the arts, and why the arts, however unsuccessful they may be commercially, do not simply fade away.

In the United States only sports receive the kind of public and community support which it would be healthy for the arts to have. Contrast the support that professional sports get in a large community with the support given its symphony orchestra, its opera company, or its chamber music organizations. And if this kind and degree of support could be instantly and permanently provided, it would still not solve the problem because these musical organizations are busy with art which stimulates archetypes appropriate to another time and place, which may or may not have any important relevance to life as it is lived here and now. The sports section of most journalistic publications is immeasurably better developed and more widely read than the arts section. And most of the critical writing in these arts sections shows very little real awareness of the meaning of this kind of relevancy.

I believe it is for this reason that there is in our culture a split between "serious" and "popular" music. Every member of ASCAP or BMI knows that popular music supports itself commercially and serious music does not. It does this partly by placing itself in near bondage to business interests but not by any means wholly so. It still exerts enormous power over its devotees, and the lion's share of that power is artistic. It is part of the entertainment industry, but its importance by no means stops there. It has been pointed out many times that the basic difference between entertainment and amusement is that the latter is an escapist activity, while entertainment at least may not be. To recognize popular music as art entails taking a look at what archetypes it activates. Much of the ongoing controversy about sex and violence in movies and on TV is an incomplete raising of this issue. In their separate and extremely contrasting cultures, both Plato and Confucius pointed out that art is not merely a symptom of culture but a contributing cause. What, then, are we doing to ourselves by our artistic habits? How many people have recognized that it is not mainly the lyrics of rock music which raise questions about the kind of influence it has upon the emotional lives of fans but *the music itself?*

As an arts council committee member I come to grips with the question of subsidies for musical performing organizations. It is frustrating not to be able to raise these issues powerfully. As a composer I tend to be more at the mercy of performing groups than influential upon them. As a teacher I come into contact mostly with other composers. I have tried to design my music so that even its technical construction raises archetypal issues, so that even its performance practice brings these into play. As a "serious" composer I am concerned to raise issues I feel as vital and important, but as a professional I am definitely not content to address an academic audience only. Any artist who is able to let his work speak from his depths and to eschew merely saying whatever gains him a wide audience or whatever his or someone else's ideology dictates is a serious artist. It is the serious artist who can help to reshape and even to help heal the society.

When President Reagan attempted to make cultural contact with Ayatollah Khomeini by sending him an autographed Bible, he acted upon an incomplete perception. It is true that Iran, like the rest of Islam, is a society in which religion exerts powerful influence by activating archetypes in its devotees; but the United States is not such a society, and is perceived as not being so by Iranians. Thus such a gesture fails in its symbolic message, and at worst suggests a hypocritical motivation. Similarly when America exports primarily its artistically irresponsible popular music and other entertainment products to the rest of the world, it projects an image of seductive shallowness. This is not perceived as hypocritical; rather it is seen as exploitative, an accurate perception. The real issue, that Iran and other radical Islamic forces are stimulating warlike and fanatical archetypal contents in their peoples, is obscured by the undeniable evidence that American business interests are stimulating self-indulgent and anarchic contents in their promotion of, for instance, rock music. Choose your poison.

Recently I listened to a TV discussion about Soviet Premier Gorbachev's *glasnost* policy. One of the American commentators said that it was much easier and less important to unleash the arts than to alter the bureaucracy. Nothing could be less accurate. Yes, it is probably easier, because Russian artists have long been champing at the bit, but it is probably even more fundamental than democratizing part of the governmental structure, because it is from the artistic sector that not only most of the dissent but also most of the positive, forward-looking criticism has come and will continue to come. It has always been more difficult for ideologues to make propagandistic use of music than of the other arts, but bureaucratic meddling in the name of ideology has long been a feature of Russian musical life. It will be most interesting to see what musical changes will follow upon *glasnost*. This kind of loosening up is unavoidable if much of Soviet society is to become computerized, because the tight rein upon information which has always characterized Soviet leadership will be impossible in the face of high-tech computerized information systems.

It is most interesting to see a parallel and even more sweeping current of change in China. That this is economic in nature can be seen as a function of the need to raise substantially the standard of living in this extremely populous country. But the opening up of the culture to the rest of the world is also transcending economic issues inevitably, and it is hard to imagine how attitudes like those of the Cultural Revolution could find any welcome in this context. It is still too soon to say what artistic ramifications will follow, but clearly the door is open to change now.

And what is our equivalent need to change? Given the closedness and ideological rigidity of these two communist societies, change moves them in a direction of freeing up. Our problem is the opposite. It is no happenstance that the drug abuse problem is one of our most serious weaknesses. And this is directly related to the self-indulgent permissiveness stimulated by our popular arts. Some kind of increase of seriousness and self-control is the only answer, and this must be given more than lip service by the arts. For rock musicians to speak out against drug abuse or even to clean up their own behavior is not sufficient, though it will certainly help. Only a change in the archetypal content of the art will really help. For us to move in a religious fundamentalist direction would produce symptoms no better than those of Islamic Revolutionism. In any case, that is too far from where most of the culture is to be at all likely on a large scale. It has been said that Russian communism abuses equality, while American capitalism abuses freedom. The archetypes we need to achieve balance are different.

The indeterminacy movement of the sixties is in this respect quintessentially American. But we have moved as far from that as from hippies. What we seek is a kind of discipline to replace the excess of freedom. What we need is a kind of discipline that leads to greater harmoniousness. The first step toward that lies in a clarification of relationships between individuals and an increased awareness and precision in our adjustments. The informational complexity of postindustrial America needs powerful organizational skills and tools to avoid anarchic dissipation of our energies. The methods of simpler societies are not adequate to the task. Thus our art needs to awaken this discipline, this awareness, this organization. It is toward this end that I have been trying to direct my art.

NOTE

1. [Ed.: At this point in the original paper, as delivered at the ASUC meeting, Johnston incorporated his "Extended Just Intonation: A Position Paper," the publication of which was then forthcoming in *Perspectives of New Music.*]

JUST INTONATION AND MERE INTONATION

1994

Any time there are two sound sources or more vibrating at the same time there are resultant patterns of interference between them. If these are simply related enough, they are intelligible to a listener. If they are too complexly related, that listener will probably try to account for them by regarding them as approximations of simpler relations. The absence of clearly related resultant patterns is perceived as an absence of power in the psychological responses which they evoke. The sharp, clear patterns made by justly related pitches evoke strong psychological responses. This clarity is mirrored revealingly in the simple arithmetic of just intonation. In contrast, the mathematics of any equal temperament is markedly more complex. This difference is symbolic of an important psychological principle.

A tone is a recurrent series of cyclic oscillations proceeding at a particular tempo. The physiological and psychological processes of our organism are also like this, recurrent and paced at different tempi. It is on this most basic of levels that music has significance for human beings. The patterns of sound evoke similar patterns of internal experiencing. The physiological processes of our organism are adjusted without the need of deliberate human volition: they proceed at tempos which harmonize to produce particular results in our bodies. But our psychological processes are not thus instinctively harmonized, requiring our conscious participation. It is here that music can be valuable, providing a model of harmonization. If the model is itself distorted, disharmonized, it may be not merely less useful; it may actually be harmful. There is then a cogent and persuasive argument for the organization of just intonation, which is precisely the adjustment of the tempo of vibrations to the simplest possible relationships.

I once relayed a request from the Tanglewood Festival to Harry Partch to lecture on just intonation. He agreed reluctantly to write a paper which I might read there. He called it "A Quarter Saw Section of Motivations and Intonations."[1] He meant that just intonation was merely a detail, a facet, of his compositional art, and he almost resented being asked to abstract it from its context. Not to mince words: he did resent it. All art has this depth of context, but this should not prevent us from studying aspects of it one at a time, so long as we do not forget the greater whole. At this twentieth anniversary of Harry Partch's death, let us recollect all the aspects of his compositional art, and let us give him thanks as well as recognition for the things he achieved.

A determination to use just intonation in composing was the most important thing I had in common with Harry. At the time I wrote to him asking for his advice and help in getting started on this, I had read his *Genesis of a Music* but had not heard any of his music. Nevertheless I knew that I wanted and needed to work with him. His book was not my first glimpse of the vistas of just intonation. I simply found in his book clear evidence that I had been preceded on this path and that I could learn much from him.

The first motivation I felt toward just intonation was a desire to adjust music theory to conform with an up-to-date scientific view of the nature of sound and tone. It was much the same as a similar urge reported by Partch in reaction to reading Helmholtz. This was followed by an impulse to eliminate the systematic approximation indigenous to temperament of any kind, again very similar to Harry Partch. But from working with Harry I discovered myself to have a negligible talent for building or designing musical instruments, and when I sought, in 1959–60, on a Guggenheim Fellowship at Columbia-Princeton, to use electronic synthesis to achieve the accuracy implied by a choice of extended just intonation, I discovered that the state of the art in electronic technology at that stage of its evolution was too primitive to permit what I needed to do. I had to turn to teaching a new performance practice to performers of traditional instruments so that they could achieve extended just intonation in performances of my music. But first I had to devise a notation equal to communicating accurately the pitch relationships I was using and to discover compositional and related theoretical techniques proper to such an aim.

This amounted to a basic reconception of the pitch theory of music. Since the basic numerical relationship of music has traditionally in all cultural contexts been the number 2, as reflected in the recycling of scales in octave spans (the octave being a ratio of 2/1), I conceived the use of each successive higher prime number as the introduction of a dimension in which the new prime number and all of its powers were compared in ratios to the powers of the number 2. So for each new prime number a new dimension is added to the lattice of ratios which has 1/1 as its center point (zero point, speaking graphically). I then devoted a lot of attention to the question of scale derivation. All of this reinforced the traditional primacy of the manipulatory techniques of inversion and retrogression and their combination. I was not seeking a radical new system, but rather a greater generalization of traditional ways of organizing tone so as to permit further evolution of the same system of organization. This search yielded microtones as a byproduct, as is the case in Partch's music. They were not a primary desideratum.

Unlike Partch, I had no wish to discredit or to replace European musical tradition, but only to free it from its own entanglements in equal temperament in order to let it develop further in its own direction. This incidentally brought it into fresh relationship with ancient and non-Western musical traditions such as Chinese, Indian, Arabic, and ancient Greek music. I first explored these relationships in the writings of Alain Daniélou, but they were to me a side issue and not a primary concern. These writings were of great aid to me in seeking a more generalized theory of music.

J. S. Bach professed to dedicate all his compositions to the greater glory of God. To translate this into more contemporary language, he saw the fundamental function of music as an aid to spiritual growth. I share this conviction. It seems to me that one's art is not or should not be a means to glorify one's egotistic vainglory, but rather an aid to self-knowledge in the pursuit of the spiritual evolution of one's interior life into a greater and no longer egotistical self. I think this is fundamental to all religions of no matter what tradition. It seems to me, as I have already said above, that just intonation is an invaluable principle in such an aim.

By now the use of extended just intonation has become a compositional movement, a development I did not earlier expect to live to see. Like all such movements it has many modes of realization exemplified by diverse composers. I welcome this context with gratitude and with considerable lively curiosity. Now that the blockage in the tradition of musical pitch usage has been cleared away, we can proceed in many directions, all of which contribute to the overreaching goal of human development.

NOTE

1. [Ed.: In the end Partch chose to record the entire lecture himself on tape, with music examples taken from his recordings or specially recorded on his Chromelodeons. The tape, which Johnston presented at Tanglewood in August 1967, has been released in its entirety on the four-CD set *Enclosure Two: Harry Partch* (St. Paul, Minn.: Innova Recordings 401, 1995).]

WITHOUT IMPROVEMENT

1995

In William Blake's symbolical work *The Marriage of Heaven and Hell,* one of the "Proverbs of Hell" reads: "Improvement makes strait roads, but the crooked roads without Improvement are roads of Genius."

In the very manner of making art there is important symbolism. Since it does not belong to a particular artist, it refers to a culture as a whole. It results from and tends to propagate a way of living and experiencing life. It has the force and function of a shaping myth. To alter in a fundamental way this myth is to induce change not only in art but in the culture itself. Cultures, like individuals, are mortal and so live for a time and die, giving way to other cultures. When this process of death and transformation is under way, cultures show just such fundamental changes of mythic content. The emerging new culture must form its own myths. Part of the available mythic raw material is contained in the mythic forms of the waning culture, but it must undergo a rebirth in order to serve a changed set of needs. It will need to mingle with yet other mythic material from other, formerly alien cultures in an analogous way.

Such a manner of making art during the period of European civilization from the Renaissance to the twentieth century was, in music, the practice known as *tonality.* It entailed the concept of key centers and modulation between them, a polarity of major and minor modes, triadic harmony with its clear differentiation between consonance and dissonance, harmonic rhythm and the organization of bars into phrases, sections, and movements, and above all the primacy of the domain of pitch in the organization of time.

During the Renaissance, as the emerging reliance upon machines began to gain momentum, instrumental music began to displace vocal music as the center of gravity of the art of composition. In particular the increasing reliance upon keyboard instruments fathered a prolonged state of experimentation with various temperaments, whose purpose was to provide a fairly wide ambitus of modulation between key centers without the seemingly inevitable concomitant of unwieldily large numbers of notes per octave of pitch span. This was widely viewed as an Improvement. Its ultimate compromise, the twelve-tone equal-tempered scale, was not firmly in place until the early nineteenth century. After that it was less than a hundred years to the crisis of tonality in the early twentieth century, which led first to atonality and then to the dethronement of pitch as a primary factor in the organization of sound.

Musical organization takes place on three scales of time: ordinary countable time (rhythm), large-scale time (form), and microtime (pitch). The most powerful emotional response to music is triggered by the perception of events in microtime. It is therefore not surprising that most of the audience for music in Western civilization has consistently rejected that music in which pitch organization has either been relegated to a minor and subordinate role or abjured altogether, either reacting toward music of earlier times in history or toward the popular music which never underwent this change. Music was ripe for this schism because owing to the compromises of temperament, the actual pitch relations underlying the design of almost all traditional Classical and Romantic music were not really audible to the listener, but were only implied by the pitch designs of melody and harmony. This greatly blunts the impact of the music, like food composed largely of synthetic substitutes for real, natural nutritional ingredients. To counteract this loss of zest, composers resorted to ever-increasing usage of chromaticism and dissonance, and it was this spate of complexity which led to the crisis of tonality. It seemed to Schoenberg that it was the bankruptcy of tonality that produced the dead end he so strongly sensed. His solution was honest and direct: to accept the true nature of the pitch spectrum Western music was using for exactly what it was, and not as the implication of something else. However, it led to a kind of complexity the typical listener did not want to deal with. This same mindset leads to "organized sound," to indeterminacy, to chance-organized compositions.

The rebirth of just intonation, spearheaded by Harry Partch, is a powerful reaction against this current of development. It makes possible the revaluation of Western musical practice in the light of just intonation, which is the true underpinning of tonality, and it also provides bridges to the musics of other cultural traditions which use varieties of just intonation. This enables the emerging culture to begin to find its own way of making art, in the shape of a new mythic formation.

The seven-tone major scale is not an arbitrary collection of pitches. It is the linear projection, into a scale, of three major triads (pitches in the proportion 4:5:6). The minor scale is an exact inversion of this, just as the minor triad is an exact inversion of the major. Modulation is usually achieved by utilizing as a pivot a common tone or more than one common tone, perhaps a chord. The patterning that results is greatly distorted by temperament, which can make possible what are in fact impossible designs, except by the use of a kind of *trompe l'oreille* distortion. A good example is the common progression C major, a minor, d minor, G major, C major, seemingly circular (or recursive) but actually spiraling away from the starting pitch, since the C you end up with is not the one you started with but microtonally distant by the interval of the syntonic comma (81/80, or 21.5 cents). Similarly enharmonic intervals are not equivalents but are microtonally distinct.

In short, the paradigm upon which the behavior of tones in Western art music rests is radically altered in important ways when tempering is brought to bear upon it. Instead of a finite and limited field of pitches which can be made to seem more varied than it is by a system of interrelationships between them which introduces ambiguity, just tuning offers a potentially infinite and open-ended system of pitches controlled by a number of relationships which are potentially infinite as well but can easily be limited to a manageable few. These relations are hierarchical, ranging from the simplest to indefinite degrees of complexity, limited only by our ability to distinguish and remember them. Also, the confusion of spiral designs with circular ones is a radical change of symbolic meaning. The most drastic of all the differences is the fact that tempering renders all intervals dissonant except the octave, radically weakening the effect both of consonance and of dissonance. Thus Schoenberg's "emancipation of the dissonance" is actually the almost total loss of consonance. There is in Schoenberg's atonal compositions an avoidance of octaves, the sole remaining actual consonance.

All of these relations of pitches, like those much less rapid ones of rhythm, are describable in simple numerical relations, referring to proportions between rates of vibration. If these proportions are quite well realized, as is not the case when they are approximated by tempered systems, they stimulate strong responses. When these proportions must be inferred by context, response is much less vivid. I once asked an Indian musician how he determined when the tuning of a raga was correct. He replied, "When the rasa is correct." *Rasa* means "emotional flavor." The strongest response to pitch is emotional. This is the secret of the power of music. Thus when the role of pitch is diminished, there is a net loss in expressive power, and the symbolic content is less clearly projected. Like a drug, the effectiveness of which diminishes with constant use, this waning of emotional expressivity resulted in an intensified effort to heighten the emotional power of music by whatever means came to hand. Not only romanticism but also the conviction that art should change progressively received a push from this effect.

Schoenberg cannot by any stretching of facts be blamed for the situation in which music found itself in the early twentieth century, but he certainly was a powerful voice in getting composers to look unblinkingly at exactly what had happened to the language of their art. And not only Schoenberg but the whole of the avant-garde pressed music in directions that eventually left the ordinary music-lover feeling a sense of radical alienation from contemporary serious music.

There can be no doubt that the effect of contemporary serious art has been, cumulatively, a radical one, lending its transformational power to the direction of fundamental change in many ways. Combining with the multiple crises and technological revolutions this effect tended still more extremely to divide conservative and radical elements, bringing out the exaggerations of both extremes which are only too familiar: radicals for whom any change is exciting and conservatives for whom any change is threatening. It is, in this climate, very difficult to maintain a position that any tradition is important to preserve or even to revivify in support of necessary and fundamental change. And even that position is capable of dangerous perversion, as in the case of Hitler.

All fundamental change must include a critique of what has been and a vision of a different future. Times when such change is incipient are turbulent to an extreme and throw up many false leads as well as some genuine ones. Only the determined search for really basic values and aims can give a reliable compass in such a storm. There are in the currents of change destructive as well as creative forces, and both are necessary, but they can balance only if reconciled in a way that enables change to proceed in continuity. I believe that the rebirth of the practice of just intonation in music is such a reconciling element. It is fascinating to see what seemingly contradictory types of musicians it brings together: radical avant-gardists, practitioners of "early music," barbershop singers, acousticians, for instance.

Much of the effect of just intonation in the United States is in the integration into our way of making music of various Asiatic traditions. Lou Harrison has made extensive use of Indonesian gamelan practices. Much of La Monte Young's music relates at its root to north Indian music. Both Terry Riley and James Tenney are as much a part of the avant-garde as of a movement to establish just intonation. My own music reevaluates many aspects of European tradition in the light of just intonation practice. In addition there is another, newer generation very much involved in this activity. It is a very varied and complex development, but at least part of its thrust necessarily is to put aside the Improvement of temperament and to return to those "crooked roads without Improvement" which William Blake so aptly indicated.

MAXIMUM CLARITY

1996

Imagine looking at home movies when the person running the projector suddenly improves the focus. It is a pleasant but definite shock to see how much clearer the images are now, even though we had accepted them before the adjustment. This is a very precise analogy to what happens when the players in a musical ensemble clean up the intonation. They do not have to compute this or even analyze the music to discover what it needs to bring it in tune. No, this is done "by ear": simply by listening for maximum clarity in the intervals that constitute the ensemble sound. Most players are scarcely aware even whether they have to raise or lower pitches in order to achieve good tuning: they make the adjustment quite directly as soon as they bring critical attention to playing in tune.

What is actually happening when such ensemble tuning is proceeding well is that the versions of the intervals which have the smallest numbers in the vibration ratios are being selected. This is what just intonation is, at its simplest. Of course, it can be more complex than that. There are usually several versions of an interval, all simple enough ratios to beguile the ear, so that one may select among them. The basis of this choice is usually what is called *expressivity.* It is what performers in the Indian tradition call *rasa,* or emotional meaning. As one becomes more and more sensitive to this dimension of performance, one begins to characterize musical styles more successfully by means of particular expressivities produced by interval choice.

This degree of sophistication is by no means unusual among fine performance artists. When they are learning this from master teachers, they rely largely on imitation of other artists who already know how to do this sort of thing well. Very little, if any, intellectual explanation is given, and frequently the language used in making suggestions is geared more toward heightening emotional awareness than toward awakening the analytical mind. For instance, "Try to play that more warmly," or "This passage needs a sense of angst."

One of the easiest style characterizations to perceive is that of blues singing. Listen to a Gershwin song sung by a jazz vocalist and then contrast it with the same song sung by an opera singer. There are perceptible intonation differences between the two. Technically, many of the blues intervals used by jazz singers involve relationships to the seventh partial of the overtone series, rather than the more "concert" sound of relationships to the fifth partial. Neither singer is at all likely to understand intellectually this difference, but by ear, the expression is quite distinct in the two unlike cases. By ear is how it is achieved and by ear is how it is appreciated. The criterion for the choice is an oral tradition: namely, the style.

When concert music draws on folk or ethnic traditions for its expressive content, various elements of performance style need to be adopted by the performer. The violin concerto of Max Bruch is a good example. These stylistic niceties are not written into the score, but a sensitive violinist learns them from oral tradition. Naturally, pitch idiosyncrasies are not the only such style traits: there are timbral and rhythmic nuances that are just as important. Jazz rhythm is not notated exactly as it is played. Play it exactly as notated and you will be accused of being "square."

There are even aspects of performance tradition that are attributable largely to the problems of the performer, which are created by compromises made by theorists, instrument designers, and even composers. When temperaments of various kinds were introduced during the sixteenth through the eighteenth centuries in Europe, they were theoretical constructs intended by theorists to make keyboard instruments feasible and to accommodate the design problems of instruments that were newly emerging as the main element in musical performance ensembles. Up to that era, art music in Europe had been predominantly vocal, and each part was performed by a single musician, with no massed unison as in a modern chorus or in the string section of a modern orchestra. In the earlier vocal style, vibrato was used only as a melodic ornament, exactly analogous to a trill or a mordant. Its use, like all ornaments, depended upon an oral, not a written, tradition. But the great difficulty of performing the pitches of these subtly comprised temperaments accurately, and the additional burden created by mass unison performance (which inevitably caused minute differences of tuning from player to player), made vibrato gradually adopted as a way of concealing these intonational imprecisions. In addition, there is a far more subtle but far more serious obscuring factor involving the practice of composers. The concept of consonance and dissonance, fundamental to Western music, strongly implies that consonance should be just tuned, and in performance practice, this is what is normally attempted. But as notation developed, it preserved a visual distinction between an E♭ and a D♯, for instance, but none between the fifth of a dominant triad and the added sixth of a subdominant one. The former is the enharmonic equivalent or diesis, the latter the syntonic comma (or the comma of Didymus). As composers accustomed themselves to temperaments, they began to disregard the differences of a syntonic comma. Thus there are passages in which the pitch will gradually go flat or sharp if all the consonances are carefully kept to just tuning. In more complex harmonic passages, it is impossible for all intervals to be consonant: somewhere in the context, an interval or several intervals will have to be tuned as dissonances. Vibrato helps conceal difficulties such as these.

It is a perfectly workable premise to base an artistic system upon a compromise such as this, as the successful existence of Western music demonstrates. However, there are consequences, some of which have yet to be squarely faced. Every aspect of an artwork is potentially symbolic, or to be more precise, the symbolic content of an artwork can be read to various depths. The symbolic meaning of a compromise like this is not a flattering commentary about a culture that imposes it upon every artwork a priori. It is rather like covering up emotional insecurities with superficial politeness, a not uncommon practice.

Plato said, "The soul is a harmony." Since the *harmoniai* were the modes of ancient Greek music, this formulation indicates a comparison not to a chord of musical tones but to a scale upon which melodies are formed. This view of the inner life is not only an ancient one: G. I. Gurdjieff called his school the Institute for the Harmonious Development of Man. In Gurdjieff's view, man does not have a soul unless he nurtures one in himself and, in this process, beginning with merciless self-observation of all one's habits, attitudes, and weaknesses, leads into a gradual process of what could be accurately described as a bringing in tune of one's interior life and a unifying of what is exterior and what is interior. In his teaching, he laid great stress upon both music and movements as significant aids in this difficult effort. The emotional life, with its addiction to all kinds of negative states, is greatly in need of such tuning, so that it can become the means to further growth instead of the principal blockage preventing it.

Plato also viewed music as a producer or inducer of inner states, in sharp contrast to Aristotle, who viewed the effect of art as purgative. Plato's view accords, by the way, with that of Confucius. In this view, to expose oneself to art charged with violent and negative emotion is to tend to induce these feelings in oneself. This does not mean that such art is destructive, but rather that it brings one into contact with disharmony in need of resolution. If this resolution takes place in the art itself, the danger is lessened, but when the perceiver of the art is left to himself to resolve the conflicts induced by the art, there is tangible danger that he may not or cannot or even may choose not to make this effort. Such art arouses the tensions and leaves one with them.

As an art of time, music affects us on three time scales: macrotime, which is the largest portion of an unfolding event; normal time, which is countable, moment to moment; and microtime, which is the proportions of relative speeds of sound vibrations. Events in macrotime are best understood by using intellect and memory. The whole area of form and development in music partakes of this nature. Normal-time events are rhythmic, affecting us through motor perceptions. The principal effect upon emotion is through microtime events. It is here that the impact of tuning is manifest. With the reinforced vibrations that result when just tuning is achieved, there is an improvement not only in clarity and resonance but, concomitantly, a sharpening of emotional response to the sounds. This results in a much stronger attraction of the listener's attention and a consequent increase in what is retained in memory. In this way, the intelligibility of the large-scale form is more accessible to the listener.

Tonality can be defined as a system of pitches related to each other by a set of interval relations that can be followed by the ear. It implies harmonic relations, not simply melodic or motivic ones, which can be appreciated in terms of linear contour. In traditional Indian music, all the pitches are played in front of a drone, so that the rasa results from a fluctuation of just intervals against one single pitch level. In traditional Western music, melodies are accompanied by, or intersect in such a way as to constitute, a series of simultaneous pitch aggregates (chords) connected by common tones or by simple interval relation from a tone in one harmony to a tone in the next. When all the harmonic pitches are tuned in simple just ratios, harmonic intelligibility (actually, a series of mathematically simple relationships) is at a maximum. The typical listener is certainly not capable of performing a harmonic analysis by ear as he listens, but all listeners respond, with a fluctuation of feeling states, to this ongoing process. When the ear is defeated in its effort to follow the harmonic flux because of the complexity of the harmonic relationships, the sound can be described as atonal. In such a complex situation, the ear cannot easily refer all tones to a single central pitch, or tonic. There seems to be an ambience in which any tone could be focal, or no particular tone.

In Indian musical tradition, the drone symbolizes the *atman,* the individual portion of God allotted to every human being, against which all else acquires its meaning in the process of experience. Our task is to bring our inner awareness into contact with *atman,* as is the practice of yoga, a word whose root means "to yoke." It is worth mentioning that the root meaning of *religio,* from which *religion* is derived, is "I reconnect." The tonic in Western music is our nearest equivalent to the drone, but it is not overtly and constantly present, so its function in bringing meaning to all other tonal events is mediated by the network of tonal relationships that make up the fabric of the music, and the tonic serves as both a point of departure (home) and also as a goal, even if not achieved.

The symbolism of atonality can be expressed, and is painfully expressive of our modern way of life. In such music, there is no pitch that can serve as a focus of organization. Indeed, on a microtemporal level, there is no easily discernible organization. Thematic and motivic patterning is perceived on the same time scale as rhythmic patterns. This absence of harmonic organizing factors, such as tonic pitches, chord roots, and a logic of harmonic progressions, strongly recalls G. I. Gurdjieff's critique of "ordinary man," in whom, he says, there is no permanent entity which can say "I" for the whole psychic organism but, rather, an externally conditioned series of temporary and competing small "I"s, each of which is, so to speak, king for a day (in fact, only for a short moment) and none of which can really exert any will over the psychic flux. Atonal music has an "expressionist" angst that subordinates any emotional responses it may, in addition, evoke. This almost amounts to a description of what Gurdjieff called "negative emotions," which constitute the overwhelming majority of activities of the ordinary person's emotional life, preventing, by their monopolization of psychic energy, the experiencing of positive emotions. But like negative emotions, atonality is only a kind and a degree of complexity that defeats the efforts of our intelligence to analyze it. As the intensely moving music of Alban Berg demonstrates, the pushing of the effort to tonalize into such thickets of complexity awakens emotional responses. This is like the difficult and painful self-knowledge that Gurdjieff counsels modern man he must strive to acquire.

It is worth noting that Schoenberg did not like the term *atonal,* preferring instead *pan-tonal.* He did not view his harmonic usage as a means of achieving independence from all sense of tonal center, though he did indeed espouse "the emancipation of dissonance," which can even more illuminatingly be seen as a great extension of the boundaries of consonance. Even a casual reading of his *Harmonielehre* makes clear his view of the overtone series as a background source of the materials of our Western musical scale. That he not only accepted but openly espoused the use of twelve-tone equal temperament is well known, but it does not follow from this that he wished to jettison the whole phenomenon of tonality in music. This point of view can indeed be found among some of his followers, but by no means all of them.

The use of extended just intonation restores the strongest perceptual aid in perceiving the network of simple mathematical ratios that makes tonality possible. The term *extended* indicates the embracing of the great extensions made by Schoenberg and many other twentieth-century composers of harmonic and melodic interval language. The mathematics of just intonation brings the realm of microtime into exact analogy with the way metrical rhythm has worked for centuries and makes even clearer why developments such as metrical modulation, with its numerous interrelated tempi, are so precisely germane to its use.

Hard rock concerts place great emphasis upon a physical response to music. The insistent rhythm, the dominance of short, cyclically repetitive patterns, and amplified highly emotional voice stress a powerful body response. This is in sharp contrast with music that makes its primary appeal to emotion, not the physicalized emotions of body response, but the more subtle and longer-lasting emotions that have to do with our feeling responses to important events and relationships in our lives. On the lighter level, the majority of popular music is of this type, but lacks the seriousness of a Chopin, who certainly stressed emotional power and evocation. There is also an intellectual dimension to music, evident in such abstract designs as Bach's fugues or the serial compositions of Babbitt. Actually, much music lays some stress on all three of these kinds of stimulation to some extent. To the extent that these different aspects are well integrated, the music tends to acquire universality and greatness.

The harmonic innovations of the late nineteenth and early twentieth centuries have been characterized by Cowell as pushing the bounds of consonance to include higher partials of the overtone series. This is a particularly apt description of Impressionist harmony and, therefore, of jazz, and it can be a meaningful description of numerous twentieth-century styles. It was thus a very natural and timely decision for Harry Partch to include the seventh and eleventh partials in his just tuned scale, and subsequent use of the thirteenth, seventeenth, and nineteenth partials is a part of this same expansion of consonance. It is not necessary to consider nonprime numbers similarly, as any of them can be produced by compounding simpler partials (e.g., the ninth is two superimposed fifths and the fifteenth is a compound of a fifth and a major third).

Just as superimposed meters involving numbers higher than five are markedly more difficult for performers to handle accurately, so prime-numbered partials higher than five are harder to tune accurately. Add to this the unfamiliarity of these sounds to the vast majority not only of performers but of composers as well. The implication of these overtone sonorities in harmonic contexts is not an infallible guide, since these harmonic configurations are usually approximated by close relations which can be tuned with primes no greater than five. These are perfectly distinct and effective nuances of tuning. The true situation is that we have uncovered a huge variety of tuning nuances which need clarification and sorting. All of this is still further complicated by the ubiquitous use for keyboards of equal-tempered twelve-tone-per-octave scales, or near approximations thereof. Such constructs as symmetrical scales are directly based on such tuning, which means that either the symmetry or the pure consonance of the tuning must be sacrificed.

The difference between these two compromises is actually profound. A symmetrical scale is a circular pattern, while its just intonation counterpart is a spiral one. The symbolic significance of circle and spiral are fundamentally different. This is exactly analogous to the difference between a repetition and a sequence. The sequence "travels," whereas the repetition is static. This is a very different meaning, exactly as different as the distinction between change and stasis. The various microtonal commas and dieses are the differences by which the spiral misses its starting point on its next cycle, unlike the circle, which meets its starting point again. The circle is two-dimensional, while the spiral is three-dimensional. It is the difference between a process that simply repeats itself and one which evolves.

Any equal temperament, of no matter what numerosity, is a closed finite system, while just intonation constitutes an infinite system which is forever open. It is of course just this infinite openness which creates the thorniest problems in making use of it. It is important to know the exact color of each interval and to sense clearly its rasa. Even the commas and dieses can find their way into the awareness of the performer, though it is difficult to be consciously aware of the displacements of spiral designs by these tiny intervals because of the time elapsed between individual coils of the spiral. A cumulative displacement of several coils becomes unmistakably perceptible, however. For instance the progression (in a major key) I–vi–ii–V–I, which is much used, if carefully tuned in just intonation will flat by approximately 22 cents each repetition, so that after five repetitions it will be flat by more than a semitone. There is even in temperament a sense of relaxing in this progression, as if tension were being released. How much stronger is this impression if actual flatting is occurring. Or try the Romantic series of modulations by major thirds: C major, E major, G♯ major, B♯ major. In this case the pitch is flatting with each cycle by about 40 cents, which is an easily perceptible amount. Even in equal temperament this progression builds considerable tension; how much more so when the pitch level changes each cycle by almost a quartertone. In both cases the pitch is flatting, but in the first case the displacement results from an interaction of prime numbers 3 and 5, while in the second case it is caused by a unilateral action of the prime number 5. One cannot be so simplistic as to posit that flatting relaxes tension. The second example builds tension in spite of flatting. It is the rasa of the active intervals which determines emotional reaction to them.

The melodic dimension of music seems on first thought to be a linear patterning describable in one dimension. But it almost inevitably entails a hierarchical relating of pitches not only to tonic notes but also to implied chord roots. This is certainly the case in traditional tonal music and even in much nontraditional contemporary music. The tonalities involved may be much more complex than major and minor triads, but the process of tonality can still work in a way analogous to music of the European common practice period. In the music of Harry Partch, Otonal and Utonal hexads are analogous to major and minor triads and can be found in progressions somewhat analogous to the progressions of traditional tonal music. The complexity is greater, and so, therefore, are the possibilities. There is also in Partch a fondness for using pseudo-consonances as expressive distortions of more familiar chordal sounds: thus a chord tuned E♭, F♯, B♭ serves, in *Barstow,* as a distorted minor triad. Similar examples abound, and heighten the slightly raunchy ambience which Partch already delineates with his graffiti text and naturalistic speech usage. All this would be impossible without extended just intonation. The melodies of Partch are frequently those of ordinary speech, heightened no more than would be done by a skilled actor.

With pretuned instruments, like most of Partch's, one is held to a gamut of pitches which is strictly limited, sometimes severely so. The free soaring in an unlimited world of pitches organized into Otonal and Utonal hexachords linked by common tones or by simple interval relations from one sonority to the next is an idea one gets from his theories but much less clearly from his music. There is no doubt that the world he envisioned is there for the taking by anyone with the courage to leave pretuned instruments to a supporting role or else use them only in special circumstances in full recognition of the straitjacket they impose. For the ear to be one's guide, as it must be when pre-tuning is not used, there must be an unequivocally clear notation of intentions and a systematic that can genuinely rest upon tuning by ear. For this one must deal with intervals the sound of which the players either already know or can learn readily. The composer has to deal with these musical materials in such a way as to make possible finding all these unfamiliar relationships without artificial or preset means. This is quite analogous to dealing with extreme rhythmic complexity. Perhaps the future will give us the possibility to have instruments with digital intelligence which can help us to size up the situation in live performance and assist in realizing accurate decisions in adjusting the intonation of the pitch language of the music we are playing. So long as this leaves the performer in charge it will be a blessing. In the interim, computer realization of complex musical intentions leaves much to be desired. No one has yet designed a computer with emotional and intuitive abilities.

It has been demonstrated over and over that complexity generated by stochastic means is not distinguishable from complexity generated by serial complications or even by chance procedures. All that is necessary is to arrive at a degree of complexity which the human mind cannot easily unravel. But complexity that is truly intelligible, though pushing the limits of human ability, is quite another matter. This is one of the perennial preoccupations of twentieth-century music, all shades of opinion and preference weighing in. If complexity is not to be pursued for its own sake, as a desideratum, one must decide what the reason for making art really is. Certainly our world grows more complex with each succeeding generation, and this is why such a theme shows up in our art. To deal with this issue truly well, one must not only use intellect but also emotion and the intelligence of the body itself.

PART III

SOME COMPOSITIONS

ON *STRING QUARTET NO. 2*

For over fifty years the art of music as practiced in the West has been tending toward a split between an art of noise and an art of tone. Especially since the 1960s the great majority of avant-garde composers have turned their attention to the art of noise, feeling, as have also many more conservative musicians, that the organization of music in terms of tone relations is bankrupt. While some composers have tried systematically to organize the remaining possibilities of tone relations so as to squeeze more possibilities out of a diminishing field, most who have remained loyal to the art of tone have accepted anachronistic modes of sound organization.

Since I have wanted, in at least a significant part of my music, to organize sound in terms of the special properties of musical tone, this problem has been a crucial one for me. My approach to the problem has been to eliminate the closed system of pitches which has been current for centuries in the West: the twelve-tone tempered scale. Since a temperament with any number of notes per octave would have the same limiting properties, I chose the infinite system of untempered pitch relations. Not wanting to ignore or to work against traditional habits of hearing tones, but rather to build upon these, I took as a point of departure the organization of tone called "just intonation," in which the phenomenon of "beats" offers a criterion to order tonal intervals in a hierarchy ranging from the most constant, beatless intervals to intervals of all sizes which have all amounts of beating. This generates a greatly expanded vocabulary of pitch relations, one in which this implicit hierarchy can be made a basis of compositional order.

To use a system of pitch as different as this from traditional notation entails new conventions and signs. It also involves a new performance practice, one in which the relating of the tones reflects the just interval relations of the pitch system (Figure 37). Since there is also no reason why other less complex modes of organization proper to less precisely related sound materials should not be used in addition to just intonation, a comprehensive art of

FIGURE 37. Johnston, *String Quartet no. 2* (opening). Copyright 1989 by Smith Publications, 2617 Gwynndale Ave., Baltimore, Maryland, USA. Used by permission.

sound, omitting none of the properties of the medium, becomes possible. Traditional tone relations can exist side by side with totally unfamiliar ones, and with noises of all kinds without a violation of stylistic integrity.

String Quartet no. 2 concentrates upon pitch and duration relations which derive from just intonation. A range of pitch intervals from conventional-sounding ones to complex microtonal variants forms the tonal vocabulary of this composition. The rhythmic behavior of several parts of the piece applies to duration and tempo principles analogous to those governing the pitches.

ON *SONATA FOR MICROTONAL PIANO*

My *Sonata for Microtonal Piano* deploys chains of just tuned (untempered) triadic intervals over the whole piano range, in interlocked consonant patterns. Only seven of the eighty-eight white and black keys of the piano have octave equivalents, one pair encompassing the distance of a double octave and the remaining six pairs separated by almost the entire length of the keyboard. Thus there are eighty-one different pitches, providing a piano with almost no consonant octaves.

Effectively, for the listener, there are three main gradations of consonance/dissonance: (1) smooth untempered thirds and fifths, which have the least amount of harshness caused by acoustical beats; (2) compounds of these such as sevenths, ninths, elevenths, thirteenths, and fifteenths (which turn out to be slightly sharp double octaves); and (3) chromatic or enharmonic intervals comprising all the even-numbered keyboard distances such as seconds, fourths, sixths, octaves, tenths, twelfths, and fourteenths, and which sound "out of tune."

This suggested to me the possibility of two opposite systems for the deployment of pitches: one that synchronizes pitch choices with the layout of consonant and dissonant intervals on the keyboard, and a violently contrasting one in which the system for choosing pitches, a twelve-tone-row procedure derived largely from certain practices of Berg and late Schoenberg, either ignores or flaunts the consonance/dissonance keyboard layout. There are two contrasting movements of each of these types.

This makes possible a Janus-faced work, in which, with only the third movement similarly located in both versions, permutation of the placement of the other three movements creates an alter-ego relationship between the two versions, called respectively *Sonata for Microtonal Piano* and *Grindlemusic.* In the *Sonata* version, the movements correspond to the classical sonata scheme: the "sonata-allegro," the "scherzo," the songlike "slow movement," and the "finale," which is in this case a meditative adagio. All movements, however, are cast in the common ballad mold, AABA, as is each of the two entire versions, the *Sonata* and *Grindlemusic.*

All tempos, all phrase and section lengths, and in certain parts of the "finale" (which opens *Grindlemusic,* the sequence closing with the "scherzo"), even note-to-note timings conform to a proportional scheme derived from a single pattern of changes in AABA form. This pattern is associated with two distinct motivic groups at different points in the work.

Tempo and time period normally relate inversely in a proportional system, but in this composition these two sets of time proportions relate without inversion, resulting in an enormously complex rhythmic shape involving elaborate metrical modulation, interrupted bars and beats, and rapid passages of enormous virtuosity.

The *Sonata,* whether presented as beauty or as the beast, is a monstrous parody-enigma, allusive, referential, sometimes derisive, distorted, a tissue of familiarity in radically strange garb. In the *Grindlemusic* sequence the movements (arranged in the order "finale," "sonata-allegro," "slow movement," "scherzo") have these titles: "Premises," "Questions," "Soul Music," "Mood Music." Whatever the closing mood brings to mind, it is overlaid with irony and derision. The *Sonata* sequence poses the challenge: fast, faster, slow, slower. When, in the *Sonata's* finale, the knots are finally untied, will it be clear from what Houdini has escaped?

Sonata, what do you want? Candy?

THE GENESIS OF *KNOCKING PIECE*
1983

In the early 1960s Wilford Leach, with whom I had collaborated on *Gertrude, or Would She Be Pleased to Receive It?* and was later to collaborate with on *Carmilla,* approached me about doing incidental music for his play *In Three Zones,* subsequently produced at Lincoln Center.

I proposed to Leach that the music be composed of every degree of tonal organization from *musique concrète* shading into literal sound effects, through non-pitched percussion to conventionally tuned instrumental music and just tuned microtonal instrumental music held together by a microtonally tuned piano. I further proposed that the action be framed by the orchestra and sound speakers: on one side the just tuned piano and the pitched instruments, and on the other the non-pitched percussion and noise sources.

The first act of *In Three Zones* consists of a retelling of the same story C. F. Ramuz designed for Stravinsky's *L'Histoire du Soldat,* a variation on the Faust legend. In Leach's version, refugees crowd the bombed-out, muddy, rutted roads of a defeated, war-torn country. A young soldier, separated from his regiment, falls in with a sinister general, also separated from his troops. Uncertain whether the war is over or not, the soldier feels constrained to obey the general, who proceeds virtually to enslave him. The general is actually an incarnation of the devil.

At a crucial point in the action the two build a campfire and settle for the night. The soldier sleeps while the general, who never sleeps, watches. The soldier dreams, and we see his dream as a film in negative print. In the dream he reaches his home village and finds it demolished entirely except for one house, which miraculously is his home. He finds it locked and climbs all over it seeking to get in.

My idea was to have two percussionists cross the stage to the piano just as the soldier goes to sleep. They would then play on the inside of the piano. For this spot I composed *Knocking Piece.* The idea of a negative transformation pervaded the conception, suggested by the Faust theme, the film in negative, the bitter homecoming. The image of the most elaborate of instruments, and in this context the most perfectly in tune, seemingly violated by two percussionists with sticks and mallets, concentratedly focusing like surgeons, bore out this theme of destruction.

I was interested, moreover, in exploring a transfer of the ratios of the pitches in a just tuned composition to ratios of superimposed metrical patterns in a percussion piece.

I had recently composed a setting of Shakespeare's *A Sea Dirge* from *The Tempest* in which I used just intonation to control microtonal transpositions of a twelve-tone set which was accompanied by a series of freely varied twelve-toned sets. The principal set, a Webern-like segmented row composed of four trichords with identical pitch construction, was subjected to only two types of permutation: rearrangement of the order of the three pitches in each trichord, and rearrangement of the order of the four trichords. Since the principal set's trichords utilized three consecutive half-steps, a chromatic texture was ensured throughout. Because the intervals made by the combination of this set with its accompanying free sets were restricted to perfect octaves, unisons, fifths and fourths, and just tuned major and minor thirds and sixths, a relatively conservative level of dissonance was also ensured. Microtonal inflection was limited solely to the transposition levels used from one statement of the principal set to the next.

The pitch levels of the principal set sequence are determined by an interrelated pair of seven-tone diatonic sets, the pitch of which is determined by an interlocking superposition of just tuned major and minor triads. A few notes have been displaced by a syntonic comma, due to their harmonic context, and in two successive cases flat and sharp enharmonic nonequivalents have been mixed.

The conversion to metrical ratios was made as follows. Perfect unisons were interpreted as 1:1; perfect octaves as 2:1; perfect fifths as 3:2; perfect fourths as 4:3; major thirds became 5:4; minor thirds 6:5; major sixths 5:3; minor sixths 8:5. There is a metrical modulation in every bar. While one player maintains a constant note speed, the other fits different superimposed patterns onto this referential base (Figure 38).

The instructions on the score read: "For two percussionists to play on the inside of a grand piano . . ." The sustaining pedal can and should be used, ad lib. Pitch should be used only as color, if at all. Typical piano sounds should be used for successive notes which have the same speed, but contrasting sounds (to varying degrees) should enter with each change of note speed. The equal

FIGURE 38. Johnston, *Knocking Piece* (excerpt). Copyright by Smith Publications, 2617 Gwynndale Ave., Baltimore, Maryland, USA. Used by permission.

marks across bar lines mean that the same note speed should be maintained in spite of a change in notation. In general, specific kinds of sounds should predominate within a given phrase. All sounds should relate to knocking. A general dynamic level is given for each phrase (within boxes, at phrase beginnings). Changes of dynamic level are also indicated. The tempo of the opening is at performers' discretion; it is strict thereafter. Not all the notes must be played. Rests are permitted if rhythmic patterns are clear.

"If the unity and simplicity of the knocking sounds are overemphasized, the realization will be monotonous. If the rationally controlled shifting tempos are not mastered, the realization will deteriorate into feigned vandalism. If the marathon ensemble co-operation and concentration required fail, the performance will be impossible to execute. A spirit of competitiveness between the performers will destroy the piece. The players must be friends; in quick alternation each must support the other."

In the course of discussing music for *In Three Zones,* Leach decided my ideas were too elaborate for his conception, and *Knocking Piece* remains the only part of that music ever to be written. It has been widely performed, sometimes with a rather theatrical approach, at other times in a "pure music" form. Theatrical versions usually explain the concept of a "ritual attack upon a symbol of tradition," as I described it for *Source* magazine, where the piece was first published. The most thoroughly theatrical version was Jocy de Oliveira's. Performing with Rick O'Donnell, she used medical gowns and a film made to reproduce analogous rhythmic patterns with a strobe-like use of light. In Rio de Janeiro this version produced audience riots when it was repeated in response to audience demonstrating.

It was easy, in the late 1960s, to make a startling impact on an audience with a cleverly made theatrical piece. The first impact of *Knocking Piece,* beyond its quite different favorable reception in Champaign-Urbana, Illinois, was as a particularly acerbic example of this genre. When the University of Illinois Contemporary Chamber Players took the piece to Darmstadt, Warsaw, Paris, and London in 1966, I decided to emphasize this aspect of the work. I felt it would not hold its own on the concert with strong examples of the genre by Hiller and Martirano unless it made a bid in the same direction. It held its own, but the result with all critics was condemnation (and occasionally praise) of its theatrical raising of the specter of vandalism. As a last effort, in London when a critic who identified himself ahead of time as "hostile" asked into the background of the piece, I gave him a succinct summary of its genesis. The result was a scathing review which condemned the piece not only as a piece of musical guerilla theater but also as one whose composer had not assumed even elementary responsibility for making it a composition.

Thereafter, while others continued on occasion to present the piece theatrically, whenever I had any control over performance circumstances I insisted upon a rather austerely formal presentation. It affords an instructive example of the importance—and the difficulty—of presenting the symbolic content of an artwork as clearly as possible, avoiding extraneous and irrelevant context, and arranging to project effectively its truly pertinent content. I do not believe verbal program notes are a help. Rather, they divert attention from the music itself, which ought to be the most powerful vehicle of meaning.

Roger Reynolds, in his book *Mind Models,* suggests that the most significant interest *Knocking Piece* has is as an example of pushing a kind of formal perception to a threshold. The effort the mind makes to orient itself to the shifting tempi is not quite successful, since the constant metrical modulation almost defeats it, but it is not so unsuccessful as to precipitate a mental rejection. It is this, Reynolds indicates, which gives the work its peculiarly abstract sense of drama. It is also this which counterindicates a too-theatrical presentation.

As a basic étude for percussionists, a study in superimposed meter and metrical modulation, it has a firm place in repertory. As an example of proportional organization it has a staying power which thoroughly vindicates for me the original experiment: to transfer a proportional scheme that works for pitches to the domain of rhythmic organization. It can validly be regarded as a minimalist work, since its construction is stripped almost bare of extraneous elements which would distract attention from its structure. It remains the most thoroughgoing use I have yet made of proportional rhythmic structure.

QUINTET FOR GROUPS: A REMINISCENCE

2002

I was chairman of the Music Planning Committee for the Festival of Contemporary Arts at the University of Illinois during the early sixties. On the second big festival we undertook with a generous budget (for those times) to include composers and styles which in general the performance faculty neither understood nor happily wanted to cooperate with. In some cases we brought in outside groups to perform music otherwise unperformable locally. When searching for an orchestra to perform, among other difficult scores, a piece by Iannis Xenakis, we discovered that Eleazar De Carvalho was attempting to turn the St. Louis Symphony in the direction of performing really new and challenging contemporary scores. He needed an out-of-town recognition and success to underscore the feasibility of his aims. We were able to provide that success for him and the orchestra, and he was immediately and generously grateful. One of the results was that he and his wife, pianist Jocy De Oliveira, took a lively interest in my music. Jocy undertook learning *Knocking Piece* with a percussionist from the orchestra and eventually toured performances of it widely. De Carvalho offered me a commission for an orchestra piece, which turned out to be *Quintet for Groups.*

I composed it with the idea that the pianist would be Jocy De Oliveira, and with the practical idea that the difficult (aleatoric and serial as well as extended just intonation) aspects of the work could be rehearsed like chamber music by smaller individual groups. This turned out to be impossible for two related reasons: Jocy was by that time persona non grata with the symphony's board and to some extent the orchestral musicians themselves because of her championing of "far-out" music; and, even more important, there was no time or money at all available to schedule individual rehearsal of small groups. Moreover, the piece called for an enlarged percussion section, which needed particularly strong players capable of, among other things, accurate handling of metrical modulation and playing with precision specific pitched combinations inside the piano, in cooperation with the pianist. But the extra percussion players had to be pulled from the back stands of the second violins and the violas, and were anything but expert percussionists. Also, like a house of cards, this caused definite gaps to occur in the multiple divisi called for in both of those orchestral sections. So the piece had serious problems before I ever got to St. Louis.

When I arrived in St. Louis I met with De Carvalho the night before the first rehearsal. He had a lot of technical questions and had to tell me of the adjustments he'd had to make. About these he was guarded enough that I only began to see how much compromise was going to be necessary next morning at the first rehearsal. I was mostly worried about the pianos being tuned correctly, since I was not supervising the tuner's activities. He gave me assurances it would be okay but said I should check the pianos and the two harps by getting to rehearsal early next day. I did that and found, to my astonished relief, that the piano tuning was very accurate. Not so the harps, and I found the one harpist who was there very much opposed to using any kind of unusual tuning on his harp. I had to tell De Carvalho about this. He reassured me he would deal with it in rehearsal. Nothing was said about the second harpist, who showed up only for the final rehearsal but was far less intransigent than the principal harpist. All this was of fundamental importance, since all through the piece the pianos and harps are providing pitch levels to help keep the rest of the orchestra correctly on pitch—or at least that was what I had planned.

As rehearsal began I was banished to the rear of the hall, simply to be a spectator. But as the opening sections began to unfold there was what amounted to a rebellion in the string sections at multiple divisi clusters. After a very unfriendly contretemps De Carvalho grabbed a chair and set it just to his side (where a soloist might be placed), saying that this was a laboratory and we were going to conduct experiments to see how this composition could be realized and that he required my presence close to him onstage to help clarify things. With that he beckoned me onto stage and we began to work, he asking me the intention of each passage and how to resolve difficulties. It was only a few moments before I realized that the string players were rebelling because they assumed that this was a piece in the Ligeti technique and that they would not be functioning as strings like to function (expressively) but rather like sounds in tape music. I suggested to De Carvalho that we begin to rehearse by taking the very last parts of the piece where order has emerged from chaos and "music" has been rediscovered. I didn't verbalize this: but it was my motivation. And it worked. Convinced that the piece was concerned with something other than noise, the string sections began to cooperate.

As we got back into the more chaotic parts of the early part of the work we discovered that the winds (two groups: a woodwind quintet with saxophone in place of French horn, and a medium-sized brass section) would cause no trouble. The reed group had rehearsed carefully on their own and functioned much like a concertino group in a concerto grosso. The brass players immediately understood that the tuning was based on overtones, that there were improvisatory passages, that they were sometimes supposed to out-shout everyone else, and ultimately that they were supposed to back up and give depth and color to the strings at the close. The strings when trying to deal with the Ligeti-like textures had to be finally convinced that I knew exactly what I was asking for when I complained of missing notes in clusters, and it was discovered that these were due to the missing players doubling as "percussionists." That I knew what notes were missing impressed them.

But the worst rebellion had yet to happen. The second percussionist (not the one Jocy De Oliveira later worked with on *Knocking Piece*) created a would-be comic scene in protest against having to play such a piece, hoping (I would guess) to galvanize those who hated being made to play such a piece into ridiculing the composition. De Carvalho reacted immediately with a show of fierce anger and fired the player on the spot, insisting that he leave immediately taking all his own equipment with him. The manager had to intercede and so a lunch break was declared.

After the lunch break De Carvalho and the orchestra manager announced to the orchestra that the percussionist would not be summarily let go but that his staying was conditional upon his taking direction from the conductor. Rehearsals resumed. I had a second meeting with the harpist, and we worked out his tuning with the use of the pianos (my original intention). As we began to work on the percussion plus harps plus pianos sections, it began to be evident that lack of group rehearsal and the inadequacy of some of the players (the displaced string section people, mostly) would necessitate giving up in those parts of the piece any hope of precise realization of the score's specific indications. The best we could achieve was a kind of improvisation in the general spirit of what was intended. Since the role of this group had been intended to ensure the keeping in line of both intonation and rhythmic (specifically tempo) proportions, this was only partly an adequate adjustment, but it kept the piece together, and we were able at last to get the overall meaning to emerge even if imperfectly realized.

At the premiere performance the audience divided sharply between hostility and strongly expressed aggressive support. In the end at both performances the pro group won out. I was told by friends who lived in St. Louis that the hostility came from the wealthy symphony contributors and their friends, who already hated what De Carvalho was doing and who were trying to get rid of him, an effort which by the end of the year was successful. The majority of the audience who kept applauding until the hostile group gave up, a large group by ordinary concert norms in St. Louis, was composed of people who were not major contributors to the Symphony but who were excited that something lively was happening for a change. I had tried to get permission from the Musicians' Union for a tape to be made of one or both performances but was flatly refused permission. Since the performance was part of a regular series of an established orchestra, there was no grant source available as auspice for another performance. It would be necessary because of the great expense of making a new score.

Not long after the performances I was on a flight to New York from Champaign-Urbana with John Cage, who was at the University of Illinois to confer with Lejaren Hiller about their upcoming collaboration on *HPSCHD*. In fact he had been unable to go for the premiere because of important meetings about that. After I had described the experience to him he said I had acted as "a great physician, diagnosing what was wrong with orchestras and prescribing accordingly."

End of story.

ON *CARMILLA*

My opera *Carmilla,* with text by Wilford Leach, is based upon the novella of that title by Sheridan Le Fanu. The most significant departure from the source text is the ending, in which the killing of the vampire is presented as a premonition, preceding the last scene, which deals with the seduction of Laura, the victim, by Carmilla, the vampire. This of course means that Laura goes into the experience with foreknowledge, a drastically different meaning.

The entire story supposedly unfolds in a Styrian castle inhabited by Laura, her father, Laura's nurse, and Mademoiselle de la Fontaine, her father's "assistant." The action unfolds entirely upon and around a large, ornate sofa, the back of which features three seemingly carved heads which are actually three singers acting as a chorus and representing, at times, Laura's household: the father and the two hired women. Behind the bench is a screen, on which are back-projected a series of slides sometimes representing the setting, sometimes events, either actual or remembered or foreseen, sometimes commenting upon the action, but in a different vein from the chorus.

The two principals are costumed in white dresses, representing young genteel ladies of the mid- to late nineteenth century. The mountebank, who enters only in Scene Seven, is dressed as a peddler, not quite in rags, but rather in a pied costume a little like that of the pied piper of Hamelin. The action is preferably staged without proscenium, either on a level with the audience or in a well below audience bleachers. The orchestra is fully visible, but well to the side of the action, and dressed in black. Visual attention should be divided between the live principals, who remain seated except for Carmilla's entrance from behind a wing or curtain at the side. The mountebank enters by an aisle either through or beside the audience, and exits the same way. All singers have microphones, either on their costumes or on stands in front of them. There must be an offstage microphone for Carmilla to use in Scene Two. Music, slides, and lighting combine to create the different moods of the scenes.

Within this framework, the director has a great deal of freedom to interpret the story. The bench of course symbolizes the confinement of the physical, social, and psychological environment. The slides give a glimpse not only of what is outside but also what is inside the minds of the principals and also what is contained in the folkloric tradition of vampirism. This is quintessentially a collaborative artwork. The libretto delineates plot and dialogue, the music contributes the emotional context and some descriptive elements, and the slides provide poetic commentary.

In the original production, under the director's supervision, the musical performers created the orchestration as "head arrangements" in a long succession of intensive improvisatory rehearsals using lead sheets provided by the composer. The orchestration provided is based upon these "head arrangements." It is not recommended that this process be repeated for each production, but rather that the parts provided be used. However, there is some room for improvisatory freedom, under the watchful control of the musical director. The same is true of the vocal parts.

The only text other than what is in the musical score was originally presented to the audience on slides during Scene Eleven. In the University of Illinois production this text was also read aloud by an extra actress, as a voiceover.

Laura is seen alone on the bench in Scene One and provides background both in a narrative and in a descriptive sense. She tells among other things of a night visit to her bed of a young girl, seen only by Laura, but evidenced by a warm depression in the bedcovers. Scene Two introduces us to the folkloric superstitions of Laura's world, expressed by the chorus, who open their eyes for the first time, revealing that the sofa contains living faces which sing. (This scene is omitted from the commercial recording on Vanguard Records.) In Scene Three the wreck of a carriage by the castle is depicted, and the arrival of a young girl by this occurrence. In this scene the voice of Carmilla is first heard, from offstage. In Scene Four the two girls meet and discover that it is not for the first time, Carmilla resembling exactly the young visitor of her early childhood. It is before this scene that Carmilla enters and sits beside Laura. In Scene Five Carmilla commences her wooing of Laura, speaking of the paradox of love's gentleness and cruelty. In Scene Six the girls witness a passing cortège and dwell on the terror of death. This is the funeral of a young girl said to have died because of the "ompire." In Scene Seven a mountebank appears, selling amulets against the "ompire," and the girls buy these amulets. In Scene Eight Laura describes the terrifying visit to her room of a monstrous cat. Scene Eight begins the description of Laura's descent into illness. Scene Nine continues and deepens this. Scene Ten takes us into the lore of the vampire, its traditions and its symbols. Here is its text:

> One sign of the vampire is the power of the hand. This power is not confined to its grasp. It leaves a numbness in the limb it seizes, which is slowly if ever recovered from. The vampire is prone to be fascinated with an engrossing vehemence with particular persons. In these cases it will husband and protract its enjoyment with the refinement of an epicure, and seems to yearn for something like sympathy and consent. Assume at starting a territory perfectly free from the pest. How does it begin? How does it multiply itself? A suicide under certain circumstances becomes a vampire. The force field of its life is not discharged as in normal death, but radiates outward through some paranormal fear, a fear of death itself. Under such circumstances certain objects and metals may charge up as in a powerful magnetic field. Thereafter in such a place manifestations of these charges may be awesome and terrible or may be relatively minor, as in those rooms, well lit, where plants turn brown, wither and die, and songbirds fail to sing. The most terrible of these charges may be so powerful as to reenergize a corpse after normal life is past. Thus it is that a suicide, disillusioned with life itself yet terrified of the unknown, of the dark abyss that is death, lurks at the edges of life, a creature of the half-light. It knows no greater gift to offer its cherished victims than the same freedom from death that it itself has found.

Scene Eleven deals with the premonition of the killing of the vampire by a stake through the heart. Scene Twelve is Carmilla's final seduction of Laura.

ON *CROSSINGS* (*STRING QUARTET NO. 3* AND *STRING QUARTET NO. 4*)

Twice it has happened to me that during or just after the lengthy composition process required to produce a complex work (I work very slowly on such pieces, with much care and computation), an almost equally elaborate one will emerge with surprising speed and fluency. Such was the case when I interrupted, in 1964, the nearly five-year struggle to complete my *Sonata for Microtonal Piano/Grindlemusic,* sketches for which date from 1960, to produce, in little over two months, *String Quartet no. 2.* The second such occurrence came in 1966, just after the intricate effort to compose the orchestral piece *Quintet for Groups,* when I took as the single precompositional determinant for a new work the same kind of microtonally modulating, just tuned twelve-tone sets that had served as the generative basis of the string parts in the final section of *Quintet for Groups,* and also for the opening movement of *String Quartet no. 2.* The work which emerged at that time, in every other aspect almost through-composed in about a month of intensive work, was *String Quartet no. 3,* a single-movement work of about sixteen minutes' duration, here presented as the first movement, *Verging,* of the diptych-like *Crossings.*

I set the third quartet aside temporarily as perhaps needing a second movement. In 1973, when commissioned to write a quartet for the Fine Arts Quartet, I composed, as a second movement, *String Quartet no. 4,* but with the stipulation that either quartet "movement" could be performed alone. While the fourth quartet has been widely performed separately, it was not until March 15, 1976, on a Naumburg Foundation Concert at Alice Tully Hall, Lincoln Center, New York City, that *String Quartet no. 3* received its first public performance. The Concord Quartet had elected to play *Crossings,* the "double" quartet linkage of quartets 3 and 4, which has, as a middle movement, an obligatory structural silence of 60 to 120 seconds.

Crossings is a traverse, a transformation/journey from one leaf of a diptych to the other, from one rim of a canyon to the other, from one quartet to another. One is invited to try which pairings the work-as-perceived will accept: old world/new world? international style/world music? serial emphasis/proportional emphasis? personal/transpersonal? The philosophical game is still more challenging when only one leaf of the diptych is contemplated, when only one half of the mapping is known. *String Quartet no. 3*, issuing into silence, asks us an urgent question. And what is the question?

One may equally well consider *Crossings* a triptych, since *The Silence*, the middle movement, is a more than merely pregnant pause, but constitutes a tenuous and breathless traverse of a ridge or bridge between two opposite canyon walls, the nearer the post-Viennese expressionist ethos, submitted to the liberating but at the same time straitjacketing abolition of twelve-tone equal temperament in favor of ultrachromatic microtonal just intonation; the farther the deceptively simple and direct-seeming American folk hymn "Amazing Grace," generating variations of steadily increasing rhythmic and microtonal profusion, always securely grounded in new-old once more frontier-fresh modal tonality capable of wide proportional spaces: new reaches of consonance and metrical intricacy which push the boundaries of intelligible complexity beyond horizons conceivable in the confines of conventional tuning. This is the world of *String Quartet no. 4, The Ascent.* This quartet, commissioned in 1973 by the Fine Arts Quartet, was premiered by them in 1974 and subsequently played widely by that group.

May this "double" quartet herald the emergence of my present work-in-progress, *String Quartet no. 5*, earlier commissioned by the Concord Quartet and still promised to them as soon as my slower pace of exploration catches up to the anticipation and faith they so generously have extended.

ON *THE AGE OF SURVEILLANCE*

In the fall of 1978 I wrote a "Do-It-Yourself-Piece" (one of a genre of my devising which entails a typewritten recipe on how to make a piece of music). This one was the fifth in a series (actually the sixth, as one not so-called qualifies) and, like some of the others, pushes back the boundaries of what can be called music, since it is altogether verbal, spoken in the normal mode.

The Age of Surveillance was a reaction to the activities of a campus group of students and faculty whose political convictions are fairly clearly Marxist in outlook. In this context, much is made of sociopolitical significance in art, and a scornful, even at times insulting attitude to all art which has no such intentions is usually projected. Music and all teaching activity surrounding it is rather excessively verbalized. A special jargon is cultivated and forced on others whenever possible. While there are many positive effects of this concern for contextual relevance, there are also quite negative effects. The aggressiveness and doctrinaire approach are the least of these drawbacks, though they are the most evident. Perhaps the most insidious are the massive use of negative emotion in public meetings to disrupt the expression of contrary opinions. After a year or so of struggling with this situation I felt impelled to make a critical statement about abuses of freedom of expression.

Also behind the conception of this angry piece is alarm over the abuse of electronic surveillance devices, notably in the Oval Office of the Washington White House, but also by such agencies as the CIA and the FBI and their overseas equivalents in other countries. The paranoid atmosphere created by the constant suspicion that one's activities are being monitored, by one can't be sure whom, is a major cause of tension in modern life. One may add to this the vitiation of effectiveness of the expression of opinion by deliberate overloading of the public channels of communication. The first of these conditions is characteristic of police states, and any degree of it in a society is cause for alarm. The second is a uniquely American technique, possible only in an atmosphere of overt "freedom of expression." It is an insidious undermining of freedom by means of an abuse of freedom.

I decided to compose a situation which represents itself to be an open forum of controversial opinion, but which is actually riddled with both kinds of abuse. I wanted to write a piece which would demonstrate the vast difference between a truly political artistic statement and the "politicizing" of art by talking about it in a special way.

The Age of Surveillance attempts to delineate a social abuse by subjecting an audience to an example of it. It comments on fear by arousing it. It abuses communication in order to protest such abuse.

In my opinion art cannot spring from shallow sources such as the projection of ideological or political doctrines. It *may* project such content, but this is a side effect. The basic context is always more fundamental than such ideas: myths, beyond ready conscious and verbal expression. This is especially true of music. Art has some of the same functions and values as dreams: it puts us in contact with less superficial aspects of ourselves than waking ego-consciousness does. An artist cannot dictate to these sources what he wants to say. He can only dry them up by such an effort.

The power of art lies precisely in its ability to transcend natural thoughts and put us in a mode of symbolism which interconnects all of us in an exploration of the unknown in ourselves. It is only incidentally "psychiatric" or "social" or "ideological" since it transcends such categories. Such issues can be addressed artistically only by getting beyond them to the basic form of experience of which they are simply examples. This cannot be achieved merely by intellectual effort.

Art needs freedom, religion needs freedom, philosophy and science need freedom if they are to plumb such depths. Freedom, like all human conditions, is vulnerable to abuse.

Art needs control, religion needs control, philosophy and science need control if they are to plumb such depths. Control, like all human conditions, is vulnerable to abuse.

ON *STRING QUARTET NO. 5*

I composed *String Quartet no. 5* in 1979 for the Concord Quartet, but they delayed performance of it because of unrelated recording commitments. When in 1983 the piece was requested on a Chicago retrospective concert of my music, I requested that they release the work so that the Tremont Quartet could premiere it, promising them my next quartet (no. 7), which they now have. The Tremont Quartet had performed and liked very much my *String Quartet no. 4* in a retrospective concert of my works at State University of New York at Buffalo several years earlier.

This work, like the fourth quartet, is based on an Appalachian folk hymn, in this case "Lonesome Valley." It is not however simply a theme with variations, as is the fourth quartet. Its form resembles more the form of Debussy's *L'Après-midi d'un Faune,* with successive "evocations" each consisting of the same sequence of thematic ideas, but differently proportioned and developed each time. It is a single movement but has sharply contrasting tempi and treatments of the basic material, which includes the folk hymn.

The compositional style involves what I call "extended just intonation." This means that the tuning is untempered, based upon ratios of pitches derived from the first sixteen partials of the overtone series. The music is highly modulatory, thus involving a very large number of different pitches per octave, which since they are not being used as a scale, I did not bother to count. It is thus microtonal in a very particular meaning of that rather catch-all term.

ON *STRING QUARTET NO. 6*

String Quartet no. 6 was composed for the New World Quartet on the occasion of their winning recognition from the Walter W. Naumburg Foundation. It has required not only more than usual care and creative partnership from within the quartet but also, during the rehearsal period, from me. Without a spirit of true collaborative participation in realizing and projecting the artistic aims of the work, a convincing performance would not have been possible. I am permanently grateful to these four men for their understanding, dedication, and hard work.

Since this quartet explores the extended (microtonally more-than-chromatic) reaches of a harmonic and modulatory system using the same numerical raw materials as Harry Partch's "monophony" but not his modal restrictions, it can be said to be tonal in a new sense: radically new in this case. It is, however, not centric, since it also employs twelve-tone technique by the device of considering the octave to contain not twelve notes but twelve regions. Then with one pitch assigned to each region, the exact pitch class changes as the complex common-tone modulations proceed. The semicombinatorial properties of the row are made the yoke to link intonation to serial process: hexachord equals Partchian hexad, Otonality alternating with Utonality, the two hexachords related by inversion. The rows are linked in a cyclic chaining using all forty-eight forms: the entire quartet, a single movement, is a giant palindrome with respect both to pitch and to rhythm. This makes an arch form with a chordal section at its keystone position. The surrounding sections each consist of four lyric solos, one each for the four instruments. Compositionally my aim was to conceal most of these techniques as skillfully as possible.

ON *JOURNEYS*

The commissioning of *Journeys* coincided with my moving from Urbana, Illinois, to Rocky Mount, North Carolina, my wife's childhood home. My own childhood was spent in Macon, Georgia, and Richmond, Virginia, so this move has been, in a real sense, a homecoming. My wife and I had lived in Champaign-Urbana since 1951. All of our children grew up there, so in an even more basic sense, Illinois is our home. Certainly the University of Illinois was home, and more, to my musical life. The whole of my professional life has been based there, and most of my compositions until the mid-1980s were created in Illinois.

The most personal meaning of *Journeys* lies in this double meaning of the movement titles: "Going" and "Returning." The folk song in the first movement sings of the lover leaving; the section (number thirteen) from Carl Sandburg's *The People, Yes* used in the second movement speaks of Illinois birds (they were purple martins), released in Martinique, who flew home.

A much deeper meaning emerges from another coincidence, the death of Paul Fromm, the Vienna-born Chicagoan patron of new music whose foundation continues to support so many of our best composers. Paul Fromm was unwilling to identify his support with any one region, group, or faction in the music of this country but lent his aid generously wherever he perceived excellence. His death was a national, not simply a regional, event. And like all deaths, his raises profound questions. It is on this level, the ultimate going, the ultimate returning, that I have wished to meditate in this music.

The burden of my life's work as a composer has been to deal persistently and in depth with acoustically pure tunings, a process that involves relying upon one's ear rather than upon the design of conventional instruments or upon the suppositions of traditional musical theory. It is based upon a scientifically accurate description of sound from an acoustic and psychoacoustic angle. It is also the basis of most of the world's musics other than our own. It results in a multiplicity of different scales and chords with indefinitely large (or small) numbers of notes. It results also in a powerfully expressive range of familiar and unfamiliar musical nuances. It could be described as an honest treatment of artistic materials in contradistinction to our conventional musical system.

In this approach to making music even the technical details of composition and performance are significantly symbolic. The line we usually draw between form and content no longer has significance, like that other imaginary line between intellect and feelings, which disappears when both faculties are brought to bear upon the same symbols. I believe that the best art is on one level immediately intelligible, but so redolent with symbolic meaning that the initial grasp of it expands almost limitlessly into a richer significance. This cannot be achieved with merely conventional artistic means, but it can also not be achieved except in relation to them.

ON *SLEEP AND WAKING*

When Ron George approached me to compose a percussion work for him, he offered to design and build instruments capable of being tuned as I would like, and sent me recordings of his own work. I liked best the American gamelan, so we decided to work together on a gamelan composition.

I wanted to do a work that would reflect the Partch-like dichotomy of Otonality and Utonality, so I decided to base the tuning on the fourth through the sixteenth partials of the overtone series of A and the exact mirror of this. Tuned pipes, tuned gongs, tuned drums, and tuned cymbals would be joined with timpani and assorted random-pitched instruments. There would be a solo part with supporting parts. There are three movements. In the first a scale consisting of the fourth through the eighth partials of the overtones and their inversion was employed. In the second the eighth through the sixteenth overtone partials alternate with the inversion of these. In the third movement the combination of all these pitches is heard for the first time. The rhythmic structure is also based upon the proportions 4:5:6:7.

The mirror-like pitch structure suggested to me the ancient alchemical formula "As above, so below." In life there are life-oriented forces and death-oriented ones. Only in the juxtaposing and balancing of these forces can the opposites be reconciled. The title *Sleep and Waking* refers to these opposed forces.

PART IV

ON OTHER COMPOSERS

LETTER FROM URBANA

1963

The 1963 Festival of Contemporary Arts at the University of Illinois included twelve musical events as well as two lectures and a roundtable discussion which posed questions illuminated by the concert programs. Edward T. Cone's lecture, "The Irrelevance of Tonality," developed the thesis that there are musical works in the pitch organization of which the perception of a central point of reference is crucial to the heard structure of the composition, while there are others, more frequently encountered in contemporary music but not absent from the music of earlier periods, in which the structure does not so depend, though the music may in some sense employ tonality. Boulez's lecture, "Poetry—Center and Absence—Music," a reflection of his recent preoccupation with texts of Stéphane Mallarmé, reexamined various historical approaches to the problem of relating music and poetry and culminated in an expression of his own views: an affirmation of the "abstract" manner of handling texts, but with an insistence upon the idea of a symbolic common ground of meaning originating in the poem and motivating the music. The roundtable, "Approaches to Improvisation," whose participants were the composers Robert Erickson and Barney Childs and the performers Bertram Turetzky, Dwight Peltzer, and Eric Dolphy, discussed problems of improvisation and aleatoric techniques in music, questioning basic aspects of the composer–performer relationship.

From the point of view of Cone's lecture, the works performed on the first weekend, in concerts given by the Walden Quartet and the Illinois Opera group directed by Ludwig Zirner, offer interesting contrasts. The comparison between the pre-twelve-tone serial technique of Webern's op. 5 and the segmented twelve-tone organization of his op. 28; the juxtaposition of both these against Schoenberg's hexachordally organized op. 45; and the contrast of all with Mayuzumi's deliberately static pieces obviously demonstrated markedly different orientations to the question of tonality. Thus the serial "free association" of Webern's op. 5 constantly approaches total chromaticism but sometimes permits emphasis on certain tones, whereas the symmetrical set formation of op. 28 practically guarantees that this cannot happen. On the other hand, Schoenberg's *String Trio* creates a wealth of tonal ambiguity. It seems constantly to be providing "roots" and "tonics," but closer listening reveals alternative possibilities in almost every case. The situation is like that of looking at certain Abstract Expressionist paintings: they can be perceived as somehow representational, but the degree of ambiguity involved is such that one must finally conclude that the essential composition of the painting does not depend upon any such reading. Although Mayuzumi's pieces connect obliquely with Webern's op. 5 in their intense preoccupation with timbre and minute detail, the resemblance stops there; to be sure, many of the pitch structures are symmetrical, but prolonged and reiterated tones and patterns establish artificial points of reference.

This procedure is also basic to Boris Blacher's *Abstrakte Oper No. 1,* different though its style may be. Here the triadic structures provide roots, but the symmetry of polychordal root groups and of root progressions provides several alternative tonics most of the time. When Blacher breaks this symmetry to establish a prejudice for one or another tonic, it is almost always for satiric effect. The promise of tonality is also, if rather chimerically, present in Gianni Ramous's *Orfeo Anno Domini MCMXLVII.* Ramous's elusive pitch continuity, not so triadic as Blacher's, depends (to my ear) more upon microformal interval relations than upon larger-dimensioned relationships. There is, however, a striking moment at the end, when a triadic cadence seems to have been established, only to be shattered by a dissonant-percussive final codetta.

The second weekend provided a shocking contrast to the first, particularly for those listeners who prefer or even require music to engage them intellectually. The weekend began with a piano recital by Dwight Peltzer (not actually part of the festival proper) which included Salvatore Martirano's *Cocktail Music* for piano, Webern's *Piano Variations* op. 27, Robert Erickson's *Ramus-Toccata,* Ramon Sender's *Thrones,* and Boulez's *Piano Sonata no. 1.* Martirano, Erickson, and Boulez's works, in very different ways, all move beyond the limitations of serial microform into a larger-scaled, freer idiom, characterized by expressionistic extremes of violence and delicacy. Erickson's toccata included improvised passages, and Sender's piece was entirely improvised on an amplified piano against tape sounds, in total darkness punctuated by flashes of colored light, accompanied by a revolving cylindrical star chart which no one could see in the dark.

Following this, the Hartt Chamber Players gave a controversial concert consisting almost entirely of works by young composers. In Robert Ashley's *Complete with Heat,* the ensemble improvised against a quiet but very droll tape piece. In Charles Whittenberg's *Electronic Study II* with solo double bass, Turetzky battled the tape and won, and in the last piece, a realization of Cornelius Cardew's *Octet '61 for Jasper Johns,* the improvising musicians, joined by two speakers reading fragments of a wordy essay by Cardew, pitted themselves against four simultaneously played tapes. The balance of this program was divided between partly aleatoric works (Bo Nilsson's *Zwanzig Gruppen,* and Roman Haubenstock-Ramati's *Interpolations* for flute and magnetic tape realized by Nancy Turetzky) and "straight" composed works (Charles Wuorinen's *Concert* for double bass alone, Donald Martino's *Cinque Frammenti,* and Stefan Wolpe's *Suite im Hexachord*).

Saturday's "Improvisation and Indeterminacy" concert featured the premiere of Erickson's *Piano Concerto,* composed for the festival, Loren Rush's improvised *Mandala Music* for three or more performers, Barney Childs's *Welcome to Whipperginny,* a work which makes extensive use of indeterminate ensemble techniques (played by the University of Illinois Percussion Ensemble under Jack McKenzie), Stockhausen's jewel-like *Refrain* (performed by Joseph Dechario, piano, Donald Andrus, celesta, and William Parsons, vibraphone), and John Cage's *Solo for Voice 2* (sung by Grace Wieck, David Barron, and Durant Robertson), performed together with *Cartridge Music.*

Finally, the Sunday jazz concert, following an afternoon roundtable on "Approaches to Improvisation," brought together the Eric Dolphy Quartet and the University Jazz Band (John Garvey, leader). The character of this weekend was fundamentally connected with its focus on virtuoso performers. Peltzer, Turetzky, oboist Josef Marx (of the Hartt ensemble), and Eric Dolphy all project intense performance personalities. The emphasis on improvisation and aleatoric music sharpened this focus. The wish to get the performer back into lively involvement with the creative process, greatly extending his privileges and responsibilities of collaboration with a composer, pervaded all the West Coast works. The East Coast parallel (and its European reflection) seemed much more aimed at breaking the habitual patterns of the performer by requiring him to adjust to unexpected and unpredictable elements introduced by techniques of chance. Since this approach is typically wedded to experimentation with various kinds of graphic notation which are open to very free interpretation, the result is similarly to involve the performer more deeply in the act of creation.

If the Erickson pieces (and to a lesser extent the Childs) seemed more interesting than most of the improvisatory or aleatoric pieces, this was probably because the control exerted by the composers effectively determined the musical macroform of these works and guaranteed stylistic consistency in their details. The Cardew piece relied entirely on Turetzky's considerable gift as a director of abstract theater and on his performers' understanding of the need for theatrical projection. The Cage piece suffered because it had no director of comparable talent, but only an electronic technician who, however competent (as James Campbell obviously was on this occasion), had of necessity to leave the performers to their own devices. The three singers rose to the theatrical occasion, but the performers of *Cartridge Music* did not. Neither the Cage nor the Cardew work was given a viable macroform by its composer, and Nilsson's *Gruppen* also suffered badly from lack of macroformal organization, a problem inherent in its chance technique.

One might have expected the jazz concert to raise interesting questions about improvisation. The existence of a jazz-improvisation tradition of long standing and the fact that Eric Dolphy is identified with a position of revolt against some major premises of that tradition seemed to augur a lively performance. On the contrary, Dolphy's quartet seemed far less free from restraints than, for instance, Peltzer, and was also less sensitive to psychological timing and to the effect it was creating on its audience. The jazz band, though not so "far out," was considerably more provocative.

It is possible to see in these trends a reaction against the mechanization of performers by impossibly complex technical demands, and against the antitheatrical effect of synthetic music (with no performer); on the other hand, this preoccupation with chance may mean an abandonment of creative responsibility, and perhaps an improvising performer is merely a sloppy composer. The roundtable discussion of March 10 raised some important questions regarding these tendencies and—fortunately—did not pretend to have answered them.

The third weekend emphasized works with elaborate serial organization, of which three deserve special mention: Rochberg's oboe piece, *La Bocca della Verità;* Babbitt's solo cantata, *Vision and Prayer;* and Boulez's *Le Marteau Sans Maître.* Babbitt's restraint in using the legendary synthesizer for such subtle, precise, and unpretentious effects is in catholic taste, as is his treatment of the Dylan Thomas poem. The *Marteau,* on the other hand, certainly has a delicate, intricate, exotic vitality—in fact, its surface is so glittering that it is hard to see inside; but if the glitter is essential to the style of instrumentation, its length seems excessive for what it has to say. Rochberg's piece has a sober, astringent quality that makes a forbidding surface, but the virtuosity of its instrumental writing helps to counteract this severity. One might be tempted to conclude that Rochberg's polyrhythmic complexity sounds, after all, like rubato, but this would overlook the cleanness of rhythmic contour and precision of linear independence which his work has.

The final weekend began with a concert of predominantly conservative music which included performances of Harrison Birtwistle's mild *Refrains and Choruses* for wind quintet, by the University of Illinois Faculty Woodwind Quintet; Russell Smith's *Palatine Songs,* by soprano Jane Schleicher and a chamber ensemble conducted by George Hunter; Leon Kirchner's virtuosic *Sonata Concertante,* by violinist Paul Rolland and pianist Howard Karp; and Chou Wen-chung's *Metaphors,* by the University of Illinois Wind Ensemble, Robert Gray conducting.

Marilyn Mason's organ recital was again predominantly conservative. The program's centerpiece was Schoenberg's somber *Variations on a Recitative,* op. 40, and also included Ross Lee Finney's *Fantasy,* Daniel Pinkham's *Concertante No. 3* for organ and percussion, Charles Ives's *Adeste Fideles in an Organ Prelude* and *Variations on America,* John Cook's *Flourish and Fugue,* Normand Lockwood's *Quiet Design,* and Edmund Haines's *Suite for Organ.*

On the final Sunday-evening program, the University Symphony Orchestra conducted by Bernard Goodman played Dallapiccola's *Variazione per Orchestra,* Charles Ives's *Decoration Day,* and Burrill Phillips's *Perspectives in a Labyrinth* for triple string orchestra. The Phillips work exploits spatially articulated counterpoint and antiphony, and asserts its energetic character in lean, atonal textures. Pianist Stanley Fletcher with Robert Gray's Wind Ensemble gave a performance of Messiaen's *Oiseaux Exotiques,* whose virtuosity and exuberance sustain interest in what is principally brilliant texture and color for a surprisingly long time. The music festival closed with a performance of Bartók's *Cantata Profana,* under Harold Decker's direction. The soloists were tenor James Bailey and baritone Bruce Foote.

Some regrets: that Elliott Carter's *String Quartet No. 2* and Alberto Ginastera's *String Quartet No. 2* had to be canceled, although the works that replaced them (Schoenberg and Webern) were certainly not inferior; that Conlon Nancarrow's pieces could not be programmed because of the lack of a special player piano; and that Ives's *Decoration Day,* already recorded, was selected rather than a less easily obtainable piece.

TO *PERSPECTIVES OF NEW MUSIC* RE. JOHN CAGE
1969

Dear Sirs:

I have a bone to pick with *Perspectives*. If it were not that this magazine is the leading scholarly publication in the United States which deals with new music, my taking up this issue would hardly be worth the trouble, since it concerns a matter (I think) of diehard aesthetic bias. But *Perspectives* has been good to me, printing my articles when no one else was interested; so I think I should give it the courtesy of registering in its pages my objections.

I take vehement exception to *Perspectives*'s perennial one-sided treatment of John Cage, so consistent that it seems to amount to an editorial policy. Anyone confining his acquaintance with contemporary American music to what is discussed and reported in the pages of *Perspectives* would inevitably acquire the impression that Cage is (1) a charlatan, (2) an incompetent composer, and (3) a passing phenomenon of fashion. This must be considered against the background of Cage's undeniable international reputation and worldwide artistic influence: he has been for a decade the clearly recognized world leader of the avant-garde.

But *Perspectives*, vaunting its concern for serious intellectual scholarship over its role as contemporary chronicle of music, has deliberately opted to ignore and deprecate most of the avant-garde. A more serious editorial mistake could scarcely be imagined. It is not even good history, let alone smart politics. It repeats a typical American academic mistake.

The leading movement in post–World War II Europe was so-called total serialism, an ultra-intellectual movement that antedated by a decade its American equivalent, which *Perspectives* undertook to represent. In the fifties the predominant compositional influences in the United States were Stravinsky and Hindemith. Most of the composers of the country, located then, as now, in the universities, were neoclassicists in style, traditionalists in pedagogy.

But during this same period the group surrounding Cage was embarking upon altogether different paths, those of indeterminacy and chance. By the time the twelve-tone movement gained ascendancy in the United States in the early sixties, in much of Europe and in Japan these newer trends had almost entirely replaced those of serial composition. American varieties of indeterminate music have continued to spread, and with greater success than imitation European varieties. Like postwar American painting, American indeterminate music has become the vanguard of style.

How *Perspectives* can ignore a phenomenon of this importance is hard to understand. If I did not know personally many of the people involved I would suspect prejudice. I must attribute shortsightedness to them, nevertheless, since this policy indicates at the very least a *lack* of the kind of "perspective" which purports to be the aim of the magazine.

The intention to organize every detail of a piece of music according to some master plan has in it something of the totalitarian dream. Certainly the effect upon the performer bears out this comparison: almost nothing is left to his responsibility, so that he can only carry out orders. One of the main motivations toward indeterminacy was a desire to get the performer back into meaningful creative relation with the composer. Performerless music (on tape) grew up alongside totally organized music. Listening to it proved to be a somewhat alarmingly antitheatrical experience in a concert hall, thus bringing forcefully to everyone's attention the importance of presentational theater in performance. Cage has pointed out still another reason for indeterminacy, this time as contradistinguished from improvisation. Habit, especially quoting others and oneself, is an enemy of creative action. Improvisation brings habit into play, depends upon it in part. Indeterminacy can shatter patterns produced by habit, forcing adaptation to new and unexpected situations.

One of the theoretical means employed in total serialism is the division of music into many parameters, each capable of organization. But not all of these parameters are capable of all the subtleties of serial composition because we do not perceive them sufficiently precisely. This has led naturally to modes of organization which are less precise: contouring, making "sound objects." These "rough" methods can be applied as well to parameters ordinarily capable not only of serial but of proportional organization, and this has been done widely. The introduction of graphic notation was a means of communicating these new organizational intentions to the performer. Just as the negative rules in twelve-tone composition serve to rule out a tonal interpretation by ear, indeterminate use of pitch and duration serves to focus organizational attention upon other elements of composition.

Thus there is plenty to say about form in indeterminate music if you give up the insistence that only serial order has sufficient intellectual rigor to be respectable. To say it you need a new intellectual framework, one provided nicely by the singling out of modes of order described as nominal (sound object), ordinal (parameter contouring), interval (melodic and serial), and ratio (harmonic and proportional).

Cage has been a leader in bringing about these developments. It is time the academics took him seriously and stopped trying to ridicule him out of existence.

The discipline of a Cage composition is enormous. It begins with a plan to circumvent the action of habit (often described as expressing oneself) and proceeds through a complex sequence of definite actions which lead to an unexpected result: the performance. Cage is a perfectionist without peer, as any copyist who ever worked for him will affirm. He is a "conscious artist" to a degree most composers cannot claim if only because the philosophy, theory, and practice of his art have been subjected by him to such close scrutiny and discipline. It is not one jot easier to play a Cage composition than one by (say) Boulez. One can just as easily fail. When at the outset, the job is taken lightly, some degree of failure, often a high degree, becomes inevitable. The attitude inculcated by *Perspectives* is encouraging this cavalier treatment: a gratuitously irresponsible action.

What about a proper article on Cage by someone who understands his work? When will we have done with such juvenilia as the insulting review of his *A Year from Monday?*

THE CORPOREALISM OF HARRY PARTCH

1975

What was planned this past winter for Harry Partch cannot now take place, because he died last fall. But that underlines the urgency that something else has to happen: the rescue of his life work, which could easily slide into oblivion.

More than is usually the case, there is after Harry Partch's death little certainty that any continuity will result from his life's efforts. Practically none of his works are performable without his instruments, and there is only one set of these. They are quite perishable and very difficult to maintain in playable condition. If anything of his work is to survive beyond a very few years, even with dedicated efforts on the part of people now concerned, the effort will have to be well supported.

Partch did say, and then gainsaid in his recently republished *Genesis of a Music*, that perhaps recordings could be a solution for such a composer as he. If the recording became the definitive artwork, as with magnetic tape compositions, which are like paintings, otherwise unpromising undertakings such as his might become feasible. But just about everything Partch composed is not only music but also theater. Although he did some films, most of his works are for the stage. They are heavy on the visual side, and not only because of the instruments, themselves works of sculpture, but as total visual theater. Their impact is not received simply by listening to the music. You do get something, but less even than from an opera you have never seen.

Corporealism was a theory that Partch lived. It is a vehement protest against what he considered the negation of the body and the bodily in our society. It resulted specifically in an attack on *abstraction*. What that meant to him was first of all that music should not be separated from words or visible actions, whether theatrical, choreographic, or simply musically functional. He directed us to see *people doing things*. He felt that aspect to be just as much music as tones or rhythms: as any of the parameters we have abstracted from the total musical experience to serve as *elements* of music.

Not only acoustics books but also manuals on musicianship usually start out by citing these elements. They anatomize music variously, but all focus on abstract categories. Harry Partch would have been more apt to cite things that pointed to what he was saying.

He would have been more inclined to point out that in *The Bewitched* he was concerned with *liberation* than to discuss his forty-three-tone microtonal scale. This liberation (among other things from musical slavishness) is achieved by a most unpromising and unpromised means: a witch. Partch knew, as we know, that no witch is going to appear to "unwitch" us, but he insisted upon this symbol.

Why a witch? Partly in order to call to mind very ancient traditions, antedating even patriarchal society and resting upon a belief in magic and sorcery. But Partch had no such beliefs. I would compare him in certain respects to William Blake, but he was certainly no seer of visions. His visions were about as corporeal as his boiled coffee. He had little interest in or patience with the "far-out" side of life except for his affirmation that everything which happens is *that far out.* If the meaning of events is sometimes obscure, it is also sometimes obvious, and not infrequently blatant. Partch was also by turns obscure, obvious, and blatant; but he was always natural, loose, free, and uncaring of anyone's opinions. There was some defiance in that, but I think very little, since these attitudes were as integral to his artistic point of view as to his lifestyle.

We are dealing with a man who was the son of apostate missionary parents: an apt symbol. There was perhaps nothing that he rejected more vehemently than telling other people what to do. And yet of course he found himself in a position where he was, even more than most composers, doing just that. He did not accept John Cage's solution, which was to stop telling people what to do. By Harry Partch's definition this was to stop making art.

He opted instead to go back to more ancient traditions than the European. He had no use for European civilization, although willy-nilly he was in part a product of it. He was very much a "rugged individualist," more so than Ives or Ruggles. He "dropped out" to the extreme of becoming a hobo. He would not compromise even to the extent of supporting himself by means of an adjunctive career.

I am not trying to make this action seem unusually heroic. I am sure that in most respects it was no act of heroism. It was an act of necessity. He wanted very much to be an artist—a composer—neither part-time nor in a commercial context. He felt his grasp of life was at least a little different from what he found around him. Not unusually he was both fascinated and repelled by what he saw.

Whimsically but quite without guile or exaggeration, Partch cites as influences Chinese, Yaqui, and ancient Greek music. As for the Greek influence, his was a far more elaborate reconstruction than that of Renaissance artists. Partch wanted to recapture that entire view of living. Many of his works use not only the tuning procedures, instrumental traditions, and scales of ancient Greece, but also its myths and symbols.

This borrowing of traditions was, I think, much deeper than mere eclecticism. It is far removed from eighteenth-, nineteenth-, or twentieth-century borrowings from classical antiquity; and it is also neither a Romantic exoticism nor a Joycean culture amalgam. It resembles more the search for worldwide symbols and motifs of some contemporary anthropologists.

Partch returned even to the methods of Greek theory. Using monochords he reconstructed the scales of Greece; he adapted Greek instrumental types for his use. He studied Greek philosophical and aesthetic ideas. But all this pointed forward, as he knew very well, to a music which was no more Greek than it was Javanese. Exoticism aroused his scorn as much as conservative orthodoxy. He did not consider it piquant that his music does indeed occasionally sound like a Cantonese opera or a Balinese gamelan. He welcomed and thoroughly assimilated not only these influences but also Hebraic chant, Mussorgsky's *Boris Godunov,* and even (via recording) a Congo puberty rite. These things fed his growth far more than mainstream European and American concert music.

One of the reasons for this was his distaste for concert occasions, with their dress clothes, straight-backed seats, rustling programs, and music critics. It was a ritual he despised. Concert etiquette was far stuffier when he was young than now. White ties and tails were obligatory for male performers, and even the grand piano, the arch-symbol of genteel formality, was and is similarly dressed. He was as derisive about all this as Nam June Paik, but he would have rejected Paik's avant-gardism, as he did that of others, with equal vehemence.

His ordeal was those hobo years. He nearly starved or froze to death more than once. He was simply drifting, riding the rails as a vagrant. I would guess, from the few conversations I had with him on this subject, that returning to his work—building instruments, composing and playing music—was after those years a wrenching effort. The experience left a mark, and not just in the sense that a near-fatal polar trek would mark a person, but in the more important respect that after his hobo years he just had no fear of society and its opinions. It had done its worst to him, yet he was still going; so in large part he had won his freedom.

This attitude had some unpleasant aspects. He really frightened many people. He was strong enough to impress those he met even casually with his undercurrent of enormous emotional energy. Combined with disregard for anyone's opinions and with the supremely difficult undertaking that performing his music has always been, this personal energy and drive could generate an atmosphere of alarming intensity.

Why all this rebellion and dedication to the nearly impossible?

The point of asking this about Harry Partch is no different from asking it about Beethoven. But even that rebel was better integrated into his social context than Partch, who was a radical dropout in many senses of the term. Like Beethoven, he could not escape seeing himself as a kind of prophet. And that is why the comparison to William Blake is apt.

For example, in *Revelation in the Courthouse Park* Partch has two stories going at once: Euripides' *The Bacchae* set in ancient Greece with Dionysus one of the characters, and a contemporary story, set in a midwestern town and involving a rock idol named Dion. Most obviously he was saying that Euripides has a great deal to tell us about American culture patterns of the 1950s and '60s. Partch's *Revelation,* composed in the late '50s, was in that respect indeed prophetic.

That kind of concern was typical of Partch. He refused to write music the main interest of which was that it was composed with pure, just tuned ratios, and not with poisoned tempered relationships. He did indeed think them poisoned. That was symbolic, and more. If you will take Plato literally, or Confucius, that has its kickback on society, since according to both philosophers there is a causal relation between the tuning of musical modes and social and psychological behavior.

Temperament is a lie. It is not a lie if you write as Schoenberg ultimately did, although actually there is the ghost of a lie even in that: the trend cries out for "emancipation from the notes." Temperament is a lie if you write tonal music and use its relationships. It pretends to be what it is not. It deceives you into believing that you recognize what it is. It even deceives you into thinking that certain relationships are identical when they are not, and many similar psychoacoustical chicaneries.

One of Partch's aims was to unmask that deception. Remaining close to folk and other ubiquitous musics, he distrusted all types of avant-gardism on the ground that they were contrivances of overcivilized cliques. But even more deeply he rejected European traditions from the Middle Ages and earlier. For the Renaissance he had a certain amount of sympathy, not only because its artists were interested in the Greeks, but largely because of the individualism of Renaissance men and women. The spirit of finding your own answer to things, in whatever field, was a point of view he respected.

It was that independence that deeply impressed me when I first learned of his work. He had really started all over. He did not simply turn away from prevailing styles, or abjure conventional instrumentation: he threw out theories of music and tuning systems and concert customs. As far as I can see he let go almost everything in order to begin anew, on a consciously chosen basis.

His music always aimed not to be part of that formal world of concert music. And while he could be and was on friendly terms with jazz and rock and folk musicians, he never wanted to become part of a movement, especially one that implied commercial entanglements. His stance is at least as radical as John Cage's rejection of order and prediction and intention in art, and it has some of the same roots. That is curious, because those two men could not have been more different in most respects.

One of those roots is American Indian. I suppose not many people would say that about John Cage, but I would. It has specifically to do with a conviction that we are just not intelligent enough to dominate everything with our own decisions: to be violating without regard all the things that we are. I am reminded of John Neihardt's book *Black Elk Speaks,* in which the old Indian medicine man said that he felt he had failed because his mission in life was to save nature—the environment—from the white man. He failed.

You have in Harry Partch a man who asserted a style of life and a way of thinking about music and art that was handmade, carefully crafted in every aspect. He assumed nothing, took over nothing without thorough reexamination. And yet tightness and overspecificity were as remote from his ambience as indeterminacy. It is probable that much of his impact will be on music that he would have had little use for, and in musical situations which would not have interested him. Still, I think his greatest importance lies in his line of action, at once anomalous and paradigmatic in twentieth-century America: his actions say unequivocally, "The presumptions that lie behind the art of this culture are no good for me. I'm going to start all over again and make something I can live with."

It is interesting that the people who dislike his music most intensely are those most identified with formal concert tradition, in one role or another. These are the people who walk out, who say, "My God, what bad taste!"

The personality of the man is very much a part of the art, and if you are a purist, that can really bother you. Partch's art is self-revelatory. He has been called a Freudian because of this, but if he was one it was due to convergence of ideas, not to an interest in Freud. He was certainly no Apollonian, to borrow Stravinsky's categories (and in fact Partch used those categories), but he never talked about Apollo, only Dionysus. He talked a lot about Dionysus, the quintessential corporealist. Sex and the drinking of wine are traditional introductory ecstasies of Dionysus, but the god signifies much more than that: he is a chthonic god, affirming a kind of truth other than that of the sunlight part of life.

Dionysus and Apollo have a secret collusion, a highly important circumstance for art. Stravinsky can be said to have subordinated Dionysus to Apollo, while Partch put Apollo in the service of Dionysus. But these are only emphases: no fully human art can do without either beneficence. Pedantic art lacks Dionysian juice, and gross popular art lacks Apollonian seriousness. Neither Stravinsky nor Partch were guilty of these egregious extremes.

King Oedipus was Partch's first big production. He took the trouble to go to Ireland to get W. B. Yeats's permission to use his translation of Sophocles's tragedy. He got that rarely given permission, but Yeats did not put it in writing. So when Partch set about to compose *Oedipus,* the heirs of the Yeats estate denied permission. Yeats's willingness is highly significant; he believed that music, as used in drama, ballet, and opera, was destructive to theater, which must be the dominant partner in any such marriage. He wanted a much simpler music, much closer to natural speech, to underscore his legendary/mythic nationalist Irish theater idiom.

There is an equivalence between Yeats and Partch on this level, but on other levels a great contrast. Partch had little or no interest in Yeats's mystical preoccupation, theosophy; and he could not be called an American nationalist, unless in the role of gadfly. He was a typical American in two respects: his satiric impatience with such ineffables as romantic mysticism, and his self-made-man image, which was well earned.

Harry Partch had one flaw which is bad in an artist. He wanted to make his own species of *Gesamtkunstwerk* with himself as sole creator of all the artistic components, like Orson Welles. Only he was not really equipped to do that successfully.

He was a very good sculptor and a remarkable writer, within limits. The texts of *U.S. Highball* are beautiful, but Partch's translation of *Oedipus,* leaning heavily on the expertise of a Bay-area Greek scholar and on Yeats's translation, leaves much to be desired.

In putting on these theatrical works he needed what he never found: someone with a matching talent equivalent to Yeats's. But had he found such, he would undoubtedly have alienated him by his phoenix-like personality. He had a great deal of pride, a great deal of cantankerousness. It almost amounted to a Nietzschean artist syndrome. He fought against this as a mentor, but not as a collaborator. And so frequently his productions were not well realized as theater.

He interfered with choreographers, telling them which limb to move and how to move it. This would have been justifiable had he been a choreographic genius, but he was not; and so it had predictable results.

In attempting to compensate for that trait, I once committed a serious artistic gaffe. I got Partch to work with Alwin Nikolais. There could not have been a worse combination of collaborators. Partch and Nikolais were poles apart. We were unable to obtain either of the choreographers Partch preferred: Martha Graham or Doris Humphrey. I actually approached both of those august personages for him, but without success. He did earlier have Martha Graham's interest, but then he offended her. Anna Sokolow would have been a better choice, and perhaps could have been interested. I am sorry we did not try that.

At any rate, Nikolais did choreograph the first production of *The Bewitched* for his company, and it was my unhappy task to have to hold that production together with both men struggling at times, and with Partch fighting to prevent its taking place. It was nonetheless the best theatrical production he ever had of anything—a superb piece of theater. But it was not the style Partch wanted and should have had. Twenty years earlier, Charles Weidman might have done it. As it was, Partch immediately redid it with the Juilliard Dance Theater, using Joyce Trisler as choreographer. His more successful attempt to dictate to her produced another tense relationship and a far less distinguished production.

What interested me in Partch first was his use of just tuned ratios. I had been convinced after a year in music school that there was something wrong with the art if that was how it was being practiced. Acoustics, which the first chapters in various theory texts always said was the basis of music, clearly was not. And it did not seem right to me that this was true. I had begun by then to look into "the physics of music," using texts that were mostly vintage turn-of-the-century. I was trying to figure out what you could do that would not leave music in that state. I spoke about this to a musicologist, who handed me a copy of the first edition of Partch's *Genesis of a Music,* saying, "Well, *I* haven't got any use for this book, but you certainly would like it."

I did indeed. But what impressed me even above the accurately applied acoustic theory was the example of this man who, understanding all that physics and history and philosophy, had also lived as a hobo and written music about it.

I did not then hear *U.S. Highball,* Partch's chronicle of a cross-country hobo trip. He said of it that it was the most creative work he ever composed, which I think was very perceptive. And the word *creative* is much better than *original,* though the latter might underline most people's estimation of it: that it is the least like anyone else of all the music he wrote.

On the surface *U.S. Highball* is a piece of Americana. It is a true adventure that Partch underwent, composed very much in the style of the music that American hoboes were listening to and playing. It's simply chanted in his way—intoned, as he called it—on pitch, with the accompaniment of a small group of instruments. Over a period of about a decade, as he added instruments to his ensemble, he changed the arrangement of this and several other pieces. Initially *U. S. Highball* and other hobo pieces were accompanied by guitar, a little percussion, and harmonium, instruments of rural America. These pieces are like folk music in many respects.

Most of the singers and many of the poets who interested Partch, especially in the early years, were folk artists or else tremendously interested in or influenced by folk music and poetry. He did become interested in much else later. One of his pieces is based on a text of Rimbaud, and "folk artist" is not descriptive of *that* poet. Obviously what interested Partch about Rimbaud was the depth of his rebellion: that he would rebel even against sanity. I doubt if Partch ever entertained *that* idea. But certainly he was impressed. He thought the point of view deserved a statement in one of the two genres that he had adopted for himself.

These amount to the comic and the tragic, which should be no surprise. But Partch returned in comedy to the Greek satyr play, with its earthy, funny, everyman themes. He juxtaposed this directly with the highly religious, supernatural elements of tragedy, in which the gods often participate as characters. The most striking such juxtaposition is in *Delusion of the Fury,* in which a tragic Japanese Noh tale is contrasted with a comic African folktale.

I think Partch's view of "the gods" was considerably less supernatural than even C. G. Jung's; and it was certainly not what most people think the Greeks thought. But he did refer to something of great power by that symbol.

There is in Partch's work a nineteenth-century Romantic element, but it is distinctly not European. I find that important and interesting, not meaning to imply anything pejorative in being European. I am only saying that ours is an offshoot of European culture, and we still have certain colonialisms, especially in our musical attitudes. Yet here was a man who was able to transcend that. Partch said things that go against our grain in many ways but which make their own kind of sense. He assimilated traditions from worldwide sources on a number of levels, discovering and revealing some fundamental cultural interconnections. This results not seldom in the alienation of at least a segment of his audience.

On occasion, performances of his works have been painful to me. I have often felt that his productions were not good, only to realize that I was badly outnumbered. A great many people evidently loved what I winced at. It is a resistible temptation to fall back on a snobbish position and relegate the audience along with the performance and possibly even the composition to anathema. It takes real perception to differentiate between immediacy of communication to large groups and the pseudocommunication of saying only what most people already wanted to hear. That distinction finally impressed me, but it took many years, especially with the hindrance of badly flawed productions.

Partch's influence, notwithstanding this divergence of taste, was a basic one for me. Early on in our association I felt I had a role to fulfill in repayment. I was not encouraged to feel this. He told me that if I or anyone else ever claimed to have been a student of his, he'd cheerfully strangle us; and I think he meant that very literally. Partch refused the master–pupil and all but denied even the master–apprentice relationship. "Apprentice" is better, because it means something like "I need this done, and if you'll stick around and do it, you can pick up whatever you can pick up," or "If you can learn something, fine. And if you want to ask me questions, I might answer them." Actually he frequently did supply answers.

He was living in Gualala, on California's north coast, in 1949–50. Gualala is isolated and primitive, a lumbering village. He was living on a ranch loaned to him by Gunnar Johansen, in a converted nineteenth-century blacksmithy which he himself had renovated. With the owner's permission he turned over to me and my wife an old herdsman's cottage which we then had to make livable. This involved, among many lesser jobs, patching the shake roof and running in some water from a spring up the mountainside. I was totally out of my depth. Nothing he asked me to do in music was as hard as those things.

Partch did not do this in any pedagogic way. It was simply, "If you want to do it, I'm living here. Here it is—here's this house . . . roof's going to leak on you—it's going to rain . . . we'll have to fix it. I'll help you. I'll show you what to do, but you'll have to do it." He was just that direct. And I am—or was then—the sort of person who could not pick up a hammer without dropping it on my foot.

So the first thing I got from him was a fundamental attitude of "doing it yourself." He applied that to artistic problems equally.

Rather soon I felt that my eventual task would be to alter attitudes, especially theoretic currents *within* the mainstream, *from* the mainstream, *to* the mainstream. It would be my role to bring his work into relation with accepted traditions and recognized challenges to tradition, and to whatever extent necessary and possible to bring these enormous trends into relation to some of his most important achievements.

Here is a quote from Partch's *Genesis:* "Few composers will regard the total virtues of equal temperament and those of monophony"—this is what he called his way of tuning music—"as equal in value. Whichever of the two sets is accepted as superior, it can be stated unequivocally that they cannot coexist in the same musical system given the present ideas behind musical instruments or the present conception of musical values; and that, short of a mechanical revolution in the construction of musical instruments and a psychic evolution in musical conceptions, they will not coexist in the same musical system in the future. Such xenogamy is conceivable but not yet practical."[1]

It seemed to me, if this whole quixotic effort were possibly going to survive, that there would have to be a relationship between musical systems. Furthermore I recognized my own roots as European and felt no need to apologize for that, so long as I was willing to transcend it and ultimately to merge it into a more global identification. I will say emphatically that I have no intention of leaving that tradition the way I found it if I can possibly do anything about it.

It was the lie about pitch that drew me to Partch's ideas in the first place. I felt that if I could devote my career, at least the innovative central thrust of it, to making a dent in the establishment about that, it would be enough. If I could achieve that it would repay my debt to Partch in some degree. To help his immediate artistic heritage to survive it is additionally necessary to make sense to many people who can see no reason for going about making music in the way that he did, and who feel his life work is simply an incompetent effort to do something that they wish he had not tried to do where they could hear it.

To start making that kind of sense it is necessary to create a music that bridges the gulf between Partch's immensely sophisticated theoretical ideas and the whole arsenal of knowledge with which we have fortified our art music. That is in large degree what I am trying to do. It entails transcending the idiosyncratic specificity of Partch's applied theory, on the one hand, and, on the other, weeding out the acoustical malpractice of several hundred years in such a way as to leave the lineage of many fruitful traditions intact. Consequently it is not only divergences in personality, taste, and background that cause my music to differ so widely from Partch's, but more importantly a contrast of intentions. The connection lies in two areas: tuning procedure and mythic purpose. But our myths are dissimilar; our means are not alike; and above all our styles are different.

I would not say that all composers are mythmakers, but it is a venerable tradition. In that sense Partch has many forebears. He wanted to express a depth-image of the human condition, of the world, of his own experience. His very considerable adaptation of composing and performing traditions is not only ingenious and full of provocative innovations, but is also selective, carefully planned by him to match what he was trying to say.

That has served me as an example, although what I do is not much like what Partch did.

He commented upon the differences between us within the first week of my being in Gualala. He could have wished for a carpenter or for a percussionist or even simply for a fellow dropout. But he had one thing he had not counted on: someone who understood his theory almost without explanation, and who could hear and reproduce the pitch relations accurately. He began to grasp that there might be some sort of real convergence between us. But since it took me about ten years to do anything concrete with what I had learned from him, he had long since given up on me.

The design of Partch's remarkable instruments is an achievement of great scope and subtlety. Many of them call for a three-dimensional performing technique, as contrasted with the predominantly two-dimensional techniques of most common instruments. This is not a new idea. It is a basic feature of percussion technique when a mixed set of instruments is used. But Partch designed such setups into his instruments.

The Diamond Marimba, which has blocks arranged in a diamond shape set on a slant between the vertical and horizontal planes, is played largely in diagonal paths of movement. The high-pitched blocks are at the top of the diamond; the low-pitched, at the bottom. On right-to-left descending diagonals the pitches descend *Otonalities* (segments of overtone series: specifically, in descending order, the eleventh, ninth, seventh, sixth, fifth, and fourth partials). On left-to-right descending diagonals the pitches descend *Utonalities* (segments of undertone series, which are the mirror inversions of overtone series: in descending order, the fourth, fifth, sixth, seventh, ninth, and eleventh undertone "partials"). Thus the pitch arrangement is in matrix form, with an emphasis on arpeggio formations easily played glissando because of the raked arrangement of the blocks. Since ascending diagonals cannot be played in this manner, Partch invented a complementary instrument, the Quadrangularis Reversum, which provides the same arpeggios in reverse direction by arranging the blocks with the high pitches at the bottom and the low pitches at the top.

Other instruments, such as the Chromelodeons (adapted reed organs), have their adjacent pitches arranged in a stepped pitch continuum (in this case microtonal) from low to high, which is of course the keyboard convention.

Some, like the Kitharas and certain of the Adapted Guitars, use plastic rods to achieve continuous glissandi (glides). Others, like the Bass Marimba and the enormous Marimba Eroica, have only a few pitches, selected (like the bells of many carillons) because of the frequency of their occurrence in the tonal patterns used in the body of music for which they were intended. Performance on these instruments is athletic, even by a percussionist's standards, because of their large physical dimensions.

The Kitharas, unlike their Greek ancestors, have parallel banks of strings tuned in alternating Otonality and Utonality hexachords; so because of reaching in and out to gain access to various "tonalities," the technique becomes pronouncedly three-dimensional.

In some cases found objects were collected, chosen for their interesting sound capabilities, and often having complex inharmonic timbres. In such cases Partch, with a careful ear to precise harmonic relations, used the sounds specifically where they would fit into the harmonic context rationally: for example, the Cloud-Chamber Bowls, which are the discarded tops and bottoms of Pyrex carboys used in vapor trail experiments in the Radiation Laboratory at the University of California, Berkeley. These are carefully labeled with the principal pitch activated when they are struck like gongs.

In the case of the Harmonic Canons, which are made up of forty-three parallel monochords with movable bridges, the variable arrangement of their bridges makes possible any pattern of notes within the range delimited by the length of the strings. Thus, a single stroke across the raked table of strings provides a forty-three-note row or any segment thereof, and the retrograde or any of its segments. Besides, the portions of the strings on the other side of the bridges produce a complementary reversible row with interesting relationships to the "original" row.

So the instruments provide serial patterns, not only in this case, but even more complexly in the case of all of the hexachordally arranged instruments, especially those designed in matrix formations.

This procedure of reducing things to the physical, to the most obvious, to the most tangible, and the most concrete is very Greek. The whole idea of the *haptic,* the touch-oriented in art, is very much alive in Partch's work. He was quite right to be attracted to the traditions of the Greeks. He was very perceptive: he did have something in common with them, something to add to their traditions.

A very great and original artist has died leaving a rich but fragile heritage. There is a Harry Partch Foundation, but as yet that guarantees perilously little. Try to imagine the expert man-hours and diverse materials it would take to duplicate his many and complex instruments, even to get one extra set. Then, maintenance problems would supervene, including housing, storage, and rehearsal space, available over a long enough time to get beyond first performances and première productions. The problem staggers conception.

NOTE

1. Harry Partch, *Genesis of a Music,* 158.

HARRY PARTCH/JOHN CAGE
1978

The motivation to be avant-garde is a complex thing, often compounded of dissatisfaction with one's own time, enthusiasm for new possibilities, and nostalgia for the past. Artists of the Renaissance, in turning their backs on the medieval world, looked back to classical times before looking to the newly discovered larger world outside Europe. Many of the innovations of early twentieth-century art were sparked by the art of primitive cultures. It would seem that to extend toward the future, it is usually necessary to reach at the same time into the past.

In the United States there has been since colonial times a music distinct from that of Europe, characterized by its rough-hewn, experimental qualities. Such men as William Billings in the eighteenth century and Anthony Philip Heinrich in the nineteenth century still have the power to startle us.

The genteel tradition in the nineteenth century, with its worship of things European and its conservative suspicion of change, nearly stamped out this native individualism. It was this conservatism above all else against which Charles Ives struggled. It was the American past to which Ives turned, to Concord, to evangelistic Protestantism, as well as to the vernacular present. But Ives was also trying to get us to "stretch our ears," and he opened a vast number of new musical horizons.

In the generation after the First World War, it was first of all Henry Cowell who stood out as a pioneer in avant-garde music. Cowell's music not only challenged us with new sounds and performance practices, but more and more turned to a world arena for its traditions.

By this point, it was a lonely business to be an avant-garde musician. The hold of latter-day colonialism on the American musical public was strong indeed, and isolation if not ostracism was the almost inevitable cost of individualism.

Out of this rich and dubious background emerged two remarkable innovators, born about ten years apart, in the years before World War I.

Harry Partch and John Cage are surely in their generation the central figures of the American Experimental Tradition. They met on several occasions, and Cage, despite an aversion to Partch's artistic vernacularisms, has always been supportive of Partch's music. Partch, on the other hand, had no grasp of Cage's art, and even less curiosity about it.

Both men are exemplars of an artistic and philosophic independence and individualism that has few peers. But their approach to music and to life diverged almost as widely as possible.

Partch, with vitriolic and passionate condemnation, threw out all of Western musical practice and theory since ancient Greece and set about to forge for himself a wholly new system, with its own scales, melodic and harmonic conventions, instruments, and concert occasions. Cage, more good-naturedly but with equal iconoclasm, divested music first of its focus on pitch, then of countable time, and finally of *choice* itself. Far less traditional even than Partch, he launched the movement called *indeterminacy* and has remained its severest practitioner. Aspects of Dada and Zen Buddhism underpin Cage's explorations of radical aesthetics. Many of his compositions could better be described as aesthetic rather than simply musical experiments.

Cage's music is abstract to the point of eliminating the personal preferences of the composer, while Partch, vilifying abstraction, championed a mode of art he called *corporealism,* underlining at every point the personal signature not only of the composer but also of each individual performer. Partch returned music to its original fusion with speech and dance, incorporating, through his beautifully crafted instruments, sculptural expression as well. Most of his works were also theatrical and cannot be understood as "pure music."

Corporealism refers not only to the reconstitution of music and speech, music and dance, music and theater, but also a body orientation, emphasizing not only the psychological identity of the musicians, but their physical presence and appearance. Partch disliked most manners of performance because of their penchant for abstracting the act of making art from its physical basis. Traditional European singing, for instance, he saw as too instrumental, as he saw European dance as too pictorial. He preferred folk and vernacular musics and their performing traditions.

Cage, who invented the happening, also often mingled the arts, but always in such a way as either to rule out the domination of the artwork by anyone's *expression,* or to display the individual performing artists as Dada objects.

Both men are masters of the written and spoken word; but while Partch engaged in polemics and even invective along with his intellectually demanding microtonal music theories, Cage uses language to challenge the supremacy of intellect and emotion as exclusive rivals for the center stage of art. A master of anecdote and koan-like aphorism, he has often composed his lectures in an idiom that recalls Gertrude Stein.

Partch described himself as a Dionysian artist. He always aimed for the overwhelming involvement the Dionysian proposes. Cage, while certainly no Apollonian in Stravinsky's sense, aimed at a cool, detached, but irritatingly provocative effect upon his listeners. Dionysian ecstasy is as far from his art as one can get.

Both men found themselves in need of very special performers. Cage solved the problem by cementing relations with artist-collaborators whose contributions complemented his own with maximum effectiveness. Most notable among these are the dancer-choreographer Merce Cunningham and the pianist-composer David Tudor. Cage's ability to work effectively with other artists is intimately related to his effort to keep his ego out of his art as much as possible.

Partch was just the opposite. At first functioning as a solo composer-performer, he soon found he needed to undertake elaborate training of performers, requiring months of dedicated work for a single performance. It was a lifelong necessity for him to maintain a loyal, dedicated ensemble to realize his works. He had very little aptitude or flexibility for collaboration, a necessity for the kind of complex inter-arts opus he typically undertook. A long history of painful relationships with collaborators and an even longer one of efforts to be a jack-of-all-arts resulted. Many of the flaws in Partch's work are due to this. He was, however, an artist of incredibly strong charisma; so he managed to triumph over even these obstacles.

Partch aimed at the widest possible audience, while remaining as uncompromising as Beethoven. Cage has aimed at an exclusively unspecified elite who would be capable of transcending the limitations of traditional and popular art. It is a tribute to Partch that in spite of the extreme unavailability of most of his work, he remains a provocative and challenging figure. It is a tribute to Cage that despite a truly esoteric aesthetic position, he has become one of the world's best-known and most influential composers, far outstripping the "controversial" label that seemed for a time inevitable for him.

HARRY PARTCH'S *CLOUD-CHAMBER MUSIC*

1978

The challenge provided by Harry Partch's pitch usages is much stronger than it appears, lost as it is among half a dozen more radical-seeming elements in his work. In particular, the impressive array of sculptural new instruments of the plectra and percussion types, whose sound has a strong attack component followed by a relatively sharp decay, obscures rather than dramatizes Partch's pitch designs.

It is not the melodic element that gets short shrift but rather the harmonic. In Partch's art, both are overwhelmingly important parameters, along with metrical rhythm. Far from dethroning pitch as a major organizing element in music, as much radical twentieth-century music does, Partch gives it a very powerful new lease on life. His microtonal melodies, particularly those so close in sound to spoken language, have attracted much notice, but entirely too little attention has been directed to Partch's return of harmonic practice to a just intonation basis.

Expanded just intonation is not simply a particular scale used in lieu of twelve-tone equal temperament. It is a radical, though by no means new, principle of ordering sounds by systematic use of numerical proportions. The same principle, applied to metrical rhythm, is one of the main elements giving provocative newness to the music of Elliott Carter, or in interesting juxtaposition, to the earlier music of John Cage and Lou Harrison. This practice was pioneered by Henry Cowell and Charles Ives. While this list gives the practice a conspicuously American pedigree, a similar usage occurs in the music of Alban Berg, Stefan Wolpe, and Luigi Nono. With respect to large-scale time divisions, the same can be said of Krzysztof Penderecki's music.

In respect to pitch, the proportional system has consistently dominated not only all Western art music before the Baroque era but the music of several major Asiatic culture groups, notably the Indian, the Chinese, and the Arab. While it may once have seemed that Western art music would dominate such cultures, the trend for a long time seems to be aggressively in an opposite direction.

The unique and typically Western aspect to Partch's pitch system is its inclusiveness. He attempts a generalized theory of proportional pitch systems in his book *Genesis of a Music.* While I do not feel he achieved this completely, he gave powerful impetus in a direction in which no other Western composer of any stature had moved for centuries.

Partch often claimed not to have any compositional expertise or ability. This was a facet of his self-taught artistic position. He felt defensive against the monolithic establishment of Western European music and its entrenched United States wing. In fact he developed highly original and effective techniques of composition which were, however, so thoroughly integrated into his total artistic effort that he disliked discussing them. But because almost all of his pitch notation is in the form of instrumental tablatures, his work has been neither published nor studied by musicologists.[1] It has so far received too little serious attention from other composers.

Cloud-Chamber Music is the eleventh of *Eleven Intrusions,* a set of small-dimensioned pieces, composed by Partch in 1949 and 1950. They were recorded in 1950 at Gualala, California, by Partch, my wife Betty and me, and Donald Pippin, with recording engineer Harry Lindgren. Several of these works were later released on records in the album *Thirty Years of Lyrical and Dramatic Music,* on Gate Five Records, a private label. *Cloud-Chamber Music* is among those *Intrusions* released in this recording.[2]

The "Cloud Chambers" referred to in the title are "found objects," the bottoms and tops of Pyrex carboys used in vapor-trail experiments to explore the behavior of subatomic particles. They were obtained, as castoffs, from the Radiation Laboratory at the University of California, Berkeley. Partch cut off the tops and bottoms by soaking a string in kerosene, tying it around a carboy, and then lighting it. Upon being chilled by immersion in water, the Pyrex broke along the line heated by the burning string.

The bowls were chosen and used specifically because of the pitches which they produce when struck and thus were integrated into the harmonic fabric of the works in which they are used. Like these, many of Partch's instruments provide a limited selection of pitches rather than a gamut, falling in the tradition of percussion rather than of keyboard instruments.

In an analogous way, voices are treated as if they were "found objects" in Partch's compositions. A Partch vocal line is an abstraction, in the sense that it is a heightened manner of speech. But especially as performed by him, such lines are uncannily accurate transliterations of natural speech. The use of this technique in characterization is far closer to legitimate theater tradition than to lyric theater or opera.

The use of the voice in *Cloud-Chamber Music* is in imitation of American Indian chant. Partch uses the Zuñi chant "Cancion de los Muchachos," which he heard himself as a boy in New Mexico.[3] Partch has spoken of his recollection of the Indians of the Southwest as a tattered remnant. Something of his concern and compassion is here evident.

The music begins with a carillon on the Cloud-Chamber Bowls and quickly settles into a mournful lament set for Adapted Viola and Guitar with Kithara and Marimba accompaniment. Resonant chords on the Kithara supported by chimes from the Bowls and Diamond Marimba back up the dialogue between the two principals.

After several phrases the Diamond Marimba introduces an accelerated tempo, ushering in the Bass Marimba and Viola, which present the "Cancion" in a defiantly affirmative mood. This leads to a dance-like passage for the two marimbas, followed by a second presentation of the "Cancion," this time by solo male voice, a part intended for Partch himself in the original version. The dance-like duo again intervenes, following which the Viola and a chorus of all the musicians sing the "Cancion" accompanied by all the instruments except the Kithara, whose player now takes up an Indian deer-hoof rattle.

This climaxes in a cadenza for Cloud-Chamber Bowls, after which the ensemble expresses its aroused state in guttural vocalization, culminating in a shout of solidarity.

The "scenario" is thus relatively simple and clear: the outburst of Cloud-Chamber Bowls first inspires a lament led by the Violist, who then, aroused by the high-pitched marimba's insistent beat, presents the magical "Cancion," first instrumentally, then vocally (on the original recording this vocal part is taken, unhappily, by the Guitar), alternating with the lively marimba duo. Then the whole ensemble joins in, with the ritual deer-hoof rattle, provoking another outburst of the Bowls, which this time arouses defiance and group fusion. Bearing in mind the origin of the Bowls in the atomic-energy program and the role of the Southwest in that development, Partch's exhortation to the downtrodden is not hard to read. His music is seldom even this far from direct verbal and theatrical meaning, resting solidly as it does on corporeal aims.

It is of significance that Partch cast himself, an aging man, in the role of inciter, with the Viola, by far the most "traditional" of his instruments from a Western musical viewpoint, as the agent undergoing the change first. The lower solo voice drops down a fourth from the G pentatonic scale to the C pentatonic (with four common tones), only to be answered by the more youthful ensemble in the higher scale, again dramatizing the difference in roles as well as ranges of voice.

Partch persistently saw himself as an inciter of youth, having little hope for the flexibility or perceptiveness of older, more culturally fixed people. He was opposed to our culture as he found it, and if he was undoubtedly first a dropout, he never relinquished the role of reformer, even in the actions and attitudes of his old age. He saw our social conditions as those of an advanced stage of decay, and looked to earlier and more "primitive" cultures not with nostalgia but with hope and exhortation.

Cloud-Chamber Music begins as a depressed reaction to a false clarion, but then seizes American Indian incentives as a reinvigorating antidote. The future is, in a certain sense, the past. We are not to be saved by science fiction become fact but rather by ancient myths and rituals, which retain intact the dignity of human life as an inseparable part of nature.

The musical means Partch uses are in a fascinating way an illustration of this same allegory. Beginning with the "nature sound" of the found object, the instruments weave a microtonally chromatic web out of materials related to their sonorities, only to be elbowed aside by the resurgence of elements simpler not in a "natural" but in a cultural context, aligning not only the instruments (a late flower of civilization) but also the voices, a primal material of music. At the end the mood is one of battle, and the microtones are subordinate to the easily perceived and sung pentatonic scale, serving as its aura and support.

In translating Partch's tablature notation into something approximating "ordinary" notation, I have used accidentals I devised for my own use in presenting ratio-scale-derived music. In such notation, uninflected notes refer to C-major just intonation (tonic, dominant, and subdominant triads tuned in 4:5:6 ratios). ♯ and ♭ raise and lower, respectively, by a ratio of 25/24 (ca. 70 cents). + and - raise and lower, respectively, by a syntonic comma 81/80 (ca. 21.5 cents). ∠ and 7 raise and lower, respectively, by the ratio 36/35 (ca. 49 cents). ↑ and ↓ raise and lower, respectively, by the ratio 33/32 (ca. 53 cents). (A full list of these newly invented accidentals is given as Figure 36 in this book.)

Partch's theory of harmony categorizes pitches in tonalities of two kinds: Otonalities, corresponding to major chords, and Utonalities, corresponding to minor chords. In Partch the term *tonality* does not refer to a scale, and not at all to a system of progressions. The ratios of an Otonality stand in the proportion 4:5:6:7:9:11 (referring to partials of a single overtone series). The Utonality is the inverse of this, referring to the same partials of an "undertone" series. Thus 1/1 Otonality consists of the ratios 1/1, 5/4, 3/2, 7/4, 9/8, 11/8. The 1/1 Utonality consists of 1/1, 8/5, 4/3, 8/7, 16/9, 16/11.[4] Note that the 1, 5, and 3 identities of these two tonalities do not give parallel major and minor. In traditional tonality, the tonic and its fifth are the focus of inversion rather than simply the tonic. Partch uses only the tonic, though he does not call it that. It is also interesting to note that in 1/1 Otonality all the denominators of the ratios are powers of 2, while in 1/1 Utonality all the numerators of the ratios are powers of 2. In Partch's terminology 2 is the *numerary nexus* of each of these tonalities. In all Otonalities, the numerary nexus is in the denominator while in all Utonalities it is in the numerator.

By letting 1/1 serve as each of the identities in an Otonality and in a Utonality, Partch generates what he calls a Tonality Diamond (Figures 39 and 40).

When "evened out" with a few "secondary ratios" which add missing identities to some of the incomplete tonalities as well as filling in scale gaps, this selection is the basis of Partch's forty-three-tone scale.

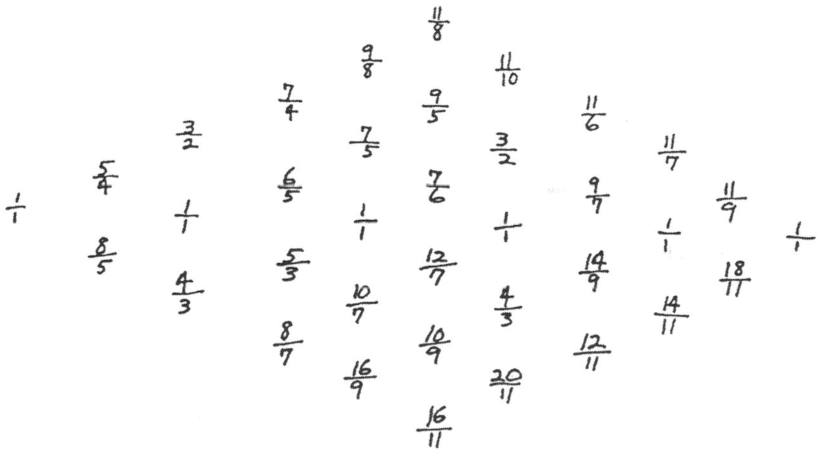

FIGURE 39. An 11–limit Tonality Diamond. The layout of pitches as given here corresponds not to the Diamond as configured in Partch's book *Genesis of a Music,* p. 159, but to the layout of pitches on Partch's Diamond Marimba; on that instrument the pitches in each hexad are spaced, as here, in "thirds" (for example, in the case of 1/1 Otonality, 1/1–5/4–3/2–7/4–9/8–11/8).

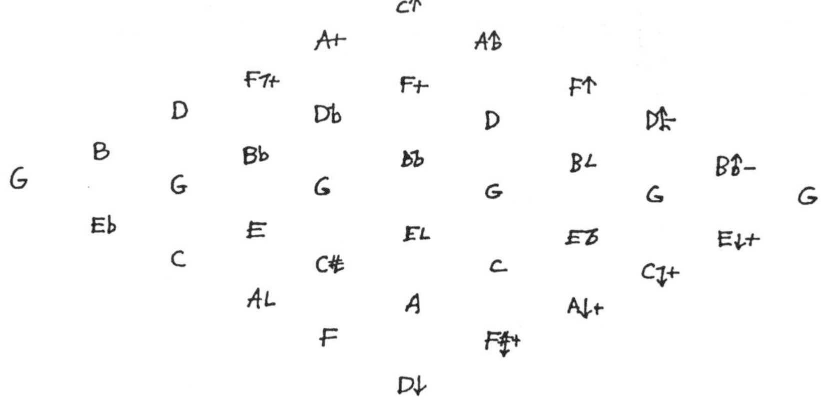

FIGURE 40. The 11–limit Tonality Diamond of Figure 39, expressed in Johnston's nomenclature for extended just intonation. In this diagram, following Partch's practice, G is taken as 1/1.

The Tonality Diamond is the basis of design of the Diamond Marimba, the blocks of which are arranged in raked tiers, with 11/8 at the top and 16/11 at the bottom, so that a glissando stroke descending from right to left gives an Otonality and a glissando stroke descending from left to right gives a Utonality.

The Bass Marimba, by contrast, has only eleven blocks, arranged from low (cello C) to high (7/6 below middle C). The notes are 4/3, 3/2, 5/3, 1/1, 8/7, 16/11, 8/5, 16/9, 11/6, 9/8, 7/6, or C, D, E, G, A∠, D↓, E♭, F, F↑, A+, B⅂♭.

The Adapted Viola has an elongated neck and is pitched an octave below the violin. It is performed gamba-style, held between the knees.

The Adapted Guitar used in this piece is stopped with a plastic rod, Hawaiian style.

The Kithara has twelve banks of six strings each ranged parallel, vertically. Each bank is a hexachord. Bank 1 is A∠ Otonality, minus the eleven identity. Bank 2 is C↑ Utonality. Bank 3 is F Otonality. Bank 4 is A+ Utonality. Bank 5 is D↓ Otonality. Bank 6 is F7+ Utonality minus the eleven identity. Bank 7 is C Otonality. Bank 8 is G Utonality. Bank 9 is E♭ Otonality. Bank 10 is B Utonality. Bank 11 is G Otonality minus the eleven identity. Bank 12 is D Utonality minus the 9 and 11 identities. Bank 1 and bank 12, against the arms of the Kithara, are equipped with plastic rods between the strings and resonators, for creating glissandi.

The pitch content of the bell-like Cloud-Chamber Bowls is complex. I have determined what seems to me the predominant pitch of each bowl, but I doubt if these are the pitches Partch heard, since the tonalities do not always match. He did designate such found objects by pitch, though not in his score. His practice was to integrate them into the sound fabric harmonically. But given my interpretation the four bowls used in this piece constitute the 5, 3, 7 and 9 identities of D$^{\angle}$- Otonality. This, plus the complex penumbra of tones surrounding it, is the opening sonority created by the Cloud-Chamber Bowl flourish at the opening of the piece.

The tension and melancholy of the opening duet is achieved by the use of the higher (7, 9, 11, and in a few cases even 15 and 21 identities) of the tonalities, largely without their triadic (1, 5, 3) identities. When these identities are subordinated to the simpler one and grouped around a simple scale structure, as they are once the "Cancion" is introduced, the effect is exuberant and strong.

The melodic style of the lament imitates the glides of spoken inflection. Partch frequently "drops off" a note to a neighboring tone before moving to the next important melodic tone. He mixes tonalities sometimes, as earlier-twentieth century composers often mix triads and sevenths in "pile-up" combinations with multiple pitch references. His use of nonharmonic dissonances is perhaps a little freer than in common-practice-period style but is essentially similar both in procedure and in effect. The chord tones cohere because of their smoother blend.

An analysis of the tonalities and nonharmonic tones yields the following insights:

Successive tonalities are usually related by common tones, either actual or implied (as missing members of a tonality). Seldom does Partch use "unrelated" successions of tonalities. The melodic lines follow stepwise designs basically, but one must remember the presence of almost four times as many notes per octave, so that the variety of "step" sizes varies considerably. Much of the expressive power of the music rests in this aspect of the melodies. In other works Partch calls for these inflections for voice, usually with a spoken quality. Here the Viola and Guitar imitate this vocal "intoning."

Cloud-Chamber Music lacks the rhythmic complexity of many of Partch's works. Even in those works such as *The Bewitched* where complications of meter abound, the effect is dance-like, never "ametrical." Similarly, even in complex microtonal melodic passages accompanied by relatively dissonant combinations of higher identities of superimposed tonalities, Partch's music never sounds atonal, but rather tonal in a totally new way.

Cloud-Chamber Music is a work in which the simple and the complex meet in an expressive way. Partch has made their meeting "part of the plot."

NOTES

1. [Ed.: While true when this paper was written, this statement is no longer the case. Partch's scores are now published by Schott, and several books about him and his work have now appeared—see bibliography.]

2. [Ed.: The original 1951 recording was released on CD in 1997 by Composers Recordings, Inc., New York, on *The Harry Partch Collection* vol. 1, CRI CD 751, and reissued in 2004 by New World Records, NW80621–2.]

3. [Ed.: In fact, recent research has shown that the "Cancion de los Muchachos" is an Isleta song, not a Zuñi one, and that Partch's acquaintance with it probably came not from his childhood but from the wax-cylinder recordings he transcribed at the Southwest Museum in Los Angeles in 1933. See Gilmore, *Harry Partch: A Biography,* 93, 195.]

4. [Ed.: In Partch's system of just intonation the note G is always taken as 1/1, regardless of the actual "tonic" or pitch center of a given passage of music. In Johnston's notation system, however, it is C that is defined as 1/1 (likewise regardless of the implied or stated "tonic" in any given musical context). Whereas Partch's rationale and Johnston's are clear, this difference has occasionally given rise to confusion. An example of the difference can be seen in Figure 40, in which the pitch layout of Partch's Diamond Marimba is expressed in Johnston's notation system. The ratio 9/8 in Partch's scale must here be written as A+; in Johnston's notation system the (uninflected) A is a 10/9 above G, hence the note must be raised by a syntonic comma (symbolized by a +) to make it a 9/8 above G.]

BEYOND HARRY PARTCH

1981

Most of American culture sees art as a variety of entertainment, and "serious" art as a not very successful variety of high-class amusement. Note the adjective: an interest in serious art is seen as a credential for identification with a higher social class. The government, and the majority of the people, thinks that art should support itself like any other commercial enterprise and that if a minority wants to indulge in aristocratic pretensions it should pay for these without subsidy.

A minority, mostly wealthy, has never given up an aristocratic stratification of society and supports an art which imitates European culture in competition with it. With the decline in Europe of political institutions directly based on aristocratic models, the artist, freed somewhat from servility to patrons, tended to become a kind of culture hero. It is as though aristocratic behavior retreated into the arts. The moneyed minority in America which supports, for example, symphony orchestras and opera companies, keeps this view alive in the face of its rejection by most of the society.

But for generating a sense of belonging to a comfortable elite, or for purposes of upward mobility (which at a certain altitude becomes social climbing), Beethoven or Debussy or Tchaikovsky or anyone else whose music has undergone the metamorphosis into museum pieces will serve much better than a living composer. And Europeans are vastly better than Americans, even if they are still alive, because it is understandable if they are aristocratic. As a result, most composers in the USA are supported by the only widely acceptable form of subsidy: posts as teachers in college and university music schools.

While the general musical life of the country mirrors the state of the world by reminding us constantly that there are many musics, most music schools still operate as if European music (and mostly that of the eighteenth and nineteenth centuries) were the only music of significance. This hegemony is challenged by jazz programs that transcend the "fun and games" state, and in a few places by performing groups growing out of ethnomusicological programs. Its most serious challenge has come from active groups of composers, who may be bent upon perpetuating the traditions of concert making and attendant musical activities but who are committed to overcoming the resistance to new repertory and to changing musical performing practices. But this activity only affects the professional world indirectly except in rare instances. Even the efforts of composers' societies seem to have relatively weak effects.

Sufficiently resourceful people can always create enclaves and cliques, but how much wider than that will the interested listening public ever grow to be? Just how long does the cultural lag have to get before we ask ourselves seriously if the gap will ever close? These questions were raised by Gunther Schuller in an address to the American Society of University Composers in the spring of 1980. But where I part company with Schuller is that I heard no hint of a way out of this cul-de-sac in his address and I have heard none in his music, unless what he proposes to do is to abandon concert music in the European tradition for jazz or ragtime or some other more popular music.

These seem to me weighty questions, and the finger pointed at us composers by Schuller to accuse us of having helped to bring about this situation seems not altogether unjust. Much so-called new music does not really deserve the wider audience it complains about being denied. If the only alternative to this is the endless replay of "the classics" or an attempt to rewrite them or to quote them or even to parallel them, we have already abandoned the serious effort to keep concert music alive.

I would be unhappy to see this happen. I would like the tradition of Western concert music to continue to develop among the world's musics in a future in which its dominance will have ended. But can we possibly regard the present state of concert music in this country as a state of health?

Questions of this kind assailed me right from the outset of my composing career, not least because of my contact with Harry Partch. I remember writing to him soon after I read his book, *Genesis of a Music,* that I had long felt that the very scale we were using had condemned contemporary composers to an ever-narrowing effort to exhaust the remaining possibilities in a closed system. Partch's determination to throw out almost the whole of Western traditions of composing, performing, theorizing, and bringing music to an audience impressed but also alarmed me. I could see even then how unlikely it would be that his work would even reach a wide public, let alone precipitate changes of so sweeping a nature.

I have never felt that the tradition of European concert music was either worthless or hopeless, though I have come more and more to see that we have allowed it to become an albatross around our necks. How and why it became so began to interest me extremely.

Among the early strong impressions pushing me toward becoming a musician was a lecture I heard at the age of twelve at Wesleyan Conservatory of Music in Macon, Georgia. It concerned the importance of the acoustical findings of Helmholtz in the development of Debussy's music. The lecturer used a monochord to demonstrate the basic premises of just tuned intervals and the phenomenon of overtones. I never lost the feeling of mystery and unfolding new possibilities that world of simple mathematical ratios opened to me. Debussy instantly became a figure of importance to me, though I had previously paid his music little attention.

Later, when I studied music theory, it was a disappointment and finally a disillusionment how cavalierly it sidestepped the principles of acoustics. By that time I was determined to master it and to acquire the tradition of European concert music, so I did not reject it, as Partch had done earlier. What happened to me was a gradually strengthening conviction that the tradition had gone awry a long time ago and was in need of rechanneling. This initially gained impetus from the impact of *Genesis of a Music* and subsequently six months' apprenticeship in Partch's studio at Gualala, California, in 1950.

It took me about ten years to digest that experience. When I finally decided to act upon these stimuli I set out to learn electronic studio techniques at Columbia-Princeton Studio while on a Guggenheim Fellowship in 1959–60. I quickly discovered that this medium was not ready for the use I wished to make of it and that my aptitude for that kind of composing was not high. It gradually became clear that neither that route nor Partch's was the best path for me, but rather the forbidding one of getting traditionally trained performers using conventional instruments to alter their performance practices sufficiently to play just tuned music elaborated to the point of microtonality. As soon as I returned to Illinois after my sabbatical, in 1960, I set about trying to compose such music.

I was convinced that this freeing of music from the artificial shackles of twelve-tone equal temperament would prove to be a key to why most twentieth-century concert music has seemed intelligible to so limited an audience. I am today more than ever convinced of this. It is a very important change I think composers could make in the unhealthy situation of music today.

Partch's aversion to European musical values originated in a rejection of

American education as well as of traditions of "classical music." Since he spent his childhood and early youth in a part of Arizona very near to the Mexican border at a time when the region was only just emerging from the condition of frontier life, the urban culture of America was as exotic to him as a foreign country. When he encountered it he did not identify with it, but rejected it passionately, stubbornly maintaining against it an art and a lifestyle drawn directly from his early influences. The fact that his parents were apostate Protestant missionaries to China and maintained something of what they had absorbed of Chinese culture, and the circumstance of living in American Indian country, figured importantly in his formation.

Even after he plunged into twentieth-century America in Los Angeles, he continued to draw almost all his artistic and cultural sustenance from non-European sources rich in the California environment. He was associated with the earliest artistic community at Big Sur. During this period one of his closest friends was Jaime de Angulo, a radically unconventional anthropologist who was studying California Indian cultures largely by assimilating into them. Thus Partch's sympathies were always with what much later would be called countercultures. When you add to this the fact that he chose to live all his life on the economic margin of American culture, surviving mostly on odd jobs, handouts, and private grants, you can begin to see how his extraordinary independence came to be, and why he seemed to much of the dropout counterculture of the sixties a prophetic older brother.

But the culture as a whole has not gone in those directions, and he runs the posthumous risk of becoming a kind of antireligious patron saint of dropouts except in the Southwest, where cultural currents of the same kind as those which produced him still generate artists of a unique breed. Without in any way wishing to diminish his large importance in these contexts, I think his significance and potential value are much larger than this.

In several crucial respects Harry Partch offers directions out of the trap our musical culture has gotten itself into. He refused resolutely to be drawn into the concert music world, not even that of "modern music" or its offspring "contemporary music" and "new music." He knew he was not part of it and would never willingly consent to further its aims by affiliating with it. His association with BMI was the creation of Oliver Daniel and Carl Haverlin and amounted to a continuing subsidy of his work almost without strings attached. Partch was grateful and occasionally cooperative but remained aloof and aggressively independent.

He refused with equal vehemence to have anything more than peripherally to do with the world of commercial music, which has swallowed up almost all the music this continent has spawned. Most of his recordings were produced and distributed privately, and his few commercial record contracts were negotiated with much effort and persuasion from colleagues who saw the importance of getting his work out to a wider public as outweighing even Partch's rejection of the values imposed by commercial and corporate interests. When his work began to attract rock musicians (for instance, Frank Zappa), there was always one inevitable barrier between them: the dependence of rock music upon a world of commercial values.

Even Partch's affiliations with universities and colleges were as tenuous and temporary as he could make them, and suspicion on the part of musical conservatives and reactionaries that the institution was harboring a cultural subversive was only marginally overbalanced by the recognition from a determined minority that this was an artist of major importance.

Even more basically, Partch saw the identification of European artistic traditions with wealth, power, and social position in American society, and fought it at every opportunity. He looked to other cultures in the world for sources and influences in his own work, and he looked behind modern European culture to its sources to discover where it went wrong. In his work he set out to correct these errors in cultural, philosophical, and artistic values. In his life he stayed as independent of the economic and institutional forces that mold cultural attitudes as he could while still forced to derive his sustenance indirectly from them. It was for that reason that he was willing to accept support from individuals who had demonstrated a belief in his work, but only rarely and with misgivings from corporate entities and institutions.

It must have looked to Partch as if the European heritage in American culture was impervious to change and insensitive to influence, and indeed this is in many respects very nearly true. But there is vastly more in our culture than that one component, and world trends are clearly running counter to a continued dominance of that particular strain. It is in fact a long time since the art music of Europe and its onetime colonies such as the USA was of anything like the strength or importance either here or in most of the rest of the world as the various popular musics so effectively disseminated by the mass media. It is above all in this respect that the United States holds a position of artistic leadership whether we are leading in a desirable direction or not.

We already face a situation in this culture where the values of "serious music" are threatened economically as well as culturally. If we elect to preserve only the museum aspects of this tradition because of the anachronistic social and economic organization of the main channels of its dissemination, we will ensure its atrophy.

In the face of this prospect, two main problems demand solutions: how can the tradition continue to grow without losing its public, and how can it become a healthy, fruitful, and even powerful stimulus to the world's other musics rather than an adulterative and disintegrative influence? If these problems are not addressed successfully, the traditions of European concert music will not only wither in this country and elsewhere but will be displaced successfully by rival traditions of music which reject above all its aristocratic anachronisms.

It begins to look as if serious music needs Harry Partch more than he ever needed it. He addressed problems it is ignoring with far more than tentative success, and he diagnosed many of its most serious ills with uncanny accuracy. The time is long overdue when diagnosis should be followed by prescription and treatment.

In 1946, *Circle* magazine published an article by Harry Partch entitled "Show Horses in the Concert Ring." It has been republished more recently by *Soundings* magazine.[1] In it Partch launches an attack on American concert music and proposes his alternatives. Here are some excerpts:

> It need hardly be labored that music is a physical art, and that a periodic groping into the physical, a reaching for an understanding of the physical, is the only basic procedure, the only way a musical era will attain any enduring significance . . .
>
> The age of specialization has given us an art of sound that denies sound, and a science of sound that denies art . . . a music-drama that denies drama, and a drama that—contrary to the practices of all other people of the world—denies music.
>
> One does not fertilize the creative instinct by twenty year plans of practice . . . to play music written by others, mostly long dead . . . And we permit an industrialization of music on the basis of such parlous degeneracy: issuance of interpretation upon interpretation of the accepted limited repertory by the record companies; facture on an assembly line of the accepted instruments and in whatever asinine notation and implied nomenclature they require—by still other companies, and so on, perennially sporting a bloom of pride over the magnificent spread of our culture. The "so on" stands for literally thousands of scholarly magazine articles, . . . ubiquitous classes in music appreciation, multiplex radio programs, all deliberately calculated to weight us permanently with the incubi and the succubi of an interpretive age: that is, with a facti-

> tious, non-creative art. The only real vitality in this entire picture is exuded by the men who are out to make money in the deal . . . Value of intrinsic content—value of human beings, of human works and attitudes—never enters the picture . . .
>
> Some very drastic remedies are called for in order to bring vitality to a body of theory that rejects investigation and a physical poetry that excludes all but purely metaphysical poets. A period of comparative anarchy, with each composer employing his own instrument or instruments, his own scale, his own forms is very necessary for a way out of this malaise.

As a first step, Partch's work can be and must be brought before a wider public and his significance correctly assessed, not diminished to the level of a cultural oddity. As an even more important second step, those of us who can must carry on aspects of his work in directions of which, perhaps, he never dreamed or felt himself ill-equipped to deal with.

During his life I helped Partch to get his work before the public for as long as he permitted. I was responsible for getting him to the University of Illinois, where he produced *The Bewitched, Revelation in the Courthouse Park,* and *Water! Water!* and where he met Danlee Mitchell, his heir. When we came to odds as a result of his delegation to me of choice of choreographer for *The Bewitched* and my subsequent holding together of the production, it was necessary for me to leave to others the active job of carrying out his work. I never ceased to be a supporter.

Since his death I have again tried to help, though I have no direct affiliation with the Harry Partch Foundation or with the ensemble which continues to produce his works.

With the aid of several other people, most particularly Thomas McGeary, a young musicologist from San Diego, I have begun to gather together oral history and other data on his life from people who knew and worked with him.[2] I do not have the intention of producing a biography of Partch, but such materials will be important to anyone who does. More recently, with the aid of a team of young researchers, Glenn Hackbarth, Larry Polansky, Janet Cameron, Mark Culbertson, Mark Behm, and Christopher Granner, I have initiated the preparation of three works of Partch for publication in a notation designed to be as little different from ordinary traditional notation as possible. The works are *Seventeen Lyrics by Li Po, Eleven Intrusions,* and *Daphne of the Dunes.* Our aim is to make Partch's scores as accessible as possible to the ordinary musician.[3]

The most significant aspect of my own work as composer is a very extensive development of microtonal just intonation. I have developed a theory in support of this which greatly extends Partch's. Since I am dealing with traditions of performing and with instruments and players which are in the European tradition, I have steeped myself in that music and have studied the techniques and aesthetic attitudes of all its phases of development up through the present. But my purpose has not been to Europeanize Partch's ideas. Rather it has been to alter that tradition so as to render it pervious to his way of thinking.

Lastly, I will not identify myself with Harry Partch. Early on in our association he paid me a compliment I did not recognize as such. He said I would never be a follower of his. Stung a little by what I took to be a rejection, I asked him why not. He said I was too much like him and I would have to find my own way.

NOTES

1. [Ed.: Partch's "Show Horses in the Concert Ring" has been republished even more recently in Partch, *Bitter Music: Collected Journals, Essays, Introductions, and Librettos,* edited with an introduction by Thomas McGeary (Urbana and Chicago: University of Illinois Press, 1991), 174–80.]

2. [Ed.: The resulting Oral History Project on Partch, conducted mostly in the years 1978–79 by Johnston and McGeary, with occasional additions thereafter, is housed in the Harry Partch Archive, Music Library, University of Illinois at Urbana-Champaign.]

3. [Ed.: The published edition of transcriptions of Partch's works into Johnston's notation system ultimately never took place as intended. Some of the work done toward the project is, however, accessible in other forms: cf. Janet Cameron, "Transcriptions of Seven Li Po Settings by Harry Partch from 'Eleven Poems by Li Po'" (M. Mus. dissertation, University of Illinois at Urbana-Champaign, 1981); and Glenn Allen Hackbarth, "An Analysis of Harry Partch's 'Daphne of the Dunes'" (D.M.A. thesis, University of Illinois at Urbana-Champaign, 1979). An article derived from the latter, Glenn Hackbarth, "*Daphne of the Dunes:* The Relationship of Drama and Music," is included in David Dunn, ed., *Harry Partch: An Anthology of Critical Perspectives.* The largest undertaking of this sort in print is Richard Kassel's transcription of Partch's *Barstow* into Johnston's notation system: Harry Partch, *Barstow: Eight Hitchhiker Inscriptions from a Highway Railing at Barstow, California.* Edited by Richard Kassel. (*Recent Researches in American Music,* 39.) (*Music of the United States of America,* 9.) Madison, Wisc.: Published for the American Musicological Society by A-R Editions, Inc., 2000.]

REGARDING LA MONTE YOUNG

1995

My relevance to La Monte Young is that I am a composer who is involved, as he is, in just intonation. About this much more later. But as a writer on him I could function as a critic, which is a variety of journalism, or I could reminisce and comment about my relation as another composer to La Monte, and try to give some insight into why he does as he does when dealing with music. On the whole, I feel much more inclined to the second alternative, though doubtless some elements of the former will from time to time enter the mix.

I first met La Monte Young in the fall of 1968 on the occasion of the Whitney Museum's presentation of works by Harry Partch. It was after the second evening of performance, the one open to the general public, that I went with Harry and a group mostly of other musicians to the Esquire Bar, near Lincoln Center. Among the group were La Monte Young and Marian Zazeela. Harry introduced us, and La Monte, anxious to have an extended time to spend with Harry, invited him to his studio the following day. I was included in the invitation. The next day, I went to the studio on Church Street. We became acquainted, and as time went on and Harry did not show up, La Monte offered to play me some of his music. As I learned later, Harry had become embroiled in some kind of personal controversy with a friend and had to settle matters in that context before thinking about anything else. La Monte was, of course, deeply disappointed that Harry had not come, and I was aware of this. Aside from my own genuine interest in his work, which would have been motivation enough, I wanted to make up as much as I could for the letdown occasioned by Harry's absence, so I encouraged La Monte not only to play as much music as he would, but to talk as much as he was willing. As it turned out, we went on all day, and La Monte quite exhausted himself. Marian invited me to stay for dinner, and we went to get some takeout Indian food.

Needless to say, I learned a great deal about La Monte and about his music.

La Monte, having grown up in rural Idaho among Mormons, had not been overexposed, as many Americans are, to European concert customs. But even to the extent that he had been exposed to them, he rejected them later, becoming a highly visible avant-garde composer in New York City in the '60s. Whether this rejection included religion or even whether religion was a major factor in his early years I did not ask and he did not volunteer. But by the late '60s, he and Marian had much more than a passing interest in yoga, and within a few years, they were both students of the north Indian musician Pandit Pran Nath, whose involvement with music has an unavoidable spiritual component. I had the distinct impression that La Monte had withdrawn at least interiorly from the iconoclastic avant-garde, seeking a much more serious and meditative musical art. From his famous burning of a violin in a performance of a Richard Maxfield work to his drone pieces with light environments by Marian Zazeela is a significantly long inner journey.

The tenor of most of the avant-garde during the '60s and '70s was not notably spiritual in nature, and La Monte Young was a not atypical avant-gardist until his development of the drone pieces. Those works have been labeled minimalist, and for very good reasons, but they lead in quite a different direction from most of the minimalist works of that time. I do not attribute this to the influence of Pandit Pran Nath but rather would suggest that it was the same sense of direction that led to the composition of the drone pieces that also led to Pran Nath. From many things La Monte Young said to me, I realized that much of his work related directly to his desire to pursue a meditative life.

It is my view that the function of art is, or at least could be, the education of the emotional life, and it is highly desirable that its techniques and, therefore, its intellectual component should be, like its perceptible sensory impact, symbolic of the emotional content. La Monte was, as a child, fascinated by the world of sounds. He spoke at his loft of listening for hours to the hum of an electrical power station, an experience of the overtone spectrum. As soon as La Monte Young began to search for his own individual musical language, this prolonged, steady-state sound made its appearance and has ever since remained his particular musical signature. The superimposition of chanting voices on top of this drone creates a very direct parallel to Indian classical music. With its use of high-level amplification, this music combines the meditative intensity of Indian music with the theatrically overpowering impact of hard rock music. In effect, Young invites the listener to concentrate with him upon a relentlessly repeating pattern of vibrations for long periods of time. This is usually presented in an art museum, rather than in a concert hall, with the audience seated on the floor. I have seen people at the University of Illinois in Urbana-Champaign doing tai chi, meditating in lotus position, even sleeping on mats during a La Monte Young performance. As an Indian musician once said to me, "It matters very little whether you fall asleep or not; the musical message will get to your mind either way."

The structure of music in extended just intonation is that of time itself—the intersecting of cyclically repetitive sequences of events, so that duration is articulated in mathematically precise resultant patterns, which become the focus of meditative concentration. Each composition is the focus upon a specific set of interlocked speeds of vibrations, experienced over a long enough period of time, and at a sufficiently high volume, to hypnotize the mind. The value of this exercise of the mind is quite analogous to that of many traditional forms of meditation. John Cage once expressed to me his divergence from this kind of artistic aim. He said he was convinced that reality, or "truth," or art, is wherever you are, always available to experience at any time, whereas La Monte's music implied, and made a requirement, that you make a special effort to be present at a ritual-like event of overpowering strength, which would compel your mind to look at reality in a particular way. If this is a criticism, and I think it is, it simply makes especially clear the very divergent aims of these two musical artists.

This intersection of time cycles is the essence of just intonation, where musical intervals are refined to be mathematically precise, simple numerical proportions, or ratios. But rather than presenting melodies, harmonies, and metrical rhythms utilizing these ratios, La Monte Young focuses directly upon the patterns themselves, experienced at the rate of vibrations per second, rather than at the much slower rates of countable time, and undisguised by secondary patterning in countable time. The structure of most Western musical compositions is created by patterns in countable time, a domain commonly called rhythm. Bypassing this kind of structure entirely, Young relies upon the resultant patterns created by long sustained tones related by simple whole-number ratios. To a mind accustomed to focus on rhythmic patterning which is built up into longer time spans by phrasing and sectioning, this concentration upon very rapid patterns seems like mere stasis; but to a mind accustomed to the stilling of surface mental activity, it opens the door to long spans of concentrated listening. This produces lengths of listening time unusual for most music: much more lengthy. I believe that this is due to the meditative state induced by the music.

Marian Zazeela's visuals are related to mandalas and so are equally at home in the meditative ambiance. They contribute to a total artwork which is like an oriental version of Wagner's ideal. In fact, Wagner's use of myth seems to me a quite parallel effort to lift the mind out of an everyday context into a world of symbolism. The constant interplay of leitmotiv counterpoint in Wagner's orchestral writing has led to the critical observation that his drama is almost entirely in the orchestra, rather than onstage in the action. The psychological states and motivations of the characters are better portrayed by this than they are by any action, vocal or bodily, by the singers. Further, the philosophical ideas behind the drama are thus dramatized. This takes place on an emotional level much more than on a verbal, intellectual one. One may understand far more deeply and also more quickly the archetypal flux of the drama by listening than by reading the program notes many people believe are the only way to "understand" Wagner's music dramas. Still, the myths Wagner uses are stories with characters and events, however saturated they may be with emotional commentary in the form of music. The symbols in La Monte Young's work are very much more abstract and mathematical than Wagner's symbols. It seems to me that is the most significant difference. Both are very much concerned with power, and that, I think, is where John Cage took umbrage.

La Monte Young's use of extended just intonation is at least as fully saturated with symbolism as Wagner's music dramas, but the symbolism is number symbolism, directly perceived as affective reactions to musical pitch ratios. There could be said to be an innate symbolic meaning to the use of each prime number as a factor in ratios. The number 2 is fundamental, since its meaning is cyclicity; it indicates a repetition of the same thing on another scale of magnitude. The octave (2/1) indicates that notes having this relation will be called by the same name even though they are higher or lower in absolute pitch. All scales in traditional music are recycled at the octave, so that one octave of a scale is all that is needed to define what it is, all higher and lower octaves being the same in ratio makeup.

The number 3 is traditionally symbolic of stability and strength. A music composed exclusively of fifths and fourths (ratios of 3/2 and 4/3), such as medieval organum, has, preeminently, those qualities. The numbers 1 and 3 are traditionally symbols of God, whereas 2 is the number of creation. Thus the interrelation of 2 and 3 is the symbol of the intercourse between God and the created world, the express subject matter of medieval religious art.

The number 5 symbolizes and evokes man's personal emotions. The introduction of triadic harmony in Renaissance music coincided with the secularization of music, which became expressive of the emotions of life.

The number 7 is not used in the classical tradition of Western music, but it is the characteristic interval component in blues music. It could be said to symbolize sexuality.

In his earlier drone pieces La Monte Young concentrated on complexes of tones involving only the prime numbers 2, 3, and 7. Since then, under Pandit Pran Nath's suggestions, he has included the number 5, and under his own impetus, higher primes. I interpret the aversion to the number 5 as a rejection of traditional Western musical values, and this attitude may well reach beyond musical values to the emotional underpinnings that are so well symbolized by triadic music. I also interpret the meditative nature of La Monte Young's performances as a reaching beyond conventional religious usages of whatever tradition toward inner psychological wellsprings. It is observable that many musicians who found their voices during the sixties have found that the only real way to grow beyond the particular kind of radicalism that characterized that revolutionary time was to seek out some form of transcendental religion.

In La Monte Young's case both aspects of this search are evident. In a strictly superficial aspect, his dress and behavior suggest strongly the image of a guru. On a deeper and quite genuine level he sought meaning and stability in a kind of meditation. That he practices this in a highly theatrical setting is very different from traditional ways, but it is clearly no less effective for him. At the best, it can open the eyes of an audience to the meditative power of musical sound. At its worst, it invites cultism. Both reactions to La Monte Young's music are common.

This music could certainly be called minimalist. But *minimalism* is one of those critics' terms that serve as labels to categorize a most diverse collection of musics. Such labels serve to close the mind, rendering further thought both unnecessary and unlikely. Most people want a pigeonhole into which a disturbing new phenomenon can be dropped so that it need not be thought about. Abetting this is one of the worst things critics do. If art is to awaken and stimulate us, it must not be shorn of its power to shock us.

This reduction to basics is admirably suited to an exploratory art. When one is presenting thoroughly unfamiliar materials, it is wise to give an audience plenty of time to absorb and digest them, and it is well also to present these unknowns as unadorned. The extra symbolic content of musical parameters other than pitch is kept to a bare minimum in order to focus our attention irresistibly. Because no interplay of different levels of symbolic meaning is encouraged, it is not necessary or even desirable to have any preconception about what these new materials will evoke. This is true even of the composer. He can evoke emotional meanings which are as much discoveries for him as for an audience.

To verbalize about these meanings is to translate one's emotional perceptions into an intellectual mode. This may or may not be an accurate process, especially if one has not the benefit of a large number of other such translations by other people. In describing the emotional meaning of the number 7 in pitch ratios as symbolic of sexuality, I am giving a personal interpretation, but also reporting a widespread musical practice observable in blues music. I am not personally acquainted with musics dealing with the numbers 11 and 13 except for the few rare experimenters with intonation such as Harry Partch and Lou Harrison and James Tenney. There are also a few younger composers who are dealing with these relationships. This is not enough for me to extrapolate symbolic meaning with confidence based upon their work. I can rely essentially only upon my own insights based upon my own work.

The use of the number 11 in ratios yields an interval in between the size of a perfect and an augmented fourth. In another combination it yields a neutral third. These are intervals similar to some available in quarter-tone equal temperament. This suggests a symbolic meaning related to ambiguity. An example in traditional symbols is androgyny.

The number 13 provides an augmented triad sound, either a minor sixth added to a major triad, or a major seventh added to a minor triad. These are poignant combinations. This observation, combined with the traditional ominous meaning of the number 13, leads me to associate the meaning with death, or at least with the emotions commonly associated with the possibility of death.

To meditate on sexuality, as sharply contradistinguished from sexual fantasizing, or from the function of sex in reproduction, leads one to the recognition of the importance of this psychic energy in inner spiritual growth. This is a position traditionally recognized in Islamic tradition as contrasted with the Christian tradition, which tends to demonize sex except in reproduction.

To meditate on androgyny is to begin to recognize the existence in each human being of whichever sex of opposite sexual characteristics, and to see the importance of bringing these into harmonious inner relationship with the dominant characteristics.

To meditate on death is to begin to accept its inevitability, its supreme importance, and its relevance to daily living. As one of the most important life experiences it ought to occupy a correspondingly large place in the values of each person, and not simply as an overwhelming dread.

What I am suggesting is at least the potential content of La Monte Young's meditative music. But like all music, this music invites a kind of thought which is only secondarily intellectual and verbal. It is preeminently emotional and purely sensory. As in the case of Wagner, the intellect's verbal formulations are the least helpful of any human abilities in understanding the symbols presented. The music speaks directly to the emotions via the senses.

In May of 1973, La Monte Young and Marian Zazeela did a performance at the University of Illinois at Urbana-Champaign. It was on a revival of the once-annual Festival of Contemporary Arts, calling itself the Phoenix Festival in honor of its resurrection. I was chairing the planning committee. To save money, I decided to house Young and Zazeela, as well as their assistant, a young girl, at my own home. Other faculty housed other invited artists; the budget was generous but not equal to the aims of the festival. We installed La Monte's electronics and projectors in the Architecture Building's museum space, a large open area with hardwood floors and tall windows. There had to be someone guarding the equipment day and night. The group was in residence about a week.

The houseguests were not typical ones. They all got up an hour before dawn and chanted with sitar accompaniment until about an hour past dawn. Days were spent at the installation rehearsing and checking the equipment. The group was friendly but very businesslike about indicating their needs and preferences.

Watching them perform and rehearse showed me what discipline and what high standards of excellence they had. I had gained some idea of La Monte's aims from listening to tapes, but the impact of the live performance, though it was largely electronic, was very much greater than I had imagined. There was a large attendance, and the event created a real stir. Not only the overtly meditative behavior already mentioned, but the general behavior and demeanor of the audience, indicated to me that they were aware of the meditative aim, even when some were not in sympathy with it. Most of the negative reactions, it seems to me, stemmed from a resistance to being so powerfully manipulated by the sound environment rather than to a failure to get the message. Perhaps this reaction is an index to the degree to which an admixture of ego-driven aim has got into this art. But no one's art is for everyone. I would guess that most of the cultish following has resulted from the weakness or immaturity of the followers than from any deliberate aim of the artist.

While La Monte and Marian were staying with us, their relationship to Pandit Pran Nath was clearly that of pupils to a guru. This is of importance, it seems to me, because it indicates the degree to which music is to La Monte Young a means to a spiritual end, and not, on some level or other, an ego-driven undertaking. It is tied into his own inner growth and is not simply his artistic vehicle to success in the world. Surely his behavior indicated that, and his manner of presenting his art to the public, while theatrical in means, did not interfere in any way with such an aim.

No evaluation of La Monte Young as an artist could possibly be a true one unless it took this dimension very much into account. To see him as one of a large number of avant-garde minimalists is to falsify his aim on a fundamental level.

I do not think there is a great deal of importance in the idea of increasing the number of notes per octave in our scale. In other words, I do not see microtonality, as such, as an important musical movement. The real importance lies in the rediscovery of just tuning. There is little interest in this in Europe, but it is fundamental in most of the other major musical traditions in the world, especially in Asia. Most of the push in this direction in Western civilization comes from the USA. La Monte Young is one of the major exponents of this movement. His direction, as indicated, is minimalist and meditation-oriented. Harry Partch built instruments and had his own variety of *Gesamtkunstwerk.* Lou Harrison relates his music overtly to oriental traditions. La Monte Young focuses primarily upon the aim of music to be a meditative medium. The music of James Tenney has much more direct relationship to the rest of avant-garde music than has La Monte Young but in most respects is more traditionalist than Young, paradoxically. My own music deliberately attempts to relate the practice of extended just intonation to mainstream currents in traditional Western music, to reassert continuity. Young's position is that of a radical innovator; but radical or not, he does fit into a context to which he gives meaning and from which he receives meaning in return. He will probably be very influential, but I do not think he can be imitated with any degree of success. He will remain unique.

NOTES ON SOURCES

"Aesthetic Theory; Philosophical Background for Mathematical Theory; Musical Background for Application of Mathematical Theory": Previously unpublished.

"Scalar Order as a Compositional Resource": First published in *Perspectives of New Music* 2 no. 2 (Spring–Summer 1964), 56–76.

"Proportionality and Expanded Musical Pitch Relations": First presented as a lecture at Illinois Wesleyan University, 1964. First published in *Perspectives of New Music* 5 no. 1 (Fall–Winter 1966), 112–20.

"Microtonal Resources": First published in John Vinton, ed., *Dictionary of Contemporary Music* (New York: E. P. Dutton, 1971), 483–84.

"Tonality Regained": First published in the *American Society of University Composers Proceedings* 6 (New York: Department of Music, Columbia University, 1971), 113–19.

"Music Theory": First published in *Encyclopaedia Britannica,* fifteenth ed. (1974), vol. 12, 746–49.

"Rational Structure in Music": First published in the *American Society of University Composers Proceedings* 11/12 (1976–77), 102–18; reprinted in *1/1: The Journal of the Just Intonation Network* 2 nos. 3 (12–15) and 4 (12–18).

"A Notation System for Extended Just Intonation": Written especially for this volume.

"Musical Intelligibility: Where Are We?": Previously unpublished.

"A Talk on Contemporary Music": Previously unpublished. First presented as a lecture at the Festival of Contemporary Arts, University of Illinois at Urbana-Champaign, 1963.

"Festivals and New Music": Written for the program booklet, Festival of Contemporary Arts, University of Illinois at Urbana-Champaign, 1965.

"Three Attacks on a Problem": First published in the *American Society of University Composers Proceedings* 2 (New York: Department of Music, Columbia University, 1967), 89–98.

"On Context": First presented as a lecture in 1968. First published in *Source* 4 (1968); reprinted in the *American Society of University Composers Proceedings* 3 (New York: Department of Music, Columbia University, 1968), 32–36.

"Contribution to IMC Panel": First presented as a lecture in 1968. First published in *The Composer* (June 1970), 6–8.

"How to Cook an Albatross": First published in *Arts in Society* 7 (1970), 34–38; reprinted in *Source* 6 (1970), 63–65.

"Art and Survival": First published in *The Composer* (Fall–Winter 1971), 9–16.

"On Bridge-Building": Previously unpublished.

"Seventeen Items": Previously unpublished.

"Art and Religion": Previously unpublished.

"Extended Just Intonation: A Position Paper": First published in *Perspectives of New Music* 25, nos. 1–2 (1987), 517–19.

"A.S.U.C. Keynote Address": First published in *Perspectives of New Music* 26, no. 1 (1988), 236–42.

"Just Intonation and Mere Intonation": First published in *1/1: The Journal of the Just Intonation Network* 8, no. 4 (November 1994), 18–19.

"Without Improvement": Written especially for this volume.

"Maximum Clarity": First published in *Contemporary Composers on Contemporary Music,* ed. Elliott Schwartz and Barney Childs with Jim Fox, expanded edition (New York: Da Capo Press, 1998), 430–39.

"Some Compositions": The texts in this category, with two exceptions, are all short program notes written for the first performance and/or recording of the works they describe. Therefore no formal citation has been given. The two exceptions are: "The Genesis of *Knocking Piece,*" first published in *Percussive Notes Research Edition* (March 1983), 25–31; and "*Quintet for Groups:* A Reminiscence," written especially for this volume.

"Letter from Urbana": Review of the 1963 Festival of Contemporary Arts at the University of Illinois. First published in *Perspectives of New Music* 2, no. 1 (1963), 137–41.

"To *Perspectives of New Music* re. John Cage": Originally written as a letter, May 27, 1969. First published in *Perspectives of New Music* (Spring–Summer 1972), 175–77.

"The Corporealism of Harry Partch": First presented as a lecture at the University of

California, San Diego, January 1975. First published in *Perspectives of New Music* 13 no. 2 (1975), 85–97.

"Harry Partch/John Cage": First published as liner notes for *Harry Partch / John Cage,* New World Records NW 214, 1978. The text as printed in this volume is a shortened version of the original liner notes. The LP featured recordings of Partch's "The Rose," "The Wind," and "The Waterfall" (from *Eleven Intrusions*), "The Intruder," "I am a Peach Tree," "A Midnight Farewell," and "Before the Cask of Wine" (from *Seventeen Lyrics by Li Po*), "The Street" (from *Eleven Intrusions*), and *The Dreamer That Remains;* and parts III and IV of Cage's *Music of Changes* (performed by David Tudor). Johnston appeared as performer on the LP, playing Diamond Marimba and Bass Marimba, in the extracts from Partch's *Eleven Intrusions.*

"Harry Partch's *Cloud-Chamber Music*": First published in David Dunn, ed., *Harry Partch: An Anthology of Critical Perspectives* (London: Harwood Academic Publishers, 2000), 41–47.

"Beyond Harry Partch": First published in *Perspectives of New Music* 22, nos. 1–2 (1984), 223–32.

"Regarding La Monte Young": Previously unpublished.

BIBLIOGRAPHY

This bibliography lists those works mentioned in the text, together with a selection of writings about Johnston's work by others.

Babbitt, Milton. "Who Cares If You Listen?" *High Fidelity* 8 no. 2, 38–40, 126–27; reprinted in Elliott Schwartz and Barney Childs with Jim Fox, eds., *Contemporary Composers on Contemporary Music* (expanded ed.). New York: Da Capo Press, 1998, pp. 243–50.

Barbour, James Murray. *Tuning and Temperament.* East Lansing: Michigan State College Press, 1951.

Barraclough, Geoffrey. *Introduction to Contemporary History.* London: C. A. Watts and Co., 1964; repr. New York: Viking Press, 1991.

Bergson, Henri. *Matter and Memory* (authorized translation by Nancy Margaret Paul and W. Scott Palmer). New York: Macmillan, 1911.

Blake, William. *The Marriage of Heaven and Hell.* London: Oxford University Press, 1975.

Bush, Philip. "Ben Johnston: Music for Piano." Liner notes to the CD *Ben Johnston: Microtonal Piano,* Koch International Classics 7369, 1997 (see discography).

Cage, John. *Silence.* Middletown, Conn.: Wesleyan University Press, 1961.

———. *A Year from Monday.* Middletown, Conn.: Wesleyan University Press, 1967.

Campbell, Joseph. *The Masks of God* (4 vols.). New York: Viking, 1969.

Chase, Gilbert, ed. *The American Composer Speaks.* Baton Rouge: Louisiana State University Press, 1966.

Childs, Barney. "Ben Johnston's *Quintet for Groups.*" *Perspectives of New Music* 7 no. 1 (Fall–Winter 1968), 110–21.

Daniélou, Alain. *An Introduction to the Study of Musical Scales.* London: The India Society, 1943, repr. 1979.

———. *Traité de Musicologie Comparée.* Paris: Hermann, 1959.

Duckworth, William. *Talking Music: Conversations with John Cage, Philip Glass, Laurie Anderson, and Five Generations of American Experimental Composers.* New York: Da Capo Press, 1999.

———. *20/20: 20 New Sounds of the 20th Century.* New York: Schirmer, 1999.

Dunn, David, ed. *Harry Partch: An Anthology of Critical Perspectives.* London: Harwood Academic, 2000.

Elster, Steven. "A Harmonic and Serial Analysis of Ben Johnston's String Quartet No. 6." *Perspectives of New Music* 29 no. 2 (Summer 1991), 138–65.

Fonville, John. "Ben Johnston's Extended Just Intonation: A Guide for Interpreters." *Perspectives of New Music* 29 no. 2 (Summer 1991), 106–37.

Gagne, Cole, and Tracey Caras. *Soundpieces: Interviews with American Composers.* Metuchen, NJ: Scarecrow Press, 1982.

Gann, Kyle. *American Music in the Twentieth Century.* New York: Schirmer, 1997.

Gibbens, John Jeffery. "Design in Ben Johnston's Sonata for Microtonal Piano." *Interface* 18 (1989), 161–94.

Gilmore, Bob. "Changing the metaphor: ratio models of musical pitch in the work of Harry Partch, Ben Johnston, and James Tenney." *Perspectives of New Music* 33 nos. 1–2 (Winter–Summer 1995), 458–503.

———. "The Climate Since Harry Partch." *Contemporary Music Review* 22 nos. 1–2 (2003), 15–34.

———. *Harry Partch: A Biography.* New Haven, CT: Yale University Press, 1998.

Gurdjieff, G. I. *Meetings with Remarkable Men.* London: Routledge and Kegan Paul, 1963.

Helmholtz, Hermann. *On the Sensations of Tone* (translated and with additions and notes by Alexander J. Ellis). London, 1875; repr. New York: Dover, 1954.

Hiller, L. A., and L. M. Isaacson. *Experimental Music.* New York: McGraw-Hill, 1959.

Hindemith, Paul. *The Craft of Musical Composition* (2 vols.; trans. Arthur Mendel). London: Schott, 1942.

Joyce, James. *Finnegans Wake.* New York: Viking, 1939; repr. London: Faber and Faber, 1964.

Kassel, Richard. "Ben Johnston," in the *New Grove Dictionary of Music and Musicians.* London: Macmillan, 2001, 13: 170–72.

Kazantzakis, Nikos. *The Poor Man of God* (first published in English as *Saint Francis*). New York: Simon and Schuster, 1962.

Keislar, Douglas. "Six Composers on Non-Standard Tunings." *Perspectives of New Music* 29 no. 1 (1991), 176–211.

Krahenbuehl, David, and Christopher Schmidt. "On the Development of Musical Systems." *Journal of Music Theory* 6 no. 1 (1962), 32–65.

Langer, Suzanne. *Feeling and Form.* New York: Charles Scribner's Sons, 1953.

Mandelbaum, Joel. "Multiple Division of the Octave and the Tonal Resources of 19–tone Temperament." Ph.D. thesis, University of Indiana, 1961.

Meyer, Leonard B. *Emotion and Meaning in Music.* Chicago: Chicago University Press, 1956.

Moles, Abraham. *Théorie de l'Information et Perception Esthetique.* Paris: Flammarian, 1958.

Ouspensky, P. D. *In Search of the Miraculous.* London: Routledge and Kegan Paul, 1950.

Partch, Harry. *Bitter Music: Collected Journals, Essays, Introductions, and Librettos.* Edited with an introduction by Thomas McGeary. Urbana and Chicago: University of Illinois Press, 1991.

———. *Genesis of a Music.* First ed., Madison: University of Wisconsin Press, 1949; second ed., enlarged, New York: Da Capo Press, 1974.

Perle, George. *Serial Composition and Atonality: An Introduction to the Music of Schoenberg, Berg, and Webern* (2nd ed., revised). Berkeley: University of California Press, 1968.

Plantinga, Leon. "Philippe de Vitry's *Ars Nova:* A Translation." *Journal of Music Theory* 5 (1961), 204–23.

Read, Gardner. *Twentieth-Century Microtonal Notation.* Westport, Conn.: Greenwood Press, 1990.

Reynolds, Roger. *Mind Models: New Forms of Musical Experience.* New York: Praeger, 1975.

Schenker, Heinrich. *Neue Musikalische Theorien und Phantasien* vol. 1, *Harmonielehre.* Stuttgart, 1906; Eng. trans. by Oswald Jonas as *Harmony,* University of Chicago Press, 1954.

Schoenberg, Arnold. *Harmonielehre* (1911). English translation as *Theory of Harmony,* trans. Roy E. Carter, third ed. Los Angeles: University of California Press, 1978.

———. *Style and Idea.* New York: Philosophical Library, 1950; expanded ed., Berkeley: University of California Press, 1975.

Schwartz, Elliott, and Barney Childs with Jim Fox, eds. *Contemporary Composers on Contemporary Music.* Expanded ed., New York: Da Capo Press, 1998.

Shinn, Randall. "Ben Johnston's Fourth String Quartet." *Perspectives of New Music* 15 no. 2 (Spring–Summer 1977), 145–73.

Stevens, S. S., ed. *Handbook of Experimental Psychology.* New York and London: John Wiley and Sons, 1951.

———. "On the Theory of Scales of Measurement." *Science* 103 no. 2684 (June 7, 1946), 677–80.

Stockhausen, Karlheinz. "How Time Passes." *Die Reihe* 3 (1959), 10–40.

Strunk, Oliver, ed. *Source Readings in Music History from Classical Antiquity through the Romantic Era.* New York: W. W. Norton and Co., 1950.

Tenney, James. *A History of 'Consonance' and 'Dissonance.'* New York: Excelsior Press, 1988.

Underhill, Evelyn. *Mysticism.* London: Methuen and Co., 1911.

Vinton, John, ed. *Dictionary of Contemporary Music.* New York: E. P. Dutton and Co., 1971.

Von Gunden, Heidi. *The Music of Ben Johnston.* Metuchen. NJ: Scarecrow Press, 1986.

Yasser, Joseph. *A Theory of Evolving Tonality.* New York: American Library of Musicology, 1932; reprinted New York: Da Capo Press, 1975.

DISCOGRAPHY

This appendix lists all the commercially available recordings of Ben Johnston's music and is divided in two sections: LP recordings (from 1964 to 1987), and CD recordings (from 1987 to 2003). Twenty-two of his works are featured here, some of them recorded more than once. Whereas these works represent only about a quarter of Johnston's total oeuvre, the range is sufficiently broad that anyone listening to all or most of these recordings would encounter a fairly representative selection of his work. To these commercial recordings should be added the quite large number of live performances that have been taped over the years for archival purposes, whether on reel-to-reel tape, cassette, or DAT. These include performances of some of Johnston's major works that are not yet available commercially, such as the first, third, and fifth string quartets, *Knocking Piece, Mass, Duo for two violins, Two Sonnets of Shakespeare, Diversion, Songs of Loss,* the *Chamber Symphony,* and many others. The process of making digital transfers of some of the older recordings has been begun by Andreas Stefik. Readers interested in obtaining further information on this unreleased material are welcome to contact the editor.

LP RECORDINGS

Carmilla. Original cast recording of the off-Broadway musical performed by the ETC Company of La MaMa, New York, directed by Wilford Leach and John Braswell. Musical direction by Zizi Mueller; orchestrations by the ETC Company. Vanguard Records, VSD79322, 1972.

Casta Bertram. Performed by Bertram Turetsky, double bass, on *The Contemporary Contrabass: New American Music by John Cage, Pauline Oliveros, Ben Johnston.* Nonesuch H-71237, 1969.

Ci-Gît Satie. Performed by the New Music Choral Ensemble. Ars Nova Ars Antigua Records, AN-1005, 1968.

Duo for flute and string bass. Performed by Nancy Turetzky, flute, and Bertram Turetzky, string bass. Advance Recordings, FGR-1, 1964.

Duo for flute and string bass. Performed by John Fonville, flute, and Thomas Fredrickson, string bass, on *American Contemporary Music from the University of Illinois.* Composers Recordings Inc., CRI 405, 1979.

Sonata for Microtonal Piano. Performed by Robert Miller, piano, on *Sound Forms for Piano.* New World Records, NW 203, 1976.

Sonnets of Desolation. Performed by the New Swingle Singers on *Ben Johnston.* Composers Recordings Inc., SD 515, 1984.

String Quartet no. 2. Performed by the Composers Quartet. Nonesuch H-71224, 1969.

String Quartet no. 4. Performed by the Fine Arts Quartet. Gasparo 205, 1980.

String Quartet no. 4. Performed by the Kronos Quartet on *White Man Sleeps.* Nonesuch H-979 163–1, 1987.

String Quartet no. 6. Performed by the New World String Quartet on Naumburg Prize Winners Perform Naumburg Commissions. Composers Recordings Inc., CRI SD 497, 1983.

Visions and Spels. Performed by the New Verbal Workshop directed by Herbert Marder on *Ben Johnston.* Composers Recordings Inc., CRI SD 515, 1984.

CD RECORDINGS

Calamity Jane to Her Daughter. Performed by Dora Ohrenstein on *Urban Diva.* Composers Recordings, Inc., CRI 654, 1994.

Five Fragments. Performed by Stephen Kalm, baritone, with Music Amici on *Ben Johnston: Ponder Nothing.* New World Records NW 80432, 1993.

Gambit. Performed by Music Amici conducted by Charles Yassky on *Ben Johnston: Ponder Nothing.* New World Records NW 80432, 1993.

Ponder Nothing. Performed by Susan Fancher, alto saxophone, on *Ponder Nothing.* Innova Recordings 564, 2002.

Ponder Nothing. Performed by Charles Yassky, clarinet, on *Ben Johnston: Ponder Nothing.* New World Records NW 80432, 1993.

Progression. Performed by Michael Cameron, double bass, on *Progression.* Zuma Records 304, 1996.

Saint Joan. Performed by Phillip Bush on *Microtonal Piano.* Koch International Classics 7369, 1997.

Septet. Performed by Music Amici on *Ben Johnston: Ponder Nothing.* New World Records NW 80432, 1993.

Sonata for Microtonal Piano. Performed by Robert Miller, piano, on *Sound Forms for Piano.* New World Records NW 80203, 1995.

Sonata for Microtonal Piano. Performed by Phillip Bush on *Microtonal Piano.* Koch International Classics 7369, 1997.

String Quartet no. 4. Performed by the Kronos Quartet on *White Man Sleeps.* Nonesuch 79163, 1987. Same recording also available on *Kronos Quartet: Released 1985–1995.* Nonesuch 79394, 1995.

String Quartet no. 9. Performed by the Stanford Quartet. Laurel Records 847, 1998.

Suite for Microtonal Piano. Performed by Phillip Bush on Microtonal Piano. Koch International Classics 7369, 1997.

Three Chinese Lyrics. Performed by Dora Ohrenstein, soprano, Marti Sweet and Matthew Raimondi, violins, on *Ben Johnston: Ponder Nothing.* New World Records NW 80432, 1993.

Trio. Performed by Charles Yassky, clarinet, Matthew Raimondi, violin, and Mark Schuman, cello, on *Ben Johnston: Ponder Nothing.* New World Records NW 80432, 1993.

Twelve Partials. Performed by John Fonville, flute, and Virginia Gaburo, piano, on *John Fonville: Temporal Details.* Einstein Records, EIN 005, 1995.

INDEX

BEN JOHNSTON was born in Macon, Georgia, in 1926. He is emeritus professor of music at the University of Illinois at Urbana-Champaign, where he taught from 1951 to 1983. His large body of compositions includes opera and musical theater, music for dance, orchestral and chamber works, choral and solo vocal works, piano music, tape pieces, and indeterminate works. He is a pioneer in the use of microtones and in the application of extended just intonation to contemporary composition.

BOB GILMORE is a senior lecturer in music at Dartington College of Arts, Devon, England. His writings on contemporary music have appeared in a variety of international publications. He is the author of *Harry Partch: A Biography.*

MUSIC IN AMERICAN LIFE

Only a Miner: Studies in Recorded Coal-Mining Songs *Archie Green*

Great Day Coming: Folk Music and the American Left *R. Serge Denisoff*

John Philip Sousa: A Descriptive Catalog of His Works *Paul E. Bierley*

The Hell-Bound Train: A Cowboy Songbook *Glenn Ohrlin*

Oh, Didn't He Ramble: The Life Story of Lee Collins, as Told to Mary Collins *Edited by Frank J. Gillis and John W. Miner*

American Labor Songs of the Nineteenth Century *Philip S. Foner*

Stars of Country Music: Uncle Dave Macon to Johnny Rodriguez *Edited by Bill C. Malone and Judith McCulloh*

Git Along, Little Dogies: Songs and Songmakers of the American West *John I. White*

A Texas-Mexican *Cancionero:* Folksongs of the Lower Border *Américo Paredes*

San Antonio Rose: The Life and Music of Bob Wills *Charles R. Townsend*

Early Downhome Blues: A Musical and Cultural Analysis *Jeff Todd Titon*

An Ives Celebration: Papers and Panels of the Charles Ives Centennial Festival-Conference *Edited by H. Wiley Hitchcock and Vivian Perlis*

Sinful Tunes and Spirituals: Black Folk Music to the Civil War *Dena J. Epstein*

Joe Scott, the Woodsman-Songmaker *Edward D. Ives*

Jimmie Rodgers: The Life and Times of America's Blue Yodeler *Nolan Porterfield*

Early American Music Engraving and Printing: A History of Music Publishing in America from 1787 to 1825, with Commentary on Earlier and Later Practices *Richard J. Wolfe*

Sing a Sad Song: The Life of Hank Williams *Roger M. Williams*

Long Steel Rail: The Railroad in American Folksong *Norm Cohen*

Resources of American Music History: A Directory of Source Materials from Colonial Times to World War II *D. W. Krummel, Jean Geil, Doris J. Dyen, and Deane L. Root*

Tenement Songs: The Popular Music of the Jewish Immigrants *Mark Slobin*

Ozark Folksongs *Vance Randolph; edited and abridged by Norm Cohen*

Oscar Sonneck and American Music *Edited by William Lichtenwanger*

Bluegrass Breakdown: The Making of the Old Southern Sound *Robert Cantwell*

Bluegrass: A History *Neil V. Rosenberg*

Music at the White House: A History of the American Spirit *Elise K. Kirk*

Red River Blues: The Blues Tradition in the Southeast *Bruce Bastin*

Good Friends and Bad Enemies: Robert Winslow Gordon and the Study of American Folksong *Debora Kodish*

Fiddlin' Georgia Crazy: Fiddlin' John Carson, His Real World, and the World of His Songs *Gene Wiggins*

America's Music: From the Pilgrims to the Present (rev. 3d ed.) *Gilbert Chase*

Secular Music in Colonial Annapolis: The Tuesday Club, 1745–56 *John Barry Talley*

Bibliographical Handbook of American Music *D. W. Krummel*

Goin' to Kansas City *Nathan W. Pearson Jr.*

"Susanna," "Jeanie," and "The Old Folks at Home": The Songs of Stephen C. Foster from His Time to Ours (2d ed.) *William W. Austin*

Songprints: The Musical Experience of Five Shoshone Women *Judith Vander*

"Happy in the Service of the Lord": Afro-American Gospel Quartets in Memphis *Kip Lornell*

Paul Hindemith in the United States *Luther Noss*

"My Song Is My Weapon": People's Songs, American Communism, and the Politics of Culture, 1930–50 *Robbie Lieberman*

Chosen Voices: The Story of the American Cantorate *Mark Slobin*

Theodore Thomas: America's Conductor and Builder of Orchestras, 1835–1905 *Ezra Schabas*

"The Whorehouse Bells Were Ringing" and Other Songs Cowboys Sing *Guy Logsdon*

Crazeology: The Autobiography of a Chicago Jazzman *Bud Freeman, as Told to Robert Wolf*

Discoursing Sweet Music: Brass Bands and Community Life in Turn-of-the-Century Pennsylvania *Kenneth Kreitner*

Mormonism and Music: A History *Michael Hicks*

Voices of the Jazz Age: Profiles of Eight Vintage Jazzmen *Chip Deffaa*

Pickin' on Peachtree: A History of Country Music in Atlanta, Georgia *Wayne W. Daniel*

Bitter Music: Collected Journals, Essays, Introductions, and Librettos *Harry Partch; edited by Thomas McGeary*

Ethnic Music on Records: A Discography of Ethnic Recordings Produced in the United States, 1893 to 1942 *Richard K. Spottswood*

Downhome Blues Lyrics: An Anthology from the Post–World War II Era *Jeff Todd Titon*

Ellington: The Early Years *Mark Tucker*

Chicago Soul *Robert Pruter*

That Half-Barbaric Twang: The Banjo in American Popular Culture *Karen Linn*

Hot Man: The Life of Art Hodes *Art Hodes and Chadwick Hansen*

The Erotic Muse: American Bawdy Songs (2d ed.) *Ed Cray*

Barrio Rhythm: Mexican American Music in Los Angeles *Steven Loza*

The Creation of Jazz: Music, Race, and Culture in Urban America *Burton W. Peretti*

Charles Martin Loeffler: A Life Apart in Music *Ellen Knight*

Club Date Musicians: Playing the New York Party Circuit *Bruce A. MacLeod*

Opera on the Road: Traveling Opera Troupes in the United States, 1825–60 *Katherine K. Preston*

The Stonemans: An Appalachian Family and the Music That Shaped Their Lives *Ivan M. Tribe*

Transforming Tradition: Folk Music Revivals Examined *Edited by Neil V. Rosenberg*

The Crooked Stovepipe: Athapaskan Fiddle Music and Square Dancing in Northeast Alaska and Northwest Canada *Craig Mishler*

Traveling the High Way Home: Ralph Stanley and the World of Traditional Bluegrass Music *John Wright*

Carl Ruggles: Composer, Painter, and Storyteller *Marilyn Ziffrin*

Never without a Song: The Years and Songs of Jennie Devlin, 1865–1952 *Katharine D. Newman*

The Hank Snow Story *Hank Snow, with Jack Ownbey and Bob Burris*

Milton Brown and the Founding of Western Swing *Cary Ginell, with special assistance from Roy Lee Brown*

Santiago de Murcia's "Códice Saldívar No. 4": A Treasury of Secular Guitar Music from Baroque Mexico *Craig H. Russell*

The Sound of the Dove: Singing in Appalachian Primitive Baptist Churches *Beverly Bush Patterson*

Heartland Excursions: Ethnomusicological Reflections on Schools of Music *Bruno Nettl*

Doowop: The Chicago Scene *Robert Pruter*

Blue Rhythms: Six Lives in Rhythm and Blues *Chip Deffaa*

Shoshone Ghost Dance Religion: Poetry Songs and Great Basin Context *Judith Vander*

Go Cat Go! Rockabilly Music and Its Makers *Craig Morrison*

'Twas Only an Irishman's Dream: The Image of Ireland and the Irish in American Popular Song Lyrics, 1800–1920 *William H. A. Williams*

Democracy at the Opera: Music, Theater, and Culture in New York City, 1815–60 *Karen Ahlquist*

Fred Waring and the Pennsylvanians *Virginia Waring*

Woody, Cisco, and Me: Seamen Three in the Merchant Marine *Jim Longhi*

Behind the Burnt Cork Mask: Early Blackface Minstrelsy and Antebellum American Popular Culture *William J. Mahar*

Going to Cincinnati: A History of the Blues in the Queen City *Steven C. Tracy*

Pistol Packin' Mama: Aunt Molly Jackson and the Politics of Folksong *Shelly Romalis*

Sixties Rock: Garage, Psychedelic, and Other Satisfactions *Michael Hicks*

The Late Great Johnny Ace and the Transition from R&B to Rock 'n' Roll *James M. Salem*

Tito Puente and the Making of Latin Music *Steven Loza*

Juilliard: A History *Andrea Olmstead*

Understanding Charles Seeger, Pioneer in American Musicology *Edited by Bell Yung and Helen Rees*

Mountains of Music: West Virginia Traditional Music from *Goldenseal* *Edited by John Lilly*

Alice Tully: An Intimate Portrait *Albert Fuller*

A Blues Life *Henry Townsend, as told to Bill Greensmith*

Long Steel Rail: The Railroad in American Folksong (2d ed.) *Norm Cohen*

The Golden Age of Gospel *Text by Horace Clarence Boyer; photography by Lloyd Yearwood*

Aaron Copland: The Life and Work of an Uncommon Man *Howard Pollack*

Louis Moreau Gottschalk *S. Frederick Starr*

Race, Rock, and Elvis *Michael T. Bertrand*

Theremin: Ether Music and Espionage *Albert Glinsky*

Poetry and Violence: The Ballad Tradition of Mexico's Costa Chica *John H. McDowell*

The Bill Monroe Reader *Edited by Tom Ewing*

Music in Lubavitcher Life *Ellen Koskoff*

Zarzuela: Spanish Operetta, American Stage *Janet L. Sturman*

Bluegrass Odyssey: A Documentary in Pictures and Words, 1966–86 *Carl Fleischhauer and Neil V. Rosenberg*

That Old-Time Rock & Roll: A Chronicle of an Era, 1954–63 *Richard Aquila*

Labor's Troubadour *Joe Glazer*

American Opera *Elise K. Kirk*

Don't Get above Your Raisin': Country Music and the Southern Working Class *Bill C. Malone*

John Alden Carpenter: A Chicago Composer *Howard Pollack*

Heartbeat of the People: Music and Dance of the Northern Pow-wow *Tara Browner*

My Lord, What a Morning: An Autobiography *Marian Anderson*

Marian Anderson: A Singer's Journey *Allan Keiler*

Charles Ives Remembered: An Oral History *Vivian Perlis*

Henry Cowell, Bohemian *Michael Hicks*

Rap Music and Street Consciousness *Cheryl L. Keyes*

Louis Prima *Garry Boulard*

Marian McPartland's Jazz World: All in Good Time *Marian McPartland*

Robert Johnson: Lost and Found *Barry Lee Pearson and Bill McCulloch*

Bound for America: Three British Composers *Nicholas Temperley*

Lost Sounds: Blacks and the Birth of the Recording Industry, 1890–1919 *Tim Brooks*

Burn, Baby! BURN! The Autobiography of Magnificent Montague *Magnificent Montague with Bob Baker*

Way Up North in Dixie: A Black Family's Claim to the Confederate Anthem *Howard L. Sacks and Judith Rose Sacks*

The Bluegrass Reader *Edited by Thomas Goldsmith*

Colin McPhee: Composer in Two Worlds *Carol J. Oja*

Robert Johnson, Mythmaking, and Contemporary American Culture *Patricia R. Schroeder*

Composing a World: Lou Harrison, Musical Wayfarer *Leta E. Miller and Fredric Lieberman*

Fritz Reiner, Maestro and Martinet *Kenneth Morgan*

That Toddlin' Town: Chicago's White Dance Bands and Orchestras, 1900–1950 *Charles A. Sengstock Jr.*

Dewey and Elvis: The Life and Times of a Rock 'n' Roll Deejay *Louis Cantor*

Come Hither to Go Yonder: Playing Bluegrass with Bill Monroe *Bob Black*

Chicago Blues: Portraits and Stories *David Whiteis*

The Incredible Band of John Philip Sousa *Paul E. Bierley*

"Maximum Clarity" and Other Writings on Music *Ben Johnston; edited by Bob Gilmore*

The University of Illinois Press
is a founding member of the
Association of University Presses.

University of Illinois Press
1325 South Oak Street
Champaign, IL 61820-6903
www.press.uillinois.edu